Victory over Nazism

THE JOURNEY OF A HOLOCAUST SURVIVOR

VICTORY OVER NAZISM

THE JOURNEY OF A HOLOCAUST SURVIVOR

Third Edition

writings by and about
Bronia Sonnenschein

compiled and edited by
Dan Sonnenschein

Memory **P**ress

Vancouver, B.C.

For information, please contact:

Dan Sonnenschein
601 — 1089 W. 13th Ave.
Vancouver, BC V6H 1N1
(604) 681-1827
dans@portal.ca

Third edition, February 2013

Cover design by Jan Westendorp

Library and Archives Canada Cataloguing in Publication

Sonnenschein, Bronia.
   Victory over Nazism : the journey of a Holocaust survivor /
writings by and about Bronia Sonnenschein ; compiled and
edited by Dan Sonnenschein.
— 3rd ed.

Includes bibliographical references.
ISBN 978-0-9736517-1-3

   1. Sonnenschein, Bronia. 2. Holocaust, Jewish (1939–1945)—
Personal narratives. 3. Holocaust survivors—Canada—Biography.
I. Sonnenschein, Dan Jacob. II. Title.
D804.196.S66 2013   940.53'18092   C2012-907891-3

Dedication

To the memory of my parents and my sister,
and to my family today,
with special thanks to my son.

The past cannot be erased.
Memories of it stay with you forever —
the good ones, as well as the sad ones.

Table of Contents

Introduction to the Third Edition

Dan Sonnenschein

HERE IS the long-contemplated third edition of this book, one I had hoped to present to my mother. This was not to be, as she died on January 26, 2011, six days after suffering a stroke in the early evening of January 20th, just as the Jewish holiday of Tu B'Shvat ("the New Year of the Trees") had ended. Another significance of this date I realized only months later, in looking at a "letter to the editor" of hers I re-discovered (printed here on page 122), calling for the commemoration in the Jewish community of January 20th as the anniversary of the notorious Wannsee Conference, whose purpose was to officially set in motion the so-called Final Solution.

Four days before, we had attended what was to be our last event together, a movie she had very much wanted to see, commemorating the annual Vancouver Raoul Wallenberg Day. This was the excellent French production *Désobéir* (Disobedience), a dramatization of the struggle of Portuguese diplomat Aristides de Sousa Mendes to save Jews while he was posted in France. We appreciated this tribute to a hero of the Holocaust, and my mother enjoyed seeing several friends at the event, who complimented her on how well she looked, despite serious injuries she had suffered the previous summer. It was a significant finale.

As three is a traditional number of completion, I had planned this edition to be the last one — "the last of the Mohicans" (as my mother, the last of her generation in our family, sometimes wistfully called herself). She had retired from public speaking as a Holocaust educator in June 2008, after giving arduous talks many times each year since 1987.

In 2005, I read a letter by renowned historian Sir Martin Gilbert in the International Jerusalem Post newspaper asking for witnesses to Kristallnacht to contact him for research he was then doing into a book on the subject. My mother did so, and was quoted several times in his *Kristallnacht: Prelude to Disaster*. A gentleman as well as scholar, Sir Martin sent her an inscribed copy of the book in addition to corresponding with her. In reading this book I discovered a fascinating though tragic fact: the fate of "Tante Mary" at whose kindergarten my mother worked when she was forced to leave her job as a legal secretary soon after the Nazi annexation of Austria (see page 48). Tante Mary was murdered in the Riga Ghetto in Latvia to which she had been deported with her mother (and possibly her sister). This information about her was credited to Holocaust historian and survivor, Gertrude Schneider, originally from Vienna.

I subsequently contacted Dr. Schneider, who then got to know my mother through some telephone conversations, and we all continued to keep in touch. We sent her the second edition of this book, and she sent my mother a warmly inscribed copy of *The Unfinished Road* — one of a series of her books on the Holocaust in Latvia. Another of her books, which I ordered and we read, is *Exile and Destruction* about Austrian Jews during that terrible time. We were very interested to learn about other similarities in their experiences: both had been in Stutthof, both women's fathers had been killed during the Holocaust while each had survived the war years with her mother and younger sister. She wrote to me in a condolence note, "I grieve with you ... [M]y only regret is that I never met Bronia in person."

Later, I got in touch with another historian of the Holocaust, Michal Unger at Bar-Ilan University in Israel, a specialist on the Lodz Ghetto. This came about after I read the book *Ghettostadt* by Gordon Horwitz in which I learned that the name of the German administrator I had spelled in the previous editions as "Scharnulla" was actually "Czarnulla" (his first name, Erich). An Internet search on this name turned up a summary of a talk by Dr. Unger called *After an Alibi: Hans Biebow and the Rescue of Three Jewish Groups from the Lodz Ghetto (1944-1945)*. This is discussed here on pages 282-283.

Since the second edition of this book, a highlight relating to Holocaust commemoration was at Vancouver's prestigious Chan Centre, where my mother gave an introduction to a performance by klezmer group, *Brave Old World* of their concert, *Songs of the Lodz Ghetto*. Her elegant appearance alone on stage, delivering her brief but meaningful speech by memory, made a deep impact on many in the audience. Her words are included here, along with the introduction of her by an event organizer.

Another significant development was for us to be notified that Bronia's videotaped testimony in 1995 for the Shoah Foundation was thought well enough of to be distributed for educational use to two school districts: in Jackson, Mississippi and in Little Rock, Arkansas. We also learned from a Shoah Foundation content specialist, Sheila Hansen, that she was using it in a course at the Foundation's Los Angeles headquarters.

In her personal life since the second edition, Bronia was blessed to attend happy family events, including the Jewish marriages of her younger granddaughter, Claire, to Lou Kolman in August, 2008, and of her grandson, Jonathan, to Jackie Berger in May, 2010. She was also proud and thrilled to become a great-grandmother, her elder granddaughter Emily giving birth to a daughter, Annie, and later a son, Leo, and Claire in between having a daughter, Makena. Posthumously, in 2012, two more of her great-grandchildren have been born: Claire's son, Asher, and Jonathan's daughter, Felicity.

In the two years of good health she enjoyed after retirement from her 21-year, late-life career as a Holocaust educator, Bronia continued to count her blessings, greatly appreciating the every-day pleasures of her home (inside and on her patio, her "summer residence"), walks in a nearby park, and the company of family and friends, to whom she continued to bring joy and cheer.

She read two new articles intended for this edition, one by Markus Schirmer, and the other by Chris Friedrichs, called *The Uniqueness of Bronia*, which has been replaced by the text of the eulogy he delivered at her funeral. The obituary has been re-printed, along with some condolence comments and letters. This edition also benefits from warm reminiscences by Peter Kavalek, Paulette Cave, and Susan Cox, and an insightful essay by Diane Rodgers, also to be thanked for finding in the online Yad Vashem archives photos of Bronia and her sister Paula taken in the Lodz Ghetto (p. 285). I am also grateful to all others whose thoughtful words have contributed to this book, as well as to Paulette Cave for proofreading, Sharon Meen for advice, and Jan Westendorp for her cover design. And thank you, my beloved mother.

Introduction

Dan Sonnenschein (1999)

O NE DAY IN 1945 IN NAZI-OCCUPIED EUROPE, a certain Herr
Czarnulla (an official representative of the Aryan "master
race"), said to my mother, "One day Herr Czarnulla will be so
small" — he illustrated with two fingers close together — "and
Frau Strauss will be so big" — and his hands spread apart. Herr
Czarnulla was drunk. He had some cause to be, as the prospect
of the defeat of Nazi Germany was becoming clearer by the day,
except to the most fanatical. We don't know whatever became of
Herr Czarnulla, who in effect saved my mother along with her
mother and sister on one occasion (recounted in the Epilogue).
We do know that his prophecy about my mother came true.
My mother overcame tremendous obstacles to achieve some
great things, in her personal life and as an educator.

She has spoken at such places as the annual Holocaust
Symposium for high school students since 1990, at dozens of
schools around Vancouver and the Lower Mainland, some
several times. She also spoke twice at a similar symposium in
Victoria, and has traveled to schools and public meetings in the
interior of British Columbia, in Salmon Arm, Kelowna, Prince
George, and Creston. This last presentation, in a part of B.C.
near the Idaho border, led to an invitation for her and a fellow
survivor to speak in Sandpoint as well as Bonners Ferry, Idaho,
to local citizens concerned about the bad reputation their area
had been given by nearby white supremacists.

It is important for understanding my mother's character that
this book is not her idea. She has excellent communications skills
in both writing and speaking, and over the years has written
some brief pieces on her Holocaust experiences as well as her
current educational activities, mostly in response to requests.
She has also contributed some "letters to the editor" over the
years, most of which are reprinted here. I felt it important to
collect many of these writings, along with such related material
as articles, letters or excerpts from correspondence, and various
comments. Bronia Sonnenschein never fails to pay tribute to her

mother, who encouraged her daughters to carry on one more day, or to the German lady who risked her life to give my mother a special letter. My mother is too modest to mention a time when she, in effect, risked her life to save her mother and sister. This event is recounted in the Epilogue. Typically, she says she had "no choice" since she knew she wouldn't survive without them.

Most material here was never intended for publication in book form, and is not designed to be a literary or strictly chronological account. By necessity, there is some repetition of key events and details, but it is hoped that this will add some emphasis and different perspectives. It is important to note that my mother is very capable of writing for herself, and any editing I have done is only slight polishing (on the order of changing an occasional 'had' to 'has'). There has been no ghostwriting: everyone's contribution has been their own. The Notes provide some additional detail, as well as translations of some words that may be unfamiliar.

Fortunately, much of my mother's story has already been told in a variety of ways which are described here. Regrettably, some forms of communication are more likely than others to result in misunderstanding. For example, responses on questionnaires sometimes indicate that a student believes that my mother has forgiven the Nazis; this is not the case. Therefore another purpose of this book is to provide a definitive account, as well as to add and preserve some little-known details.

This book is a tribute to my mother, a historical record, and an album of memories to be cherished by our family and passed on to future generations. Perhaps some scholars, educators, and others will find it of interest too. I consider my mother to be an emblem of the Jewish people — small, vulnerable, a victim of persecution, but surviving, enduring, and contributing to the world. Not just a survivor physically, her zest for life and Viennese-flavoured joie de vivre were not crushed. Her story deserves to be told.

Prologue

*A Happy Life
in Vienna*

A Happy Life in Vienna

Bronia Sonnenschein

I LIVE WITH THE MEMORY of having grown up in one of Europe's most beautiful cities, of having the kindest, most loving parents any child could wish for, and a large loving family of aunts, cousins, uncles, and a grandmother I adored. Thanks to them, my childhood and youth were the happiest years. They provided me with love, and taught me dignity and handed me values to live by. They also made sure to provide me with a good education. I was well equipped or so they thought. But never did anyone tell me what hatred was. Nor did my parents know what hatred was. Hitler's rule, his Nazi regime, taught us well.

Our origins were in Galicia, Poland, where my parents had grown up and where all my mother's family had lived. My father's parents later on moved to Romania. Galicia was known in those days as "Austrian Poland" since it was ruled by the Emperor of Austria, Franz Joseph, and the "intelligentsia" spoke German. My father had studied law in Lemberg. My parents and all of my mother's relatives, including my grandparents eventually moved to Vienna. I was at that time four months old and have, of course, no recollection of those days, since I was raised and educated in Vienna, together with my sister Paula who was born in that city.

I will forever cherish the memories of my happy childhood and youth, of our happy home life and of a world that was for me filled with hope and belief. I was always encouraged by my loving parents, my sister and other close relatives. I enjoyed my school-years; both my sister and I went to public schools from kindergarten to high-school and graduation. We got along easily with our non-Jewish friends. Nobody at that time thought me to be inferior by being Jewish. Yet antisemitism has been around for 2,000 years. Every so often it makes itself visible. Maybe I was fortunate not to have been touched by it at that time.

There was also the effort and wisdom of my parents to give me a well rounded education besides the basic one I was taught at school. At an early age, while attending kindergarten (a French one), we, the young students, were taken to the Museum of History of Arts. We probably did not understand the magnificent art of old Masters, but it opened up a window. I still remember it. Being musical herself, my mother insisted on piano lessons, introducing me slowly to music, whereas my father insisted on language lessons, French and English, therefore providing a "key" to the world. Later on in high-school I continued with English. As students we were given the opportunity of attending the Viennese State's Opera House, where a whole new world of music opened up before me. We obviously did not have the "best tickets in the house", it was on the fourth gallery, but the acoustics were splendid, and even though we had to stand during the whole performance, it never hampered my enthusiasm for music. It stayed with me. Opera-glasses helped us on the fourth gallery to also see the singers, of which Vienna had so many talented ones. And there was so much joy in everything I did: visits to the Vienna woods, swimming in the Danube or in one of Austria's lakes, family get-togethers for holidays and birthdays, and other occasions to celebrate our holidays so rich in tradition, being passed on from generation to generation. The many friends I had also contributed greatly to being happy. It was a happy life indeed.

Bronia wrote this in reply to a request from Fran Teisch, daughter of Rose Tillinger (née Garfunkel), the sister of Bronia's aunt, Blanca, to reminisce about Fran's family. A comment from Fran's sister, Harriet, is on page 277.

AS CHILDREN WE (Paula and I) were told to be on our very best behaviour when visiting the Garfunkel family, the gentlest, finest people who came to be our family when their daughter Blanca married Uncle Zuima, my mother's brother. I instantly loved Tante Blanca who gladly would have given the shirt off her back had you needed it. She also had a gentle sense of humour. Both she and my uncle belonged to my dearest family members. I loved Rosl (your beloved mother), a typical Garfunkel child, dearly beloved and cherished by everyone. I felt so privileged having visited her and her husband Joe in San Mateo.

I was a child when your aunt Annie died. I believe it was leukemia. I did not know Loni that well, maybe I did not see her as much. But I sure remember Salo and his brother Felix. Salo was a bon vivant, he loved girls (and why not), he was good looking and a sharp dresser. For a while he dated my friend Martha's sister Kate (older than me) who was a smart, pretty woman and it seemed quite a serious involvement. Yet the moment Salo met Hilda, he dumped Kate. Just a pretty face, that's all she was. "Love is blind" so they say. Felix was an adventurer.

We went each year for summer holidays to Gars am Kamp. No sooner was school over than our yearly "pilgrimage" to this lovely place on the river Kamp started. Tante Blanca and family, by that time they had a daughter Phyllis, were included as well as my cousins Roman and Marcel, sons of Janek and Mila Kawalek. It was a hectic holiday because we kids fought constantly — mainly with Phyllis. My sister and Phyllis were close in age and were fighting like cats and dogs. Phyllis was a "whiner", Paula a tomboy. I stayed out of it, being older and presumably "wiser". I had my juicy fights with cousin Roman (the one who was buried with full military honours in Arlington). Tante Blanca was the referee, the one that restored peace for a little while. I loved Tante Blanca and Uncle Zuima, I always will.

In these ideal surroundings, Felix once appeared. As told by my mother, he once appeared in Gars having *walked* from Vienna to Gars. I forget how long it took. He took my mother's breath away when he appeared at the door looking like a tramp (no wonder), unshaved, stumbling into the hall, tired and hungry. But he became instantly famous and got t.l.c. from our family. I also remember Felix and my mother having once climbed a mountain, the Rax, again admired by everyone.

Rosl, your mother, invited all of us to celebrate our visit to New York after the war. It was in summer of 1950 and frightfully hot. Your wonderful mother wanting her guests to be comfortable suggested for all of us to sit on the floor, believing it to be cooler. I was not, but we had lots of fun. I'll never forget this beautiful family — they all added to the joy of being alive, having survived the tragedy of the Holocaust.

Editor's Note: More happy memories are recorded on pages 234-5.

Cecilia Kawalek (née Fischbach) and Philip Kawalek,
Bronia's maternal grandparents.

Emilia, middle daughter of
the six Kawalek children.

Abraham Schwebel, Bronia's father,
was also from a large family.

Bronia's extended family in Vienna. Front: Unknown, Bronia, Paula, Roman and Marcel Kawalek. Middle: Blanca Kawalek, Clara Hauslinger, Cecilia Kawalek, Unknown, Emilia Schwebel, Mila Kawalek. Standing: Ann Kawalek, Unknown, Phyllis and Zuima Kawalek, Z. Hauslinger, Unknown, Unknown, Abraham Schwebel, Janek Kawalek, Hella Hauslinger.

Bronia at an early age.

Bronia and Paula from previous family photo.

The Schwebel family in Vienna, in the early 1920s.

"My first schoolday" — Bronia.

"My first schoolday" — Paula.

Bronia as a teenager.

The Schwebel sisters.

The Schwebel ladies in 1938.

Emilia with her daughters.

Bronia as a young woman.

Bronia in the Vienna Woods.

Part 1

Years of Horror

Five Years of Horror

Bronia Sonnenschein (1985)

O N MAY 8, 1945 a young Russian soldier rode on his horse into the courtyard of the barracks in Theresienstadt (Czechoslovakia) bearing the greatest gift — freedom for the barely alive survivors of German concentration camps. "You are free, you can go home now to your fathers and sons, husbands and brothers, you are free!"

After five years of endless suffering, of having been stripped of our dignity, this priceless gift — freedom — overwhelmed us. We had waited for it for so long and now it was ours. There was no strength left in the undernourished bodies to shout wildly with joy. Some approached the young soldier kissing his boots. He was, after all, the messenger of peace. But where was home? Where were the graves of the countless men, women and children who had perished? Did freedom mean we could lift up our heads again, become members of the human race and be treated as such?

It all started on March 13, 1938 when German troops marched into Vienna. From that day on nothing was ever the same again. What we had taken for granted, being a free people in a democratic country, had been taken away from us by brutal force. Vienna was not home for us anymore; it became more like a battleground and, leaving everything behind us, we sought refuge in Poland. Little did we know that this was the first step to hell from where millions of innocent people would never return.

It was January 1939 and we waited anxiously in the city of Lodz for the promised papers from our sponsors in the United States to enable us to emigrate to America. When they finally arrived it was too late — war was being declared on September 1, 1939 and it hardly took any time at all for the Germans to conquer Poland. Again we witnessed German troops marching into the city where we had sought to be safe for a little while.

There was no escape route, we were trapped. And again we were driven from our home. Germans entered our apartment and within ten minutes we were on the street — it was February 1940. Having expected it to happen — we had experience by now — a small suitcase with only the most essential clothes, a blanket and a pillow was prepared to take along with us.

And so we entered the ghetto in Lodz, renamed by the Germans Litzmannstadt. Crammed into it, the smallest and poorest part of this city, were 160,000 Jews. The control of the ghetto was in the hands of the Gestapo. The ghetto itself was hermetically closed off to the outside world on May 1, 1940.

Chaim Rumkowski, the "Elder of the Jews", was appointed to 'rule' the ghetto by the authorities of the German *Ghetto-verwaltung* (ghetto administration) whose leader was Hans Biebow.

The starving inhabitants of the ghetto, under the iron rule of Chaim Rumkowski, produced in the workshops every imaginable product the Germans demanded. In return they supplied the ghetto with meager food-rations — rotten vegetables, rotten potatoes, flour that seemed to contain sawdust, brown sugar, and occasionally horse meat. Our diet never contained milk, cheese or eggs. A loaf of bread had to last for eight days — since there was not much more to eat we were never able to hold on to it for eight days. The workshops supplied us with two watery soups a day. A working day lasted twelve hours. This diet was from time to time topped off with a ration of potato peels.

The death rate in the ghetto was staggering, yet the demand for excellence in producing everything from furniture, machinery, clothing, toys for the German children — while ours were dying of hunger — never stopped. And so we lived and toiled from day to day. It seemed as if the war would never end. We had no information whatsoever as to how the war progressed and days turned into weeks, months, years. They were only interrupted by other great misfortunes.

In 1941 approximately 20,000 Jews from Vienna and Prague were sent to the Lodz Ghetto. Our food ration did not increase —

we had to share with them what we had. But it did not last long. The majority of them were deported, killed right in the trucks that took them away. It was by now 1942 and deportations from the ghetto never stopped. Firstly the children and old people, then the sick ones followed by those that were too weak and from whom no more work could be extracted. The bread ration was lowered; the demands for work increased. Hunger and epidemics had taken their toll in the ghetto. Yet it was still too slow for the Germans to achieve the "final solution". That blow came for us ghetto survivors in August 1944 when the liquidation of the ghetto began. All that was left were about 60,000 Jews.

The ghetto years had been hard ones, hard beyond any imagination. But families were together. We were still able to comfort each other. We were still together when we were herded into cattle wagons. For four days we could still draw strength from each other despite lack of food, lack of air to breathe, lack of proper facilities. There were about 50 of us in each wagon on the long journey that took us to Auschwitz.

The dreaded segregation started to take place. Men were separated from women, children from their mothers. Stark naked we stood before the SS men, one of them being Dr. Mengele. The slightest blemish on our body, an insignificant scar, grey hair, and the death-sentence was pronounced by just moving to the left side as indicated by the finger on the SS man's hand. Those moving to the right were taken into showers, our heads were shaved, we became totally bald and lost our identity. They handed us rags to cover our bodies and with this our initiation into the death camp of Auschwitz was completed. Those that were marked for death — the "blue death" by gas, were taken into "showers" containing the lethal gas while the Auschwitz band, all dressed in white, played Bach and Beethoven. Their suffering did not last long. Their bodies were fed into the ovens. The smoke never stopped coming from the ovens which turned to ashes innocent human beings.

There are no words to describe the terror, the humiliation, the sadness and the hopelessness of this situation. How could

God, whose chosen people we were, permit actions against us of this magnitude? The reason, and I believe it to be the only reason that the three of us survived, was the fact that we were together — unknown to our tormentors. Had they known that there was a mother and her two daughters they surely would have separated us.

And so the three of us faced the days in Auschwitz, slept side by side on the bunks in the camp that was overflowing with inmates, stood at attention at roll-calls — roll-calls that seemed to go on forever and ever. We stood at them when the sun was beating down on our bald heads and we stood at them when it rained and the first snow fell. We never talked much, afraid that they might find out our well-guarded secret. And we endured the gnawing hunger, the lice, the fear.

Stutthof was our next destination. Since the camp in Stutthof was a fairly new one, it was not prepared for masses of new inmates. As a result we sat and slept on the floor so close together that not even a hand could have been put between us. There was only one watery soup a day, one slice of bread, and a bowl of coffee to be shared by five people. Everything had to be done by a group of five. We marched in a group of five, stood at attention in groups of five, were taken to the latrines in groups of five. And then there were the constant beatings by the "Kapos" (camp police). They held us responsible for the bad smell, the lice, the overcrowding. Yet only in the rarest instances did they let us use washrooms. Not having towels, we had to put the same old dirty rags on our cold and wet bodies. No wonder we were covered with lice adding to our torment. Thousands around us died but we were still holding on by sheer willpower. And when Paula came down with scarlet fever we had to use every ounce of willpower to shield her from the Kapos. Had they known, they would have taken her to the so-called "sick-room" from where nobody ever returned. We propped her up every time she fainted during roll-call; yet she miraculously survived this dreaded disease, without any medication, without the slightest comfort to ease her pains. Our stay in Stutthof lasted four months.

In December 1944 we were again transported, this time to the forced labor camp in Dresden. It must have been around Christmas, as we were forced to sing Christmas carols to amuse the commandant of the ammunition factory in the Schandauerstrasse 68, our new location. But things started to look up for us, or so we thought. We could actually take a hot shower (the first one in many months), our 'rags' were disinfected and we felt reasonably clean. We still suffered from hunger, but we slept in bunks with one blanket for five and the roll-calls were being taken inside. Since we were given work, sorting bullets, we were even permitted to use inside toilets, a luxury denied us for so long. The days were long — they started at five in the morning — but we felt there was a ray of hope for our survival.

Only for us there was more tragedy still ahead. On the night of February 13, 1945, the allied forces and the Russians attacked Dresden. Whatever they did not destroy in that first night, they did the following night. Dresden went up in flames and thousands perished. But the Germans were still holding on to us. They did not want to be deprived of the macabre pleasure of killing us themselves. Being hit by bombs was in their opinion too good for us. The factory where we worked had been partially destroyed so they 'saved' us from the fire, the incredible hail and storm produced by the bombs, and led us towards the river Elbe where we stood all night waiting for the attack to end. And although we were frightened to death, not even comprehending the impact of the attack, hope was surging through us that this attack might signal the end of the war and free us.

And we were wrong again. Our darkest hour had still not come. Since we could not return to the damaged factory, the diabolical plan of the Germans was to take us to another camp near Dresden, Pirna. Although it must have been quite clear by then to them that they had just about lost the war, they still exercised their authority over us, they still tormented us, starved us, and showed their contempt for us in any possible way. We were only a few weeks in Pirna, yet hundreds from our transport died there. I am at a loss to understand how it was possible for us to survive. But we did. The original transport of about 60,000 people had shrunk considerably, yet there were still enough of us left to be considered for working on the reconstruction of the factory in Dresden.

It was March 1945 when we returned to Dresden and on April 12, the Russians having advanced towards Dresden, we were again being driven out of this city.

Accompanied by SS men, we started our "death-march." We had no idea of what our destination would be. We marched for 12 days with no food, no shelter, bombs flying above us. We mostly walked along the river Elbe. Those, and there were so many, that died on the way, were simply thrown into that river. To quench our thirst we drank from the very same river. The will to live had finally left us. Paula and I decided to end it all. Being so close to the river, drowning in it seemed to be the simplest way. We confronted mother with it. She agreed, but begged us to wait just one more day, the 24th of April, Paula's birthday. On that very day we entered Theresienstadt; the Germans left us there and we were taken over by the Jewish community of Theresienstadt — the model ghetto. The plan was to concentrate all concentration camp inmates in that ghetto which was to be blown up later on. But they ran out of time and so it was God's will that we lived to hear the young Russian soldier tell us on May 8, 1945 that we were free.

On May 8, 1985 it will be 40 years since this memorable day in Theresienstadt. There are only two of us from our family left to tell our story. It will be up to you, the second generation, to carry the torch for us who survived and never to forget those that did not.

Epilogue

Five Years of Horror was written upon the encouragement of my beloved sister, Paula Lenga. She was the driving force behind many important steps I had taken in my life.

I am dedicating this account of our experiences during the Holocaust to her memory. She passed away on February 6, 1986, and her memory will be cherished not only by me but by everybody who knew her.

Note

There is one special event not mentioned in my account. Yet I have never failed to tell the students during my presentation of this special event.

It happened while we were lined up to leave the factory in Dresden — the Russians having come closer and closer to Dresden — when a German woman who was in charge of the camp kitchen, approached me thrusting a letter into my hands whispering "this is a 'Schutzbrief' — it will protect you."

It only took a few seconds for her to do so and for me to hide this letter in my blouse. (I had worked in the office typing all day long where she had noticed me, since I occasionally was asked to do work for her as well.) She never knew my name — we had no names only numbers; I knew hers and have never forgotten it.

In all that terrible hatred and violence surrounding us there was this one woman who actually took pity on a half-starved Jewish inmate.

Without knowing the contents of this letter, I carried it with me during our death-march remembering only her words that it will protect me and those next to me. Maybe it did. I believed in it then and I believe in it now. I still have my 'Schutzbrief' carefully wrapped in rice paper. It is my dearest possession.

They say "Faith can move mountains" — maybe it is true. Besides, I had a "why" to live.

The Schwebel Family's Journey in Nazi-occupied Europe
(March 13, 1938 to May 8, 1945)

Bronia's mother and sister also survived the journey.
Bronia's father perished in Stutthof in September, 1944.

Testimony on the Lodz Ghetto

Bronia Sonnenschein (c. 1947)

THE GHETTO IN LODZ (Litzmannstadt) consists of a small part (*Stadteil*) on the periphery of the city. It is enclosed by barbed wire, and guarded by German and Jewish guards. It is forbidden to leave or enter, punishable by death.

About 180,000 Jews were taken into the Ghetto in February 1940. On the orders of the mayor of Litzmannstadt, an "Elder of the Jews" was installed in charge of the Ghetto. M. Chaim Rumkowski, a man of 65, a Lithuanian Jew, who could hardly speak German, nor really correct Polish, only Yiddish. A man of native intelligence and energy, driven by ambition, rich in ideas and fantasy. Rumkowski is a "dictator" in the Ghetto. His words, regardless of his weakness in speaking the official languages, are understood and accepted. He wanted to build the largest ghetto and he succeeded. He would provide labor in order to get food for the Ghetto.

Rumkowski began to build up the Ghetto. A Jewish police would be set up, an office for registration, statistics, food administration, postal administration, and so on. The Ghetto would receive its own currency, the Ghetto mark. And factories began to work. There were dress factories, carpenters, metalworkers, shoe manufacturing, paper manufacturing, lingerie, hats, textiles, art supplies, watch repairs, laundries, laboratories. In short, everything that is done by a well-functioning state. The work done in those factories would have passed the most critical eyes of a jury.

And the machines started to work, operated with swollen feet and laborious breathing because their lungs were partly destroyed. The carpenters produced the most beautiful furniture. All of those workers were called the gray people of the Ghetto. For their work they received food supplied by the Ghetto administration (administrator Hans Biebow), two watery soups daily, once with kohlrabi, once with cabbage, occasionally a potato, and a small ration of groceries twice a month. This, which was supposed to last for 14 days, could easily have been consumed in one day. One bread (1 kg) for eight days.

And the President (Rumkowski) chased around with his horse and carriage from factory to factory, to inspect, scream at the workers and ask them to produce more and more and more. Day and night shifts were implemented, new factories were set up for: slippers, straw shoes, carpets. The motive in the Ghetto was work; only by working can we stay alive and provide for ourselves. For a little while they leave us alone. Countless people die from weakness, hunger, malnutrition. Nobody seems to care.

The workshops were enlarged, new workshops were installed, commissions came from Germany to inspect the ghetto. One of them was Heinrich Himmler. And Rumkowski succeeded in having a house of culture established where concerts were held. Recovery homes were installed so that those workers who had worked one year were sent for eight days to rest.

And a new set of devastating events began in the ghetto. The settlement of Jews from Vienna, Germany, Luxembourg, Prague that started to arrive in 1941. Bratfisch, the head of the Gestapo, informed the Eldest of the Jews during a brief meeting that within three weeks 24,000 Jews would need to be settled in the ghetto. He did not care where they would be housed, the ghetto won't be enlarged, he simply does not care. "Make room, Rumkowski, however you care to do it. There won't be more food rations for the 24,000 new people. You have to share with what you have." Bratfisch refused to accept any exclamation of Rumkowski.

Meetings were called, plans were made for housing these newcomers. In three days, a thousand people each day started to arrive. The first transport came from Vienna. The carpenters worked day and night to make bunks, schools were emptied to make some room and our meager food ration became so much smaller in order to share. And the transports came daily. The new arrivals found it immensely difficult to settle in the ghetto.

So many of them died. We had already learned to live with hunger, they could not do it. They were not given much time to think about it. They arrived during October and November in 1941; the evacuation of the new arrivals started in May 1942. It was the second tragedy — they went on transports to the concentration camp Auschwitz.

And even these tragic days passed, work continued, orders arrived from Germany to produce more and more. A new workplace was established, a metal workshop. A large hall was established for showrooms so that the work being produced in the ghetto could be shown to arriving guests from Germany. From old rags carpentry work was produced and children's clothing from remnants. Large warehouses from Berlin continued to send orders. And we worked, worked, to keep alive.

The third catastrophe befell the ghetto. The evacuation of patients from the hospital. This time Rumkowski was not notified beforehand. One day, early in the morning at about 5 a.m., cars from the Gestapo raced through the ghetto and stopped before the hospital. They threw the patients out of the window in the prepared trucks, those that had recuperated, those that were critically ill. The alive on top of the dead, children and the old people. The helpless patients who were on their way to recovery, all of them were taken away. Nobody could help them. The hospital was converted into workshops.

The next tragic event came when the chief of the Gestapo, Bratfisch, notified the Eldest of the Jews that on orders, children up to 10 years old, and men and women over 50 were to be taken to a place from where they could be selected by the Gestapo. "Do it with the help of your police, Rumkowski. If it does not succeed our commando will come to the ghetto. How it will turn out you can probably figure out yourself." And without blinking an eye he left, without even giving Rumkowski a chance to speak. The Jewish administration had to keep a clear head to deal with it. Telephones were not still for a moment, the managers of all workplaces were called to meetings, the chief of police, all sat together till deep into the night considering how to go about this devilish plan. The following day Rumkowski addressed the ghetto inmates relating the orders of the Gestapo. He asked the inmates to part with the best they have, to submit their children so that the Ghetto might be saved and the handling of this plan by the Gestapo be avoided. Also, those over 50 he asked to submit themselves on their own. He was well aware how senseless this instruction was. We had starved together, frozen in winter together, by the sweat of our faces did we work together staying alive regardless of our meager food ration, and now we were asked to rip our heart out. Those were incredibly difficult days for us. And the Gestapo did what they said they would do. An 8-day curfew was ordered; whoever dared to walk on the street would be shot. And just that time we were to collect our food ration which we could not do, and so the whole ghetto was exposed to starvation, not having any reserves.

And the commando arrives in the ghetto and certain streets are encircled by them. Those taking part in it were: Hans Biebow, Commissar Fuchs, Schmidt, Krischon, Richter (all Gestapo). In one hand the whip, they order people out of their homes to assemble on the street and without further choosing people are being selected to step forward and taken to the waiting trucks, being loaded on them like cattle. From there into cars which returned shortly — gassing does not take long. These people did not have to be taken to Auschwitz. It is all done in absolute stillness, there are no scenes, nobody is crying, there is no wailing. Stunned, absolutely stunned, like animals being taken to the slaughterhouse march these poor victims their last way. And without any pity, children are being taken away from their mothers, forced from their breasts, some women not even being aware what is being done to them. The hand that had previously held their child's hand is just hanging at their side, lifeless. Others are running after the truck, jumping on it to follow their children to their death. People are running after their parents to be with them. And so this horror lasts for eight days. Thirty thousand people were killed this way, gassed. It is a Sunday, the eighth day, when the curfew is being lifted. The food rations that had been withheld are again obtainable and can be picked up at the designated stores — as if nothing had happened and what nobody ever believed to be possible, did happen, work continued regardless of 30,000 people having been killed. And again the machines are humming in the workshops, more workshops are being established, more orders are coming in and every little bit of news coming into the ghetto is being eagerly absorbed since we do not have newspapers and hope for liberation continues. The year is 1944 and the next catastrophic event in the ghetto unfolds. The Eldest of the Jews receives the order from the German authorities (Ghetto administration) to pass on to the managers of all the workshops the orders to make lists of those working in each shop of who should be deported. Another devilish plan. We, the Jews, shall determine who should be deported, workers with whom we have shared all the sorrows. The managers who should determine whose names to put on the lists are nearly losing their mind. Those workers had worked so diligently, gave their best to sustain the Ghetto and now, the Jewish managers should declare a death sentence for them. Whoever does not comply with this order and won't show up on the designated area will receive the greatest punishment. Nobody shows up for work, everybody is hiding, sustains themselves on raw vegetables — yet, nevertheless, the Gestapo succeeds again in deporting 10,000 people. This "action" lasts four weeks. We breathe again in relief when it is over.

The Russians are getting closer to Warsaw and we have hope again that it will last only a few days before we will be liberated. There are so few of us, about 60,000 people.

And the greatest series of unhappy events starts to unfold. The liquidation of the ghetto. We had slaved and worked for four and a half years, diligent hands produced work to sustain just naked life just for the sake of freedom and independence, and what was our reward? Again the police raced through the ghetto. People go into hiding like hunted animals, going from house to house to hide. Nothing helped. Transport after transport went out, all of them to Auschwitz.

Where was God as we were being transported from the ghetto? All God's Jewish children. Their machines, their tools were left behind, all of them to be tortured and gassed? Only a few of them from all countries who were being sent to the concentration camp returned and lived to see freedom. All of us experienced the same, like the old fisherman, who dreamed all his life of a little green box, and when finally he got it said, with sorrow in his heart and deeply disappointed: "It is not the green I was dreaming of."

The happiness we had been dreaming about was not to be. What we had dreamed of in the Ghetto, when we were all together, did not bring our freedom. There are all the unknown graves and the sorrow, with which we are so deeply connected.

Correspondence on the Lodz Ghetto

August 5, 1990

Mr. Alan Adelson
Jewish Heritage Project
150 Franklin St. #1 W
New York, N.Y. 10013

Dear Mr. Adelson,

I have read the book "The Lodz Ghetto" and seen the movie "The Lodz Ghetto". I also read Mr. Dobroszycki's book "Chronicle of the Lodz Ghetto". I wish to thank you, Mr. Lapides and everyone involved in recording the Ghetto years, the pain, hardship and sufferings of the Ghetto-dwellers. I was one of them.

My name and that of my father actually appear in the "Chronicle of the Lodz Ghetto" on pages 20 and 354. My maiden name was Schwebel. (In the book it was spelled "Szwebel", which is, I believe, the Polish spelling.)

I worked as one of Rumkowski's secretaries in the Ghetto administration on Baluter Ring. As a matter of fact, "Praeses" Rumkowski, as we used to call him, officiated at my and Mary Schifflinger's wedding on September 18, 1943.

My father and husband were killed in Stutthof.

Both Mary and I were present on the day when Hans Biebow, in one of his drunken rages beat up and bloodied Rumkowski. I remember it so clearly. It was on a Sunday afternoon, just the two of us were on duty while Rumkowski sat in his office. Biebow stormed in and the ugly and frightening scene took place, right in front of our eyes. It was Schwind, Biebow's deputy, who was apparently alerted by one of our policemen and stepped in. If not, I am sure Biebow would have killed Rumkowski right on the spot.

In August 1944 I was deported, together with my family, to Auschwitz. From there later on to Stutthof and eventually to Dresden. Ironically it was Hans Biebow who was again in charge of the Munitions factory in Dresden, Schandauerstrasse 68.

In April 1945 we started on the "death-march" and arrived after marching for two weeks in Theresienstadt where we were liberated on May 8, 1945.

I am a member of the Vancouver Holocaust Centre and have given oral (videotaped) and written testimony about the Holocaust the way I experienced it. My son and daughter belong to our "Second Generation" group and are actively involved.

I would be happy to hear from you. Thank you again for having made public our sufferings. The world must know and never forget.

Sincerely yours

Bronia Sonnenschein

P.S. Since I do not have a mailing address for Mr. L. Dobroszycki I would appreciate if you could possibly forward a copy of this letter to him with my gratitude and appreciation.

The Jewish Heritage Writing Project
150 Franklin Street, #1W
New York, N.Y.

August 15, 1990

Dear Ms. Sonnenschein,

Thank you for your letter, for taking the interest and involvement to read my book and then write to me about your life in the ghetto. Can you tell me what had so enraged Biebow that he beat Rumkowski? And if there are any responses you have to my "On Rumkowski" piece, which barely articulates issues and is not even a start working on this man. But from your letter, it seems your mind and language have engaged this. If you have written anything, or would like to write to me again, I would like to read what you have to say.

Sincerely,

Alan Adelson

August 30, 1990

Mr. Alan Adelson
Executive Director
The Jewish Heritage Writing Project
150 Franklin St. #1W
New York, N.Y. 10013

Dear Mr. Adelson:

Thank you for showing interest in my letter. First of all I wish to answer your question with regard to Rumkowski being attacked by Biebow. There was no reason, no provocation, Biebow did not need any reason to beat up Rumkowski; to him Rumkowski, although the appointed leader of the Ghetto was, after all, just another Jew. Biebow was just drunk — maybe bad news from home, somebody higher up stepping on his toes, nobody knows, he just had to vent his anger, get drunk and beat up a Jew.

As to the man Rumkowski was, please let me tell you a little bit about the way I saw him. For us, his "subjects", Rumkowski was a person who demanded respect and trust, as well as total obedience. We had to trust him, he was the only one to lead us, to save the Ghetto. We realized that we had to help him in his task, to make the Ghetto work, not only to please him, but to try to stay alive as long as possible. He was obsessed with his mission, he demanded the greatest sacrifices from us — "give me the best you have, give me your children" — Biebow's orders. It was totally inhuman — the children did not go alone, needless to say. The Ghetto was in mourning and still Rumkowski extracted from us the best work, to fill every order the workshops were given to the best of our ability, just so that we might have a chance to survive.

Even a condemned man clings to hope till the very last minute, grasps at every straw. This is what we did, what Rumkowski demanded from us.

But I also would like it to be known that nobody but Rumkowski, nobody in his so-called "inner circle" would have stood up to Biebow the way he did. I did not only hear Biebow shouting through closed doors "either you give me what I want, or the whole Ghetto goes" — no idle threats, believe me — but Rumkowski's shouting and pleading as well.

Often, very often, Biebow and his troops stormed into the Ghetto, picked up people from the streets, loaded them into trucks, never to be seen again. He thought nothing of it, once storming our hospital and throwing patients out the window into waiting trucks.

That Rumkowski, his personal secretary Dora Fuchs and members of his "inner circle" did not suffer from hunger and cold the way we did, well, let history judge him on that.

On a lighter note, permit me to show you also one of the ways Rumkowski perceived his "domain", the Ghetto. To him the Ghetto was a state within a state. And a state should have a newspaper, the Ghetto-Zeitung (gazette). You mentioned in your book Szmuel Rozensztain. He was the man responsible for the newspaper and I was given by Rumkowski the task of translating this paper into German. The paper could not "hit the streets" before the Gestapo Commandant, Fuchs, had an exact translation of it for which I was responsible. And whenever Rumkowski wanted something it had to be done. If he asked "jump" you did not ask "why", you asked how high?

I remember many nights sitting up with Mr. Rozensztain laboring over this paper. It was somehow a case of the blind leading the blind. Mr. Rozensztain did not speak German and my Yiddish was rather limited. But we did it. Needless to say I was greatly relieved when the paper folded. It did not last too long.

In moments when there was a certain calm in the Ghetto, no transports coming in, no deportations, Rumkowski in a lighter mood remarked, "*das Ghetto klappt wie ein Zeigerl*" (the Ghetto functions like a clock).

A popular song "praising" Rumkowski, especially when we received a special ration of potatoes (later on only potato peels) was at such times "*Inser Praeses Chaim, is a Mensch a gitter, men wird noch essen in die Ghetto Semmerlech mit Bitter*" (Our President Chaim is a good man, there will come a time in the Ghetto when we will eat buns with butter).

It never came to that, of course. But you can see, we were still holding out, still hoping. And Rumkowski continued to be revered, hated and loved.

I personally believe that it was thanks to Rumkowski that I lasted in the Ghetto together with my family for four years — until the transport to Auschwitz.

Sure, we starved, sure, we suffered and went through agonies, but we made it.

Thank you for letting me share my memories with you, sad as they may be.

Sincerely,

Bronia Sonnenschein

Scenes from the Shoah

Bronia Sonnenschein

A Child of the Ghetto

AND I REMEMBER SHMULEK. A little four-year old boy with light brown, wavy hair and the saddest eyes I had ever seen.

Shmulek and his father, a shoemaker, lived in the same house in the Ghetto where we lived. His mother had died before. When his father left home early to work, little Shmulek was obviously left alone.

Every time I encountered him, either before going to work or returning, I said hello to him but there was absolutely nothing I could have done for this little boy. And then the day came in 1942 when the Gestapo entered the Ghetto to round up children, newborns till ten years old. Shmulek's dad was holding his little boy's hand tightly. They had only each other. It came as no surprise when little Shmulek was separated from his father and taken with the other children, becoming a statistic.

His father's hand was still outstretched, but his little boy was not clutching it anymore. When my mother looked in on him later on, this poor man was dead, mercifully so. There really was no reason for him to live. He had died of "a broken heart".

Little Shmulek — here we would have called him probably Sammy – never had the chance to grow up. I often think of him. He never in his short life tasted chocolate, had ice-cream or belonged to the Little League. He was Jewish and became one of the one and a half million children killed during the Holocaust.

Final Glimpses

WHEN WE WERE SEPARATED UPON ARRIVAL IN AUSCHWITZ, MY mother, sister and I were sure we would not see my father again. Soon after, we women were taken to Stutthof, and so was he.

It was only during roll calls, taking place on a large field,

when all of us could see across the barbed wire the group of
men. They wore striped prison clothes and strange-looking caps.
We had fleeting looks at each other, my father attempting to
wave at us. After a few days we could not spot him again, a sure sign
that he was gone. We never knew, nor will we ever know, how
he was killed. Needless to say, he became a statistic. But we
continued to "hang in" as he always told us to.
His name is inscribed on a memorial at a Jewish cemetery in
Vancouver.

Aunt Mila

MY BELOVED AUNT, "Tante Mila", was Mathilde Kawalek (née
Hollenberg). She was deported from Vienna to the Lodz Ghetto
in late 1941, where she was re-united with my family. Later, she
was transported to Auschwitz and Stutthof with us.

In Stutthof, in the barracks, several hundred of us were
sitting having our soup when the guard came, and picked out
Tante Mila and Bozena Strauss, my mother-in-law. They stood
up, proud as soldiers, and walked with her; I'm sure they knew
where they were going. They hadn't finished their soup that we'd
waited for all night (usually served around 11, after roll call) and
that was it. We sat stunned. Some people finished the soup they
had left. I guess that's the first time we lost our appetite.

In the Ghetto, Tante Mila had a deck of cards and enjoyed
playing solitaire in the evenings after work. She was a kind and
warm-hearted person with a wonderful nature, believing in a
good outcome. So it was no wonder that when the cards worked
in her favor, she would pronounce happily, "You see, I'll see my
boys again." When not, she said, "the cards are silly anyway."
She and my uncle, my mother's eldest brother, had twin sons
who were fortunate to be among the last Jewish students to
graduate from the University in Vienna, in the faculty of medi-
cine. They escaped to England and managed to go to the U.S.
One of them, Roman Kawalek, joined the American Army, be-

coming a captain as a medic. As I learned from him after the war, his mind was always on saving his mother. These thoughts were with him when he fought on the beaches of Normandy. By that time, our beloved Tante Mila was gone, also becoming a statistic. Roman became a well-known physician in New Jersey, and I renewed the warm friendship I had enjoyed with my cousin in Vienna. He visited for a couple of joyous family occasions, and regaled us with such stories as how he played tennis with Norman Schwartzkopf. Roman passed away in 1998 and was buried with full military honors at Arlington cemetery. His son and two daughters live in America with their families. Roman's twin brother, Marcel, who had gone on to become a children's psychiatrist in California (and whom we had visited there) had passed away some years before.

Until the last moment, I had frequently asked Tante Mila if she really believed it would ever end and we would survive. She would reply, "my child, it isn't dark enough yet." "Can it get any darker?", I asked. "It can ... when it's totally dark, the light will come again."

Roman in Normandy.

Mila with her sons in Vienna.

My Friend Mary

MARY SCHIFFLINGER and I worked together in a small office of the Ghetto administration facing each other across the desk. We spent more time together than with our families, since "normal" office hours were not the norm in this environment. There was a small iron heater in the middle of this room on whose top Mary used to "toast" her bread which she had sliced with a razor blade to make two slices out of one. No wonder those two slices were paper thin and no wonder that they burned nine out of ten times. Mary being my friend, I ended up sharing my bread with her.

Together Mary and I witnessed when Hans Biebow, the German administrator, once beat up Rumkowski, the Jewish administrator, by knocking his head against the heater, while being totally drunk and out of control [see pages 29 and 32]. Together we also witnessed when the children were taken away during the deportation from the Ghetto in September 1942, together we starved, together we were clinging to the only people we wanted to live for: Mary to her sister and mother, me to my family. We were together in the freight car taking us to Auschwitz and from there on to Stutthof where first Mary's sister and then her mother died (were killed). Like Shmulek's father, so too Mary had lost the will to live, and when I did not see her at the roll call, I knew I had lost my dear friend. Maybe I am the only one to remember Mary, the only one who will not forget her.

The Promise

IT WAS IN THE CONCENTRATION CAMP STUTTHOF in late fall, maybe early winter (clocks and calendars did not exist in the camps) that we, the inmates, made a promise.

All of us had already experienced Nazi brutality for four years, committed by Hitler's followers, vicious people who had descended from humanity from the very moment that Hitler created the "Third Reich".

All of us had been robbed of our spirits in Auschwitz, and fighting to stay alive by sheer willpower became more difficult with each passing moment.

The lights were turned off for the night we spent lying on the bare floor of the place, body pressed upon body wearing our rags that we never changed. Our wooden shoes replaced a pillow.

I do not know which of the women, there were so many of us, thought that we should promise to tell the world what they, the Nazis, did to us, should anyone of us survive. And we did. The promise was passed on from one of the women to the other. We did not see each other's faces, it was not necessary; we did not know each other's name, it was not necessary either. It was not signed by witnesses and lawyers and yet it was a sacred promise. We never met each other. I kept my promise and I'll keep on telling future generations what happened behind barbed wire. "Tell them." I won't forget, I'll always remember.

The Slap

ON THE DEATH MARCH FROM DRESDEN in April 1945, not knowing where it would end, not knowing when it would end, contributed greatly to our despair. We had already experienced years in the Lodz ghetto, then our stay in Auschwitz, followed by Stutthof and Dresden, and were weakened by hunger and devoid of hope.

It was not only the hunger, it was thirst as well. I was burning up. Although we were "permitted" to drink from the river Elbe, the same river where the bodies of those having collapsed were thrown, I simply could not do it. Maybe I had fallen into a stupor, maybe I had taken leave of my senses, when I asked one of the guards for a little bit of water.

His answer was a vicious slap in my face. It was not only the physical hurt, it was demeaning, an assault on one's soul. It also jolted me into consciousness — a reverse reaction. I was more than ever determined to live in the face of evil.

Glimmers of Kindness

SEPTEMBER 11, 2001 was the day thousands were killed by terrorists, evil people for whom the sanctity of life does not mean much, who know only brutal force. Many thousands since have been grieving their loved ones.

On this day the world witnessed not only hatred, but miraculously also compassion. People who risked their lives hoping to help: firemen, police, the man on the street, government officials. And my thoughts went back many years ago. I remember there were among the enemies, the Nazi killers, just a few who showed human compassion for us, the inmates of the concentration camp and death camp. One of them was from the military (I don't know or even knew then his rank) who went around the long table where we ate the tasteless, unsalted soup. He sprinkled salt that he obviously had in his pocket on the soup while whispering "it will get better." Somehow the killers found out; after a short while we heard a shot ringing out and the only person there trying to give us not only salt but a bit of hope was never seen again.

On the death march we noticed people opening their windows, clapping and shouting wildly, guards telling them we were a bunch of murderers and thieves. Yet again there was an old, frail woman, a basket with slices of bread in her hand to distribute to what she so rightly assumed were people in dire need. The guards brutally pushed us away, she nearly fell, she wanted to help. And there was one more. He was a guard in Auschwitz who whispered whenever he had an occasion, "Lasst das Wassertrinken nach" – don't drink the water. Somehow he wanted to warn us, he knew why it was dangerous. He also knew that we were burning up with thirst. There was nothing more that he could do.

And so on this first anniversary of September 11, I am thinking not only of brutal force, but am thinking of those who helped, risking their lives so that others might have a chance to live. May they rest in peace.

Stutthof

SOMETIME IN SEPTEMBER 1944 (calendars and clocks did not exist in camps so I cannot pinpoint exact dates) we, the prisoners, were taken to the camp in Stutthof, where we were placed in a very large room. All it had were windows on each side, nothing else but the bare floor where we ate and slept. This room was filled to capacity with prisoners, we slept on the floor, body pressed next to body like sardines in a tin. Our daily food-ration consisted of one watery soup (red beets, kohlrabi), one slice of bread, coffee (ersatz) to be shared by five. This food-ration was consistent in all camps. Washrooms, with a door, became distant memories.

The lice came with us from Auschwitz. We were given time during the day to have a so-called "Laus-Appel" to kill the lice on our bodies, they actually crawled on our clothing that became in time just rags since we never changed them and were not able to keep clean. We attended roll-call from dawn to dusk and to enliven it were ordered to perform exercises, like knee-bends, raising arms and so on. The guards were standing by with whips.

Arrival in Auschwitz

This and the following piece were transcribed from some of Paula Lenga's statements in a 90-minute audio interview conducted in 1978 by Meyer Freedman with Paula and Bronia: our only record of Paula speaking of her Holocaust experiences.

THEY TOOK US TO THE SHOWER AND SHAVED US. There was no mirror so we couldn't see how we looked. I was with a very good friend — we looked at each other — and started to laugh so hysterically. We looked like monkeys, it was such a hysterical laugh, I will never forget it. She was really a very dear friend.

Another incident soon after arriving, was standing at a gate and crying. A kapo talked to me and I told him my husband had been taken away on the other side. He asked my husband's name which I gave him. After the war I found out from my husband that he had all of a sudden heard his name called out. He didn't know if he should do anything, but decided to answer. The kapo told him, listen, don't be scared, I just wanted to tell you I spoke to your wife, and she is all right. He was even so good, he gave him extra clothes.

Scarlet Fever

THERE WAS A SECOND MIRACLE (the first was that I found my father in Poland) — I got scarlet fever, which can be fatal and very contagious. This was a time when we slept side by side, mother covering from one side, my sister from the other side. I had a high fever, and an inmate in the camp who was a doctor couldn't do anything. He said to mother, please don't show that she is sick — if they find out they will take her away. So with high fever, I was standing in freezing weather at 4 o'clock in the morning for that counting again. I couldn't stand very straight, and my sister was standing in front, mother in the back, to give a little support so I shouldn't collapse. It was such terrible pain, it starts in the throat, I couldn't breathe. After a week or so, my whole body started peeling, like a snake, the time when it is most contagious. Nobody caught the sickness.

Katya

This and the next two pieces were transcribed from audio interviews conducted by Bronia's son in 2003. "Granny" refers to Bronia's mother, Emily.

IT WAS 1944 AND WE WERE IN STUTTHOF, and there was a woman guard, a 17-year old, beautiful looking girl from Slovakia; Katya was her name. And Katya was extremely cruel to the inmates. Once the order came and she said that all the women — we were only women in there — over a certain age — I don't remember the age — should step forward. Later on we learned never to do anything out of our own free will. We were so used to obeying orders, and when Granny stepped forward because she was in that age group, when Katya saw her she stretched out her hand and slapped Granny — I mean viciously across the face. "What are you doing here?!", she said. "You don't belong here, get out of here!" And Granny joined the other ones, prisoners like us.

Later on, much later on, we found out these people who were really in that age group were taken to the gas chambers. And so we figured that Katya knew that Granny was at that age, and didn't want her to be taken to the gas chamber, for some reason or the other. Maybe she reminded her of her mother, I don't know the reason. Anyway, she saved Granny's life. And that was Katya, a 17-year old girl. So everybody who was lucky enough to have one person, just one, that had a conscience, had the chance to survive, that was it.

I will remember Katya forever. I know she had the most beautiful blond hair, she was a bit of a chubby girl. Everybody was scared of Katya. We figured it out that she had some resemblance ... she didn't know Granny from anyone else. Maybe God wanted Granny to live. You can figure it out anyway you choose. But we know that's how it happened.

From then on, unless we were forced to, we never raised our hand again. It's a lesson you learn the hard way.

Death March

WE MOSTLY SLEPT OUTSIDE, but once they took us to a hole, and they told us we have to go down. Obviously everyone was petrified. We were so afraid to go down there because this where they would take us down and shoot us for sure. There were stairs going down, and it turned out it was a chicken coop, and it smelled absolutely terrible. I'd never seen a chicken coop before. The supper we got that evening was a slice of bread, it was probably mostly sawdust in the bread, and very dark oil, like machine oil. And that was our supper. And we ate it — if you're hungry you eat, even bread with oil.

Another night we were in a stable, where horses used to be. There was not a single horse left. God knows whatever they did with the horses. Well, they had horsemeat. It was only sporadically that we got a slice of bread. Once, they gave us on the death march, soup. It was extremely greasy, it was cold, and not salted. No one could eat that soup because you got terribly sick when you ate it, on an empty stomach, greasy, you could cut it. That's when I found a bone in the soup. I never let go of the bone till we reached Theresienstadt. I know Granny sometimes whispered, "Spit it out, you could swallow it." I said, "Never." I wouldn't let go of that bone. I licked it so clean like a dog licks a bone clean. I imagined I'd get a smell, something out of it.

I remember also the guard, her name was Herta, if I remember correctly, also extremely cruel. Not the SS, another guard. We came to a rest spot and they probably had trucks going with food for the guards. And she said, "Lunch is ready! Noodles with nuts!" It happened to be a dish I really liked a lot. It was so frustrating...here we were starving, looking in garbage cans, sometimes we found an apple or whatever. She tormented us calling out the menu for their lunch. These are little odds and ends or pieces that point out how tremendously cruel they were.

Because they were starving, they had no strength. Today I can't imagine how anyone can march for two weeks, not eat, not sleep properly. I can't figure that out. This is a miracle that some made it, an absolute miracle.

Rita

ON THE DEATH MARCH, escape was almost impossible — it was the main ambition of the SS to prevent escapes. They had means to catch you.

There was a very beautiful girl named Rita, and Rita was very daring. Rita tried to escape. It was a totally hopeless cause. With us was that German woman guard [*see Epilogue*], that crazy woman who told us how she had left her husband and child to follow the Führer — she wouldn't have rested until she found Rita and punished her, to show her who was the boss. We knew who was the boss. This woman made it her life's ambition to catch her, she was after her. She got hold of Rita. The little hair that Rita had grown in was shaved again. The guard tied Rita to a tree, completely naked, pretending like she was Jesus Christ, in the same position, arms outstretched. This guard didn't believe in Jesus Christ or religion — she had only one god: Adolph Hitler.

And Rita stood there all night, soiling herself, and we heard her cry. That girl cried so bitterly, "Mama!, Mama!, help me!" Rita's mother was long gone. To hear that girl helpless, crying in the night, "Mama!, Mama!, help me!" — it could drive you totally insane.

I think if you talked a year about the Holocaust, you couldn't say everything. So many little hidden things ... they go through your head, watching other people ...

Rita apparently made it, I don't know how I found out. I don't know any more about Rita. She survived — God wanted her to survive.

Appointment with Death

Gretl Keren Fischer (1999)

*Following are two excerpts from the novel "An Answer for Pierre",
the first one based on an account Dr. Fischer heard from Bronia
when they were friends in Vancouver. (She now lives in Ottawa.)
Her novel is an impassioned and deeply philosophical study of the
Holocaust and reactions to it.*

"[O]NE DAY Bronia had a bellyache, and it kept her at the latrine
too long and she was late at roll-call, and the little girl-warder
with fashion-model makeup who was in charge of them told her
she'd be punished. And then the girl-warder left the yard,
ostentatiously, as if to consult with someone in authority, and
when she came back, she said to Bronia, 'Tomorrow you'll be
shot.' She said it just like that.... Everybody tried to calm Bronia.
A woman was weeping, and many were angry because Bronia
let herself go so much. They told her if she didn't get on with her
work, she'd only make things worse for herself. And the girl-
warder walked away as if to make more exact inquiries, and
when she came back, she said: 'At half past two. That's definite.
Tomorrow afternoon.'

"Most of the inmates didn't believe her. They were
convinced that girl had no influence in the camp. She was only
threatening people to make their nerves tingle. She liked to
torment them. But the thirty or more hours till half past two next
day, and even later, till three, till four, till Bronia could believe
that it wouldn't happen. ... They had no watches, of course, and
there were no clocks. When the factory whistle blew it must
have been one. She couldn't know whether it was two o'clock
now or half-past two or three. They could come even if it was
only two. And they could come after three. And how could one
be sure even after that turned out to be just an ordinary truck
that had come for the wood.... At sundown her hands were
aching from chopping and stacking wood, and in the dark one
still didn't know ... (How can one ever unmake this?!) And when

they didn't come — did this mean a reprieve? Or were they merely late? There were executions constantly. In front of a camp workshop there was sawdust on the floor, still damp and sticky and brown where police dogs had been set upon a man until he was dead. Perhaps it was only a delay, and they were still coming to take her away. And what was the time? It was driving one mad not to know exactly what the time was. But it didn't matter. They could come any time. Towards morning she began to hope. But then perhaps they had only changed the day...."

Another excerpt, in which a character speaks:

"My mother, my father, my young brother .... and all those others. They had to live with this not just for an instant but for days, weeks, months, even years — who knows?! — the constant threat to be murdered today, tomorrow, to see the people you love 'selected,' torn away to be murdered, and the only choice to die with them, to commit suicide perhaps by provoking the sadists in charge with some trifling disobedience; or to steel oneself with the hope, the desperate will to survive so that one could tell it all, so that perhaps one day one might be able to let the world know. And millions had this will and did not succeed and realized they would never have a chance to tell the world, never be able to accuse, never be able to scream it into the living day, not knowing whether anyone will be left to tell how dastardly, how agonizingly they were done to death. ...."

The Story of Tante Mary

Dan Sonnenschein et al. (2012)

VERY SOON after Germany's annexation of Austria into the Third Reich, Bronia was forced to leave her job as a legal secretary (against the wishes of her employer, who valued her highly), and found a new position as a kindergarten teacher at the school run by Mary Korwill, known affectionately by all as "Tante Mary" (Aunt Mary). Mary's sister Edith also worked as a teacher there.

Bronia very much enjoyed this work and held Tante Mary in great esteem, saying that "[s]he was the guardian angel for the children in her care while their parents were frantically trying to get to the free world after the annexation." (See page 139.) The photo below shows Bronia outside the school, whose sign says, *Privatkindergarten, Sprachschule, Kinder bis 11 Jahre* (Private kindergarten, Language school, Children up to 11 years).

It was not until much later, after reading Martin Gilbert's book on Kristallnacht wherein he quotes from a book on the Riga Ghetto in Latvia, that we learned of Tante Mary's tragic fate.

The death of Mary Korwill is described in *Journey into Terror: The Story of the Riga Ghetto* by Gertrude Schneider, who tells of how the ghetto's vicious ruler, Kurt Krause, who had previously murdered those found bartering goods, changed his policy in the summer of 1942 to lesser punishments for female offenders.

> "Unfortunately, the ghetto commandant's show of clemency came too late for many who had been found guilty of offenses before the summer. In March 1942, for instance, Fleischel, the elder of the Hanover group, caught the Vienna group's school teacher, Mary Korwill, who had owned the well-known Tante Mary Children's Camp in Austria, wearing her gold wristwatch. Just as Fleischel was berating her loudly for 'illegally' owning jewelry, Krause, in one of his bad moods, happened to come out of the big gate leading onto *Berliner Strasse*. On learning of Miss Korwill's 'crime,' he took her directly to the cemetery and shot her. Fleischel and Tante Mary's aged mother were both ordered to watch the execution."

After seeing the four films in the powerful series, *Forgotten Transports*, by Czech filmmaker Lukas Pribyl, I talked to him and we later corresponded briefly. He sent me some notes from an interview with Alzbeta Bergmannova, who succeeded Mary as teacher in the 'Viennese' school in the Riga Ghetto, and told him:

> "Mary Korwill had much experience working with children and though she lacked school materials, she always managed to keep the attention of the kids and make the lessons interesting and fun. Older children had to help younger ones study and since there was little paper, few pens and books, children memorized most of the taught subjects or learned through songs and poems."

Using Bergamonnova's Anglicized name in the following, Schneider writes:

> "The spiritual and cultural leaders of the German ghetto — not necessarily the administrative functionaries, but people like ... Elizabeth Bergmann ... never ceased to impress upon the young people that the first law of resistance was survival. The day-to-day struggle to cope with ghetto conditions required live people, not dead heroes."

Of Tante Mary, she writes that for the two months in Riga before being killed (after being deported there from Vienna along with her mother on January 11, 1942):

"[S]he was very much alive and determined to give each child the proper training for a better future. ... Children were taught poems and ballads; they learned entire passages by heart. Thus, the parents had a treat in store for them, for the children could entertain them in the evening by reciting the poems and singing the songs they had learned at Tante Mary's school. ... Since Tante Mary was an educator with years of experience, the school was quite successful; the children enjoyed going there and made progress in their studies. Tante Mary was strict, but fair. She knew several children in her charge who had attended her camp in Austria, but she did not play favorites. Her untimely death was a traumatic experience for the children, who had spent most of their waking hours each day for two whole months under her guidance."

As may well be imagined, Mary's mother (Elsa) was also very traumatized. Schneider recalls:

The old lady lived on for a long time — until late in the second winter. At times, her mind would wander and she would ask people where her daughter had gone."

My mother wrote to Martin Gilbert after learning in his book of Mary's murder: "Tante Mary's violent death saddened me a lot. She deserved the best that life has to offer and got the worst."

The fate of Mary Korwill's sister, Edith, remains a mystery. Lukas Pribyl wrote to me, "I do know Mary had a sister, that she existed but unfortunately that's about it, I know nothing more ..." My mother may have been the last one to have remembered her.

Cecilia Kawalek, Bronia's maternal grandmother, deported from Vienna to Theresienstadt, and then to her death in Maly Trostenec near Minsk.

Mathilde Kawalek, Bronia's aunt Mila, deported from Vienna to the Lodz Ghetto, and then to Stutthof where she was killed.

Abraham Schwebel, Bronia's father, who endured the Lodz Ghetto and Auschwitz, perished in Stutthof.

Erich Strauss, Bronia's first husband, perished in Stutthof, as did his mother, Bozena.

Inmates of the Lodz Ghetto on a special occasion, probably in 1943.
Front row from left: Abraham and Emilia Schwebel, Paula Schwebel,
Unknown, Bronia, Erich Strauss.

Poster by Bronia's daughter,
Vivian, for her daughter
Emily Talia Sztabzyb's play,
The Treasure, based partly
on Holocaust experiences
of Bronia and Paula, and
performed for the first time
at a Yom Ha'Shoah event
in Calgary in April 2012.

Office staff of the Lodz Ghetto's Jewish administration. Bronia is second from right, with her close friend Mary Schifflinger standing to her right (see page 38).

Paula modeling an outfit as part of her job in a Ghetto clothing factory.

Chaim Rumkowski, Jewish ruler of the Lodz Ghetto, talking to his Gestapo master, Hans Biebow. Note the badges on Rumkowski's jacket. Rumkowski was killed in Auschwitz in 1944; Biebow was hanged in Lodz in 1947.

Emily Schwebel and her daughters in
1945, several months after liberation.

Part 2

*Rebuilding
a Life*

Rebuilding My Life

Bronia Sonnenschein (1997)

MIRACLES DO HAPPEN. I survived the slaughter, the slaughter of six million Jews, one and a half million of them children. Only the three of us, my mother, my sister and I were blessed to hear the young Russian soldier liberating us, telling us that we were free, that we could go home now. It truly was a highly emotional moment. The realization that we had no home to go to, hit us later.

After I was dismissed from the hospital — years of starvation had left their marks — I somehow made it to Prague which is not far from Theresienstadt. I had been given clean clothes in Theresienstadt after finally shedding the ones I had worn in the various concentration camps. That was all I really had. Fortunately, I was able to have found temporary shelter in Prague and food was distributed in various train-stations. The moment I felt strong enough to work I applied for work in a factory that looked for people stuffing vanilla powder for baking in small packages. Not knowing Czech, that was all I could do in the beginning. It simply had to be enough so I could rent a room. Every free moment I had had to be devoted to learn enough Czech to find a better job. I was fortunate to actually be offered a good job at a hops exporting firm. My knowledge of French and English was instrumental in getting this job. I had learned both languages in Vienna.

The joy of working on a job that was challenging and interesting, besides paying reasonably well, was unfortunately short-lived. The communists entered Prague — it was almost like "deja vu" — different uniforms — Russians — different orders, dictatorship all over again. I could no longer work at my job. Yet luck was with me — or was it maybe a miracle? — that I immediately found another job in the American Joint Distribution Committee, a Jewish organization set up to help, if necessary with food, but mainly in facilitating Jewish people to reach the free world, providing they had relatives there to vouch for them not to become a burden to their respective governments. But the real miracle of finding this job was that I met Dr. Kurt Sonnenschein there who was to become my husband. We were married on December 28, 1948 and since the political situation in Prague became worse we realized that we had absolutely no future there. The state of Israel had become established and so we left Prague — it was a nightmare to get out of there — and arrived in Israel in May 1949. Our son Dan was born there in December 1949. In 1949 when we arrived in Haifa, Israel, the situation in this tiny country taking in thousands of refugees, Holocaust survivors, was immensely difficult. I loved and will always love Israel for its courage and determination, but I could not face again the prospect to struggle, especially not when having a baby. Another turn came when my late husband's brother, who had emigrated to Canada a year earlier was able to sponsor us to come to Vancouver where he and his wife had settled down.

We arrived in Vancouver, via a short stay in Göteborg, Sweden, as guests of my husband's friends, and a short stay in New York with my relatives, the ones that got away in time. The three of us arrived in this beautiful city in July 1950. My mother and sister and her husband were soon to follow. We were a family again and our happiness was great when a year later, in July 1951 our little girl was born. My husband had found a job in a lumber company, an office job. Although it did not pay all that much, we were confident we could make it, especially as I hoped to work again once the children were older. My mother always lived with me.

Yet there was still a lot of unhappiness in store for me. On September 1, 1952 we were taken on a ride, by car, to some of Vancouver's surroundings. We never completed that ride. The car we were in was involved in a head-on collision and my husband got killed. My son and I survived; the baby, our little girl, was at home with my mother.

Again I had to start to pick up the pieces of my life. I was given a job in the same place that my husband had worked in and worked there for 25 years. My greatest pride and joy are my children, proof that we made it. It was not easy, but we did. Both my children have university degrees. My elder granddaughter Emily (I have three grandchildren) will start university this fall.

After working 25 years on my job I gave in to my children's wishes to stop working — at least full time — especially since my daughter expected her first child. After a while I realized I can't just sit around. I had lost my mother in 1977; my sister, my very best friend, passed away in 1986. I was the only one left to share my story, their stories as well, about our experiences during the Holocaust with future generations. I became a member of the Vancouver Holocaust Centre Society and have addressed during the last ten years thousands of students of all ages. We have to keep the memory of the Holocaust alive so that it may never happen again.

One of my students was Markus Schirmer whom I met at the University of British Columbia. I am glad we met. We were able to cross barriers, a young German and a Jewish woman.

It is possible for us to get along if we learn to accept each other and to understand each other. Only then can we live side by side in peace. Hatred breeds violence, understanding leads to hope and peace. Let us hope and pray for peace together.

Finding Meaning Again

April 21, 1992

Dr. Viktor Frankl
1 Mariannengasse
Vienna, Austria 1090

Dear Dr. Frankl,

I read your book "Man's Search for Meaning" for the first time in 1969. It opened up my eyes to many questions I had asked myself before. I read the same book a few weeks ago again and understood it even better. My letter should have been written a long, long time ago. But, I believe it is never too late to say thank you for having opened doors for me I had never entered before.

Please allow me to introduce myself briefly to you. Until 1939 I lived in Vienna with my parents and my sister. The "Anschluss" on March 13, 1938 changed our life drastically, as it did for so many thousands of Jews. We loved Vienna deeply, but the nightmare began. We ended up in the Ghetto in Lodz, Poland where we existed (you can't call it "living") till August 1944 when we were deported to Auschwitz, from there on to Stutthof, then on to a forced labor camp to Dresden. In April 1945 we started our death-march from Dresden and ended up in Theresienstadt where we were liberated on May 8, 1945.

I am enclosing a copy of a recently published article in our newspaper describing certain events. Maybe you will find it interesting. The quote I read in your book "Man's Search for Meaning" (I had never actually read publications by Nietzsche) was and is the best answer as to why the three of us survived. (My father was killed in Stutthof.) We had a "why" to live for ...

Please forgive me for having written to you in English.
Although German, or shall I say "Wienerisch" is my mother
language, it became rather rusty after having lived in Canada
for 42 years and very little, or almost no occasion to speak or
write in German. I understand it, of course and will never
forget it. But I don't seem to be as fluent in it anymore.
I wish you continuing health and happiness.

Sincerely yours,

Bronia Sonnenschein

Translation of reply

April 27, 1992

Dear Mrs. Sonnenschein,

Many thanks for your letter which I received today — the
anniversary of my liberation from the last concentration camp.
Your words mean a lot to me, as you must have lived
through similar experiences and your praise for my book is
encouragement for me. With best wishes,

Yours,

Dr. Frankl

January 23, 1995

Dear Dr. Frankl,

I sincerely hope that my letter will reach you in good health.
The year 1995 marks a milestone for all of us who so miraculously survived the Holocaust, although it is still a few months
away from our actual liberation date, for you, as you once wrote
to me, the 27th of April, for me the 8th of May. I still think of the
day when a young Russian soldier, our liberator, told us "you
are free." I can practically hear him, feel the silence following his
words. There was absolutely no strength left to shout with joy.
Besides, all of us had forgotten what joy was. But there were
tears, an ocean of tears. Only slowly did it sink in — never a
"Zaehlappel" again, no more beatings, no more hunger, no more
Kapos, no more fear.

It is another miracle that we, the survivors of the "K.Z."
were able to take our rightful place in society. To prove to ourselves, to prove to the world, how much each one of us could
and would be able to enrich other people's lives, each of us in our
own way. I am in awe of your accomplishments. You certainly
were able to capture the world at large with your teachings, your
lectures, your books.

We fought hard not only to survive, but to keep our sanity
as well. There is you, Elie Wiesel, Samuel Pisar, the late Primo
Levi and many others, just to name a few.

This is why I so strongly felt to write to you and share with
you my thoughts on the 50th anniversary of our liberation.

I wish you health and happiness always.

Yours,

Bronia Sonnenschein

Seeing Past Hate

Claudia Cornwall (1992)

*This article was published in The Vancouver Sun's
Saturday Review on April 11, 1992. Claudia met
Bronia while doing research for her book, "Letter
from Vienna: A Daughter Uncovers Her Family's
Jewish Past" (which won a B.C. Book Prize).*

"I'VE DRAGGED IT ALL OVER THE WORLD — to Prague, Israel, the United States and now here. I really believe in it," she says.

The letter is more than 45 years old and covered by a protective sheet of rice paper. When Bronia Sonnenschein unwraps it, I see that it is typed and single spaced, about a page and half long. In the folds, the yellowed paper is torn and some sentences are obliterated. "If there were a fire," she explains, "it's the first thing I would save."

Bronia is Jewish.

In April 1945 she was in Dresden, waiting for her transport to leave. She had already survived much — the Lodz ghetto and concentration camps at Auschwitz, Stutthof and Pirna. For the previous few weeks she had been working in a forced labor camp rebuilding a munitions factory. "I still remember the address, Schandauerstrasse 68."

Bronia was standing in a long line outside the factory among about a thousand inmates. The Soviets were just outside the city and the Germans had decided to move these Jewish prisoners rather than relinquish them.

"We weren't told where we were going or why. We only knew that we had to leave." Suddenly a woman rushed up to her and thrust a piece of paper into her hands. "Take it. This will protect you," she whispered.

Quickly Bronia stuffed the letter into her blouse. The contact was over in an instant. "If the guards had seen, the consequences would have been catastrophic for both of us."

The woman who ran up to Bronia was a gentile who had been in charge of the camp kitchen, Mrs. Upschat. "She didn't know my name because we were only allowed numbers. But she knew my face because I had sometimes worked for her."

Bronia did not read the letter. It was too dangerous. "But the mere fact that someone wanted to protect me in the midst of that tremendous hatred ... I treated it like a talisman, like something holy."

Bronia had another secret beside the one that was concealed under her clothes. Her mother and younger sister were trudging along with her.

"If the guards had known they would have separated us immediately." But they never found out. "We all looked horrible anyway. Our heads were shaved, we were exhausted. No one noticed any family resemblance."

It was cold that spring as the transport moved south along the Elbe River. There was no food or shelter and the air was thick with Allied bombs. Clearly the war was coming to an end. But Bronia did not know whether she would live to see peace, and after days of marching, she hardly cared.

Her sister, Paula, asked, "Why don't we jump in the river? It would be so easy." Bronia recalls that she had agreed with her, but she wanted to tell their mother before they took the plunge.

"Just wait one more day," their mother pleaded. "Tomorrow is Paula's birthday." Bronia and her sister agreed to wait.

The next day the transport reached the Theresienstadt ghetto, near Prague. The administration was in chaos. The SS guards fled, leaving them with the few Jews still alive. "We were given sugar cubes. We could shower and put on clean clothes."

On May 8, 1945, a young Russian soldier rode his horse into Theresienstadt and said: "You are free, you can go home now."

I look at Bronia in wonder. She is slim, petite, pretty. She smiles frequently and her large blue eyes light up when she talks of her grandchildren. "Tough" is not an adjective that springs to mind.

She tells me her story in the living room of her apartment. Bright and warm, it is full of china figurines, pictures painted by her daughter and photographs of her family.

I sit on a chair covered in a small flowered print, drinking tea and eating meringue cookies. Bronia calls them *Nuss Pusserln*. This is Viennese dialect, not listed in my pocket German-English dictionary. She says it means, "A little nut kiss".

Despite all that happened, Bronia still likes Viennese music, and a waltz makes her feel like dancing. "I probably shouldn't feel that way," she says with a rueful shrug.

I touch her letter, brushing my fingers over it very slowly. It seems so old and fragile.

At the top, in German, are the words, "In the Name of the Father, the Son, and the Holy Ghost."

If you believe in its power, the letter promises, it will protect you and those around you from all harm.

"I didn't read it," says Bronia, "until after liberation. I was never alone."

"When you learned what it said," I ask, "did you think it strange that Mrs. Upschat gave you a Christian letter?"

"Oh no. I thought of it as a blessing. It could have been any religion — Chinese, Japanese."

"When I talk about my experiences, I always mention Mrs. Upschat," Bronia says. She often goes to schools and colleges. Every May she participates in a symposium about the Holocaust.

Sometimes the students ask whether she hates the Germans. "No," she explains. "I am uncomfortable with them. But I don't hate them. I have seen what hate can do."

This year, Holocaust Remembrance Day falls on April 30. Bronia will be one of six Holocaust survivors to light a candle in a commemorative ceremony in Vancouver.

Bronia Sonnenschein and Noam Dolgin light one of six candles to commemorate "Kristallnacht" at the Beth Israel Synagogue during the annual commemorative event, on November 9, 1995.

The Meaning of Yom Ha'Shoah

Bronia Sonnenschein (1991)

O N APRIL 11, 1991 we will again observe Yom Ha'Shoah. We will put a stone next to the name of a loved one which has been inscribed by us on the monument in the Schara Tzedeck cemetery, and we will honour their memory.

In unison we will recite the Kaddish and spend some time recalling not only the horror they had to live through, the brutal way in which they were killed, but also the good and happy times we shared with them.

Yom Ha'Shoah is a time to reflect, to come together, to show that we share each other's sorrow, that there is a common bond. Together we will pay tribute to the survivors in our community and together we will honour the memory of the victims of the Holocaust.

Although it is now forty-six years since the Jews of Europe have been liberated from German concentration camps and the open wounds have become scars — scars that will never quite heal — it is our sacred duty to recall the Holocaust with all its horror year after year so the world shall never forget the inhuman treatment our people suffered at the hands of the Nazis, the great sorrow of a people Hitler tried to wipe out.

In every corner of the world there are — thanks God — still survivors left whose voices can be heard; once these voices will be stilled our sons and daughters will carry on with the tradition to observe Yom Ha'Shoah. Hitler's victims shall never be forgotten and the tragedy that has befallen our people shall never be erased from our memory.

Bronia and her mother, Emily,
enjoying life in post-war Prague.

Bronia with young friends.

Emilia Schwebel
in 1948.

Emilia Schwebel enjoying life again soon after the war,
in the resort Marianske Lazny (Marienbad), near Prague.

Paula Lenga
soon after
the war.

Paula Lenga enjoying life again, in 1946.

The joy of life: Bronia in Marianske Lazny, a spa resort she loved. The upper photos may have been from another such resort, Karlovy Vary (Karlsbad).

Bronia in her new life in Prague, several years after her liberation.

Marriage to Dr. Kurt Sonnenschein in Prague.

Bronia with her husband, Kurt Sonnenschein, in Prague, Spring 1949.

Paradise in a Vancouver backyard.

Bronia and
her children.

Paula Lenga with her
niece and nephew.

Emily Schwebel and
her daughters, on a
Mother's Day outing.

Bronia enjoying a happy time with her family in Vancouver.
From left to right: Ann Morse (aunt), Bronia, Paula (sister), a guest,
Vivian (daughter), Dan (son), Emily (mother), Stan (brother-in-law).

With eldest
grandchild,
Emily.

Emily Schwebel, "Granny" as we knew her, in her kitchen (she was a wonderful cook and baker). This last photograph was taken by Dr. Ben Herman, Vivian's fiancé. Sadly, she died several months before the wedding. Her name lives on.

Stan Lenga, husband of Paula, survived similar ordeals; they reunited in Bergen Belsen in 1945. Stan was a businessman and a natural comedian.

Paula Lenga with a Russian immigrant at the Vancouver Jewish Family Service Agency. After Paula's death in 1986, this agency honored her dedication by instituting an annual Paula Lenga award for exemplary volunteer service. She was also a talented fashion illustrator and hardworking businesswoman devoted to her family.

Bronia with her grandchildren at the Bayshore Inn in July, 1991.

Part 3

*Years of
Teaching*

Letters on Oral Testimony

May 11, 1990

Dear Dr. Krell,

I wish to thank you for having encouraged me to give testimony about the five years of horror in the Ghetto and various concentration camps. As my interviewer you were extremely helpful guiding me step by step to recall my experiences during those years — starting way back in Vienna in 1938.

My only fear now is that focusing on my pain and suffering I did not pay enough tribute to all the people in the Ghetto whose life I shared, whose pain and suffering I felt, whose passing I mourned. Together we struggled to make the Ghetto work until we were reduced to animals ready to be slaughtered.

Agony can't be described. It is as impossible as describing a blue sky, vibrant colours, a flower to a blind person or music to the one who is deaf.

But I will always remember my fellow inmates whose life had touched mine. They won't be forgotten!

Thank you,

Bronia Sonnenschein

May 22, 1990

Dearest Bronia,

Forgive me for calling you by your first name without
an invitation to do so. However, I feel we have gotten to
know each other.

Therefore, you should also not write to me as Dr. Krell.
Rob, Robert or Robbie will do fine.

Your letter of May 11, 1990 expressing concern that you
perhaps did not pay enough tribute to the people of the
Ghetto, is itself a most touching tribute.

In writing your memoirs and providing an eyewitness
account you have done precisely what your fellow Ghetto
inmates would have hoped for, that someone would survive
and bear witness.

Your memories have lent new dignity to their lives and
have ensured they shall indeed not be forgotten.

I shall cherish your letter.

With respect and thanks,

Robert Krell, M.D.

Bronia Sonnenschein (July 1990)

C ERTAIN SEGMENTS OF MY ORAL TESTIMONY given on May 9, 1990 should be clarified.

In the first part of my statement regarding my upbringing as a Jewish child I wish to state that referring to my "secular" upbringing should in no way diminish the fact that I — and, of course, my whole family, was aware of the fact that not only were we Jewish, but that our faith was something to be cherished and proud of. We were raised as Jewish children living in a Christian world, yet at the same time enjoying the same living conditions, the same standards, the same "joie de vivre" as our non-Jewish neighbours, acquaintances, schoolmates did. Contrary to now we did not have to be on guard constantly. Pogroms in Russia and well before that the Spanish inquisition was something we read about, but it did not affect us. The Holocaust has changed all that. For us, the European Jews, who lived through it, we carry the scars of this unspeakable experience with us. Not only that, but I personally erected an invisible barrier between myself and the Christian world. I do not trust them anymore. I don't live in a dreamworld anymore the way I lived in Vienna when I was young. I am now much more aware of who I am and what I am. I became, in a way, the guardian of my religion, of my people.

In the second segment of my testimony referring to the Ghetto in Lodz and the deportation to Auschwitz I believe I did not stress enough the horrifying impression I had upon arriving in Auschwitz. It was difficult to talk about it, difficult to describe the feeling of standing stark naked together with hundreds of other women on the square in Auschwitz being inspected by what I later found out was Mengele, the man with the piercing eyes, the whip in one hand and with the other hand squeezing our breast in order to determine if anyone among us was pregnant. I did not quite understand at this particular moment what he meant when with a flick of his thumb he sent us either to the right or to the left. How could one understand at this very moment that it meant life or death? I was too bewildered, too scared being shaved (all bodily hair) and pushed under the shower to realize what happened to those women who had the slightest scar on their body, who had grey hair and who had children in their arms or clinging to them. Could a normal-thinking person comprehend that these women and children were in Mengele's opinion unfit to live? That they were to be gassed and burned? I referred to "bunkbeds" in Auschwitz, but I used the wrong word. There were no "beds" in concentration camps. In Auschwitz they had "bunks" in contrast to Stutthof where we sat and slept on the bare floor. Maybe it was just psychological that I thought bunks were better than the floor because they were elevated.

As far as Theresienstadt being the final destination of our death-march is concerned, I wish to stress a very important point. The Germans did not deliver us to Theresienstadt in order to get us to a safe haven. Far from that — Theresienstadt which at one point was regarded as the "model Ghetto", the one that was shown to the Red Cross, was to be the final setting to eliminate the sad remainder of the inmates of various concentration camps and labour camps. Theresienstadt with all its inmates was to be blown up at the beginning of May (I don't know the exact date). That the German guards left us at the entrance to Theresienstadt was not an act of "kindness"; it was to obey the last diabolical command.

God was with us as it was already too late in the game for the Germans to set this plan in motion.

I hope by attaching this appendix to my testimony I will have clarified a few points to the best of my knowledge and recollection.

Comments on Recorded Testimony

Bronia Sonnenschein (January, 1992)

F OR WELL OVER 40 YEARS I had not been able to share my experiences during the Holocaust with outsiders, as a matter of fact, not even talked at great length about them with my children. For us survivors the clock keeps ticking speedily. And so, upon the encouragement of my son and daughter and the encouragement of Dr. Robert Krell, I finally agreed to relate these experiences on videotape.

My interviewer was Dr. Krell who guided me expertly during this session. I must confess, it was an overwhelming experience and the only regret I had afterwards was that I might not have succeeded in relating the trauma, the hurt, the incredible suffering of all my fellow inmates as well as it should have been done.

But since then, talking about the tragedy of the Jewish people during the darkest years when Hitler was in power, I have overcome my initial fear of not only confronting an audience, but myself as well, with my past experience. To talk about the unspeakable is never easy.

With the help of the original videotape and another one that was taken recently during a session I had with high-school students, teaching them about the Holocaust has become the most important task I had set myself. I believe it justifies my own survival — we tend to ask ourselves the question "why did I survive while six million of our people were so brutally killed?"

In the light of rising anti-Semitism, Holocaust denial, hate literature, it is, therefore, of utmost importance that the voices of survivors will be heard, that our testimony will be recorded on videotape and last long after we have gone. It is, after all, the most effective, if not only tool we have to combat hate against the Jewish people.

Only then will our promise, to keep the memory of all the victims of the Holocaust alive, be fulfilled.

Holocaust Awareness Day at Camp Hatikvah

Bronia Sonnenschein (1990)

YOM HA'SHOAH DAY AT CAMP HATIKVAH STARTED WITH THE raising of the flags, Canadian and Israeli, at halfmast. A significant beginning to what became a very meaningful day. Programs for the entire day were designed by Dror Balshine and Ron Ezekiel. Both of them deserve a lot of credit, as well as the counsellors who wrote and performed by impersonating certain characters by not only talking like them, but dressing as well and looking like them. They went to great details and did a perfect job.

My part in this worthwhile endeavor was to give a talk about my experiences during the Holocaust, to relate to them as a survivor what it was all about. My first talk in the morning was directed at the younger group, eight to twelve years old. The second talk to the older group, thirteen and up, took place in the afternoon. I was given enough time, each talk was approximately two hours long, which included a question and answer period. This way I was able to explain to the children how it all started, for me way back in 1938 in Vienna. With the younger group I began by reciting the words that I had recited so many years ago during a Purim play, when nobody even had heard of Hitler. I was ten or eleven years old at that time. I will repeat it here so you too can understand the significance of it:

"And if in the distant future a Haman should rise again,
bringing death and destruction to our people, then let the memory
of this day give us hope and belief in hours of danger,
and may we never lose the conviction that God will
always be with us, as He was with us today."

I then continued to explain to the campers about another tyrant, Adolf Hitler, and what his plans for the Jews were. I described life in the Ghetto, in Poland, the way we worked so very hard for so little food we received in return. I tried to explain what hunger means, how it hurts and how valiantly we tried to keep up our spirit — and yet how many of us died in the Ghetto. I explained briefly — keeping always in mind that I had to deal with young children — about deportations from the Ghetto and finally our ride in a cattle car to the concentration camp Auschwitz. On these subjects too I touched only briefly. But it had to be said, nevertheless, and gas chambers and crematoria had to be mentioned. I moved on to my next destination, concentration camp Stutthof, without dwelling on it too much. I talked about the forced labor camp in Dresden, Germany, and the long march that took us later on from Dresden to yet another Ghetto in Theresienstadt, Czechoslovakia, where we were at last liberated on May 8, 1945 — we were told that we are free again.

The children listened attentively and asked many questions. I know no harm came to them listening to me, they were soon caught up in other programs relating to the Holocaust, and later on all of them enjoyed their lunch, a happy, boisterous affair.

With the older group I could obviously get into more details. I could actually feel the way they responded to me, how deeply touched they were and how much they appreciated learning about my experiences and my feelings living through those difficult years. I told them that we struggled hard not to let them kill our spirit during those four years in the Ghetto. I mentioned that occasionally talented musicians gave a concert for us, that for a little while we could forget the ugliness of the Ghetto, that for a "brief shining moment" we could actually enjoy their music just as much as they enjoyed playing for us. It did not happen too often. I just wanted to bring out — and I believe I did — how strong we Jews are and how strong we always have to be.

Since they were so attentive I felt they deserved also to be told about my very personal experience. The one where a German woman thrust a letter in my hand before we had to leave the forced labor camp in Dresden. This letter was called a "Schutzbrief", a letter that means to protect the person in whose possession it was and who believed in it, from bullets, from water, from fire, from enemies. I told them that I believed in it for the simple reason that it was given to me in good faith at a time when we were surrounded by hatred — and that I still have this letter. I carried it with me on our death-march from Dresden which ended when we arrived in the Ghetto Theresienstadt. I also mentioned that I strongly believed that it was the miracle that my mother had hoped and prayed for during the long march that got us finally, half dead, but still alive to this point, to live to see the day when a young Russian soldier told us that we are free, the day of liberation on May 8, 1945.

I answered all their questions as well as I could. Before concluding my talk I just asked them to be strong, to believe in themselves and to continue to be proud of who they are and what they are — I am. For the rest of the day I was delighted to listen to their excellent program and I still had lots of opportunities to talk to many beautiful young people, always discussing with them whatever it was they wanted to know. It was a great experience and I am happy to have been given this opportunity to explain what it really was like. I won't forget my day at Camp Hatikvah and I hope that some of the campers will remember me — sometimes.

Bronia gave another presentation at Camp Hatikvah two years later, and received the following two letters in response.

July 13, 1992

Dear Bronia,

Thank you very much for the visit earlier this month.

Countless campers and staff have commented to me that they were fascinated by the speeches; the focus on your life before and after really caught people's interest as it delved into portions of that time period that are often overlooked when examing the Holocaust.

As such, your speeches made Camp Hatikvah's Yom HaShoah more meaningful and educational and for that we thank you wholeheartedly.

I hope that many more can hear your insightful words.

Sincerely Yours,

Adam Levine
Program Director

July 14, 1992

Dear Mrs. Sonnenschein,

On behalf of all the staff and campers at Camp Hatikvah, I would like to extend to you our sincere gratitude for being a part of our Yom HaShoah program on Sunday July 12. We felt that the program was a huge success, mostly because of your participation. Not only did you provide the children and the staff with valuable information and insight into the Holocaust, but you developed strong personal bonds with everyone you touched at Camp Hatikvah during your brief stay here. Your warmth and kindness touched us all and brought the experiences of the Holocaust closer to home for each of us. We thank you deeply and look forward to seeing you soon. You will always be welcome at Camp Hatikvah. Thank you so much.

Sincerely yours,

Adam M. Dodek
Assistant Director

Holocaust Speech in the B.C. Legislature

Bernie Simpson, MLA (May 8, 1995)

FIFTY YEARS AGO TODAY, the Allied forces liberated Europe from Nazi tyranny. Several weeks before, the Allied forces entered the death camps of Auschwitz, Birkenau, Bergen-Belsen, Buchenwald, and Dachau. They were the sites of the destruction of six million innocent men, women and children. Their only sin was that they were Jewish. What was witnessed by the Allied forces and the world was an act of brutality that will go down in the annals of world history as the most barbaric act ever carried out by humankind. The Holocaust was the systematic, bureaucratic annihilation of six million Jews by the Nazi regime and their collaborators. In 1933 approximately nine million Jews lived in 21 countries in Europe. By 1945 two out of every three European Jews had been slaughtered.

Hon. Speaker, although the Jews were the primary victims, they were not the only ones. Hundreds of thousands of Gypsies, 250,000 mentally and physically infirm, homosexuals, thousands of political or religious dissidents such as communists, socialists, trade unionists and Jehovah's Witnesses — all were persecuted and annihilated for their beliefs. Millions of Soviet prisoners of war perished from starvation, disease and forced labour. There was a deliberate and well-planned extermination of more than fifteen million persons in what we know today as the Holocaust. This genocide of staggering proportions was carried out with scrupulous efficiency by a well-coordinated German bureaucracy, with the collaboration of the legislators in Germany, the educational system, churches, the judiciary, the medical profession, industry, business and other professions.

What did the Allied troops see when they entered those camps? A 21-year-old medical technician with the RCAF, John Doerksen, who now lives in Abbotsford, entered Bergen-Belsen. He stated: "It was horrendous to see that many people die. They were so emaciated; people were just skin and bones. Whether you are a survivor or liberator, it is an experience you will never forget." These words were echoed by Gen. Vasily Petrenko, who liberated Auschwitz. He stated: "I was totally unprepared for Auschwitz. What astonished me were the children, some mere infants who had been left behind in hasty evacuation. They were the survivors of the medical experiments perpetuated by Auschwitz camp doctor, Josef Mengele." Several victims of this doctor now live in Vancouver.

Capt. Timothy Brennan, writing to his wife and child, said: "You cannot imagine that such things exist in a civilized world." Gen. Dwight Eisenhower, Allied Supreme Commander, stated: "The things I saw beggared description." He ordered aides to ensure that as many GIs as possible saw the camps. The Supreme Commander urged lawmakers and editors to come immediately, to bear witness. In an editorial, "Gazing Into the Pit," the Christian Century stated that the atrocities showed "...the horror of humanity itself when it surrendered to its capacity for evil."

The most eloquent voice at the time was Edward R. Murrow, the CBS radio broadcaster. While he was walking through the camps, little children clung to his hands. Walking through the barracks, he was applauded by men so weak it sounded like the hand clapping of babies. He said at the time: "I reported what I saw and I heard but only a part of it. For most of it, I have no words."

Hon. Speaker, the Nazis butchered, the Jews were slaughtered, and the world watched on. How did this happen? Let there be no doubt about it: the United States, Great Britain, Canada and the other nations outside of Nazi Europe received numerous press reports that these camps existed before the Allied troops entered the camps in 1945. It is not correct to say there was liberation of the camps. Liberation would signify intent, and the questions arise: had, in fact, the camps been wilfully targeted for liberation? Had the Soviet and Western armies been directed to liberate these individual camps? It is a distortion of history to suggest there was an actual intention to liberate the death camps. Historians, after examining the available records, are influenced by the absolute surprise and shock of the officers and men who came upon the camps. As John Doerksen said, he and the others were utterly unprepared for Auschwitz. A thorough examination of British and American maps shows absolutely no mention of concentration camps. Nowhere can one find the concentration camps as part of military assignments. The so-called liberation was, at best, a by-product of military success — a never-intended result of strategic military planning. The actual liberation of the concentration camps was never once a priority of field commanders, let alone of the strategic planners in London, Washington and Moscow. American planes flew over Auschwitz to bomb military targets such as the giant I.G. Farben plant that converted coal to synthetic fuel, just a few miles away from Auschwitz. No bombs ever fell on Auschwitz, on Birkenau or on the rail lines leading up to the camps. No, the American War Department stuck to a policy of not mixing military and humanitarian objectives.

A partial proof of this unpreparedness of the military forces as they approached each camp is that they arrived with no provisions, let alone the emergency equipment that the tragic crisis of mass human suffering called for. The lack of supplies is testimony to the absence of intention on the part of the Allied forces. There's no doubt that all those who entered responded compassionately to the human catastrophe facing them, but each witness will attest that all this effort was strictly unrehearsed — the result of no original preparation. Most of those camps had been abandoned by the SS prior to the arrival of the Allied forces. Hygiene, food and medical help came later, on an improvised basis.

So let us do away with the myth of Allied liberation. Let us be critical of the lethal prewar immigration policies of Canada, the United States and other countries that denied entry to these desperately wretched people trying to flee Nazi Germany. By 1942 the governments of the United States and Great Britain knew and had confirmed reports of the Final Solution — Germany's intent to kill all the Jews of Europe. Great Britain, the United States and Canada, influenced by anti-Semitism rampant throughout their countries, feared a massive influx of refugees and turned their back on them, resulting in hundreds of thousands of deaths. Historians, working with newly declassified British and Canadian cabinet papers, have uncovered the sad truth that our country — yes, our country of Canada, hon. Speaker and hon. members — together with other countries, could have done far more. For example, there was a plan in 1943 to buy the freedom of 70,000 Romanian Jews. In response, the U.K. Foreign Office minutes, which were declassified last year, said: "Once we open the door to adult male Jews to be taken out of the enemy territory, a quite unmanageable flood may result." Because of this policy, close to 70,000 Romanian Jews were killed. On June 25, 1942, the Daily Telegraph reported that 700,000 Polish Jews had been killed, some by mobile gas vans. In September of that year, three months before the end of the year, the New York Herald Tribune stated: "Hitler has ordered four million Jews slain." Sir Anthony Eden, the British Foreign Secretary, told the House of Commons on September 17, 1942, that Germany was now carrying into effect Hitler's often-repeated intention to exterminate the Jewish people in Europe.

On July 19, 1944, it became clear that more than a half a million Hungarian Jews were about to be transported to their deaths. Chaim Weizmann, later the first president of the state of Israel, appealed to Eden to bomb the railways, and despite Eden's appeal to Churchill, nothing was done. Allied aircraft could have bombed the camps without difficulty, but the crematoria and railway yards were never targeted as Jewish leaders in North America and Britain had pleaded. Yes, anti-Semitism was rife not only in Nazi Germany but also throughout the world in the Second World War.

I am sure, hon. members, that this House will be shocked when I say that anti-Semitism was rife in this Legislature. In a book written by Irving Abella, "None Is Too Many", he discloses, after reviewing recently released Department of External Affairs records, that Mackenzie King, Canada's Prime Minister during the war years, feared that allowing in Jews would disrupt unity.

I'm ashamed to stand up here today and say that a former Premier of this province, T.D. Pattullo, then said to Prime Minister Mackenzie King that although the province was prepared to take some refugees, they did not want too many Jews. This is a matter of public record which has now been recently disclosed by our External Affairs department.

Anti-Semitism did not end in this Legislature after the Second World War. In the 1950s a prominent member of the Social Credit cabinet made a comment that the destruction of six million Jews was a fulfillment of the prophecy. There was a case of another member of the defunct Social Credit Party, who went on to become Speaker of this Legislature, who made a disparaging remark — an anti-Semitic remark — directed toward the Jewish MLA Norm Levi.

Jewish quotas existed until recently in various professions in this province — in universities, medical schools and industries. Jews and other ethnic groups such as Chinese were restricted from buying property in the British Properties, and they were restricted from joining many private clubs. Some of you may be shocked to hear that the Vancouver Club and some of our esteemed golf clubs did not allow Jews.

In 1970 I started my law career with the law firm headed by one of British Columbia's most distinguished citizens, a man whom I have the highest regard for — our former Lieutenant-Governor Walter Owen. When I joined the firm, Walter wanted to nominate me to become the first Jew to join the Vancouver Club, of which he was president. This was an invitation that I was quick to reject, but I appreciated that Walter was determined to break down the barriers of prejudice. It was several years later that the first Jew was allowed into that club — Justice Nathan Nemetz. So when we think of anti-Semitism and racism toward other ethnic groups, and we think that it is a phenomenon of the past, let us wake up and look around us, as it is prevalent in every corner of this province.

The righteous gentiles. Not everyone was indifferent to the tragedy that was unfolding during the Second World War. Many were like John Doerksen, who, after the war, enrolled in a Bible college to find answers. Last week in the Vancouver Sun, he stated: "I'm a Christian guy and I believe in God and I have a lot of faith. I'm a human guy; I get emotional. I cannot understand why God would permit something like this." During the war there were numerous righteous gentiles who saved tens of thousands of Jews and other persecuted persons.

A couple of years ago, when I, together with my young family, went to Israel, we visited Yad Vashem — a memorial to the six million Jews who perished. As we got off the bus, we walked through a beautifully treed area that had plaques on it, and these plaques had names of gentiles who, at great personal risk, saved tens of thousand of Jews. One of these righteous gentiles, of course, was Schindler, whose heroic deeds have been perpetuated by the movie "Schindler's List". I know that many of you have seen that movie and were moved by it. I recall speaking to the leader of the Reform Party in this House, who had just seen the movie, and he described what an impact it had on him.

In this House, the former member for the Abbotsford riding, Harry de Jong, came up to me after one of my speeches on this subject and told me passionately how his family had saved Jews in Holland. Yes, there were righteous gentiles. These righteous gentiles will be forever remembered in the annals of history as standing up against Nazi tyranny. However, on the whole, the world's political leaders and the world stood by with indifference.

A couple of weeks ago, a memorial took place at the Beth Israel Synagogue, of which I'm a member. Although I have attended many of these memorials, this was the most moving one. It was attended by over 400 people, including the hon. member for Vancouver-Langara. I'm sure he would agree with me that the testimony given by the survivors of the death camps and their children was most moving. One of those survivors was a prominent philanthropist and leader in the Jewish community, Mr. Leon Kahn. In his book, "No Time to Mourn" — a true story of a Jewish partisan fighter — Mr. Kahn talked about how he lost his entire family when he was 17 years old. The book starts off by listing over 30 members of his family who were slaughtered, including his father, Shel, his mother, Miriam, his brother Benjamin and his sister Frieda. I quote how he witnessed the death of his beloved sister: "I saw her fall as her pursuer posed his blade over her, and as the bayonet entered my poor sister's defenceless body."

Leon, in his book, talked about his dying father and what he said to him, while he held his father in his arms:

"Remember I loved you dearly, just as your mother, brother and sister loved you. Even though we are all gone, you are not alone, and someday you will have a family of your own. Tell them about your murdered family and what became of us. Tell your children that they had grandparents who would have loved them if they had allowed them to."

His father went on and said: "I know you'll survive and begin a new life. Never forget who you are, and be proud of your Jewish heritage. Teach your children to keep their faith and to practise it as part of their daily lives."

I urge all members to attend these memorials every year, to speak to the survivors and the children of the survivors, and to visit the Vancouver Holocaust Centre and the Jewish Community Centre. The centre has been established to break down the walls of prejudice and intolerance through education and remembrance of the Holocaust. Meet for yourself the many survivors who are now living in Vancouver and learn firsthand what it was like to go through this infamous period in our history.

I remember when I was five years old my single-parent mother took some of those survivors into our house, shortly after the war ended, and how I would hear the screams in the middle of the night as they would awaken from their nightmares. I remember only too well the discipline that one of those survivors meted out to me when he saw that I was disrespectful to my mother, and the anger in his eyes and the intensity. It probably was meant to be a well-meaning spanking. Whenever that particular survivor sees me, he approaches me and apologizes profusely, and tears come to his eyes.

Could this genocide happen again? One would have thought that the world would have learned a lesson after witnessing such unspeakable brutality. No, the answer is an obvious no. History is repeating itself before us. Mass murders continue and continue. And the world watches, just like the world watched the destruction of European Jewry. Genocidal bloodletting and mass slaughters have taken place in Cambodia, Biafra, Bosnia, Rwanda and elsewhere. They do not approach the Holocaust in scale, but they vividly show humankind's inhumanity to our fellow human beings.

One need not go any further than to your corner news-stand and pick up this week's edition of Maclean's magazine. Look at the cover, hon. members; look at the Nazi flag. Read the article "The Enemy Within." I'm sure the hon. member for Chilliwack will be appalled to read about one of his constituents, Charles Scott, the colonel of the white supremacist Aryan Nations. Listen to him talk about the evil Jews who are the literal line to Satan on Earth. Scott will be recognized for his efforts by being named, in July at the Aryan Congress in the United States, as the Aryan of the year.

Let us not forget the Scotts, the Keegstras, the Zundels, the McAleers and what they stand for. Frankly, I didn't find too much sympathy for Mr. Zundel last night, when he got on television proclaiming that he was a law-abiding citizen and bemoaning the fact that he lost his home to fire. Mr. Zundel is a Holocaust-denier who glorifies Adolf Hitler.

Hon. Speaker and hon. members, last night a survivor of Auschwitz, Mrs. Bronia Sonnenschein, came over to our house and spoke of her experiences. Bronia has spoken to thousands of school children in B.C. throughout the years. I urge hon. members to encourage their school districts to have Bronia and other speakers speak to the students in their ridings. These arrangements can be made through the Vancouver Holocaust Centre.

She was a prisoner of Auschwitz; that was the largest of the death camps. More than one million people lost their lives at this camp. Nine out of ten were Jewish. At one time, the four largest gas chambers could each hold two thousand people. Bronia related how they were transported to the camp in cattle cars. For five days they travelled, 50 in a car with no food and little water; many died on the way. When the survivors arrived, they saw the smokestacks belching the remnants of European Jewry. A sign at the entrance read: "Work makes one free." They were greeted by SS physician Dr. Josef Mengele, who decided who was to be exterminated immediately. Those were the old, the sick and the children.

Bronia is a very dignified woman. She related how those who were spared immediate death were dehumanized. They immediately had all their hair shaved off and a registration number tattooed on their left forearm [*she was not tattooed; see note on p. 288 — ed.*]. They were then ordered to strip naked and stand in the courtyard, often in freezing rain and snow. The men were forced to wear ragged striped pants and jackets, and the women workdresses. They had no change of clothing, and they slept in the same clothes they worked in. They were always hungry. Food was a watered soup made with rotten vegetables and a few ounces of bread. Each day was a struggle for survival under unbearable conditions. They were housed in primitive barracks with no windows and no bathroom, only a bucket. Each barrack held 36 wooden bunkbeds, and inmates were squeezed five or six across a wooden plank. As many as 500 inmates were in a single barrack. Most of these prisoners survived but a few months.

I asked Bronia what we as legislators could do. I told her that I was going to be speaking on the Holocaust today, and she said we must educate about the Holocaust. We must support educational institutions such as the Holocaust Centre, and we must be forever diligent on what is going on in our ridings and root out racism whenever and wherever it arises.

Let us value human life throughout the world and recognize the fact that we are responsible for the well-being not only of our family but of our neighbours and all humankind.

I wish to dedicate this reading from one of the survivors of Auschwitz [*Elie Wiesel — ed.*], which is found in the prayer book of the synagogue I belong to. This reading is dedicated to the Bronia Sonnenscheins, the Leon Kahns and the 15 million martyrs who perished in the Holocaust:

> "Not far from us, flames were leaping up from a ditch, gigantic flames. They were burning something. A lorry drew up at the pit and delivered its load: little children, babies. Around us everyone was weeping. Someone began to recite the kaddish. I do not know if it has ever happened before in the long history of the Jews that people recited the prayer for the dead for themselves. Never shall I forget the first night in the camp. Never shall I forget that smoke. Never shall I forget the little faces of the children, whose bodies I saw turned into wreaths of smoke beneath a sun and sky."

From Auschwitz to the Creston Valley

Bronia Sonnenschein (1996)

CRESTON VALLEY, a small peaceful town of about 7,000 inhabitants, a perfect spot where one expects to find tranquillity, a perfect spot to raise a family, far enough from the hustle and bustle of big city life – but also the place where unwelcome 'elements', white supremacists, have settled down to make their presence known. This too is Creston.

But these elements did not count on the determination of the people of Creston, their mayor Lela Irvine, in particular, to keep their town racist-free. Mayor Irvine is a strong determined woman; she will keep Creston Valley racist-free.

It was the Creston Valley Human Rights Coalition with the Canadian Jewish Congress, Pacific Region, who organized an Anti-Racism Outreach Program. Its theme was "The Holocaust Remembered: Linking history to contemporary issues of diversity and human dignity."

Participating in this event which took place November 19 and 20, 1996, was the Honourable Ujjal Dosanjh, B.C. Attorney General and Minister responsible for Multiculturalism, Human Rights and Immigration, and Sandy Dore, B.C. Teachers Federation – Program Against Racism. Eyewitness accounts were provided by Bronia Sonnenschein, survivor of Auschwitz, and Robbie Waisman, survivor of Buchenwald. It was Marilyn Berger, associate director of the Canadian Jewish Congress who led her group from Vancouver to Creston; under her guidance the event proved to be a tremendous success.

It is Marilyn Berger's agenda to visit outlying communities, accompanied by survivors sharing their experiences during the Holocaust. I had been privileged to accompany Marilyn Berger on all her "trips" and so did Robbie Waisman. Her government grant let her visit so far Salmon Arm, Nelson, Vernon, Salt Spring Island, Victoria, and Kelowna. All of those visits met with great success. Wherever we went we received an outpouring of love from the public and students and teachers alike, promising us they would never let it happen again, promising to remember the Holocaust and keep the memory alive. Can one ask for more?

Creston Valley was the highlight of our trip with an audience of 700 people, the local people one evening, and students and teachers the following morning. The Attorney General attended the evening session, laying out his plans to combat racism and anti-semitism.

For me, a survivor of Auschwitz, it was a long, hard road from Auschwitz to Creston, as it was for Robbie Waisman from Buchenwald to Creston.

And so, my dear friend Marilyn, should you call on me again in the future to go with you on "your trips" as you call them, I will be ready. I will try to be a part of it for as long as I can. Not even a blizzard, like the one greeting us upon our arrival in Creston, or the fog in Salmon Arm, or even getting up at 6 in the morning, will keep me away. I will be ready, Marilyn!

I would like to thank the Canadian Jewish Congress as well as anyone who goes the "extra mile" promoting Holocaust education. We are all in it together!

Letter to a Symposium Organizer

Bronia Sonnenschein (1997)

*This letter was sent in reply to Al Gribbin, a teacher
at Prince Charles Secondary School in Creston, B.C.*

January 20, 1997

Dear Al,

First of all I wish to thank you for the initiative you took in
making the symposium on Racism in Creston happen. It is
thanks to people like you that the future generation is being
taught what racism and anti-semitism is and the incredible
danger it inflicts on mankind. One of the students in her letter
thanked you for your efforts. And so do I and the rest of our
group.

You are right in stating in your letter to Marilyn that some
of the students would have liked a response. All of the students
writing the letters showed great understanding and compassion
for the victims of the Holocaust. I wish to thank them all for
having expressed their feelings upon hearing Robbie and me
giving testimony.

Here are some that I felt should be answered. I hope you
will be able to recognize them by their questions and my
answers.

— How can we prevent another Holocaust (report on the
symposium and how I felt).
Nothing can be solved by violence. Our only tool is
education. I am confident that this student will stand up
once and inform other people who are ignorant and even
resentful — like certain "elements" and their followers
who are guided by hatred, and remember our testimony
and film clips.

— As to the student of German ancestry.

I would like to tell I know exactly how hurtful it is to be
looked upon as an outcast. It happened to me, only far
worse. An open talk with her or his fellow students would
help. He or she can't be held responsible for what their
grandparents' generation did. But what this student can
do — and these things can be done — is right the wrong.
I would like this student to know that I am well aware that
not every German was a Nazi—but every Jew was a victim.
It is a big task, but it can be done. I also wish this student
would have approached me and we would have been able
to talk about it. I always welcome listeners. In this respect
I thought it would be of interest to you in future discussions
to read the enclosed article: "A Bridge to Nuremberg — the
Story of Bronia and Markus" [see p. 191], a story of friendship and understanding. He, Markus, will ensure through
his teaching that the memory of the Holocaust will be kept
alive. Nazis will never be forgiven. Good people will
always be remembered.

— The Racism symposium. My most memorable moment.

This student was obviously putting him- or herself in the
shoes of victims and was able to actually feel the pain we
endured. Thank you so much for commenting on my courage, as the student put it.
I would never doubt my religion. I might never understand
why it happened. Somehow I believe that God did appoint
a guardian angel to watch over me. I did survive by a miracle and so believe in miracles and continue to do so. It was
because of my religion, my silent communication with my
mother and sister that I did not let them break my spirit,
my will to live. I had to surrender everything I had, but not
my soul. I did not let them take away my soul. I hope this
student won't ever lose hope and courage to withstand some
of the knocks life is dealing sometime.

— Racism symposium.

I have the same answer for this student. I just wish to add: it is a gift to be able to appreciate the things we have, a family, friends, good teachers, a home, a country. It is, after all, so easy to take freedom for granted when it has never been taken away from us.

I have taught my children and grandchildren to always count their blessings. I know I do. I want all of you who wrote to me to know that I am happy to read from your letters that I have been able to influence you in such a positive way. The memory of the Holocaust should never fade. Six million shall never be forgotten. Thank you.

— Racism symposium.

Another student commented "once the Jews' soul and pride" had been taken it was easier for the soldiers (I personally refer to them as Nazis — soldiers fought on the front) to torture and kill them. I have stated before that I did not let it happen to me.

— Symposium project.

Thank you from all my heart for the standing ovation you gave "the frail little woman", as I thank all of them who did. By the way, it was the first time a student referred to me as "frail". Little, yes, much to my regret I am, but so far I am usually called "strong". Not physically, of course, but spiritually. I would have liked to shake hands with you.

— Racism symposium.

I will always pay tribute to the German woman who gave me the letter (in German it is called Schutzbrief). I wish I had been able after the war to thank her and to tell her I have her "Schutzbrief" (translated into English it is a letter to protect the person it was given to and who believes in its power, as I did).

To the general public, listening to us with such expression of warmth and understanding, to all the teachers, the organizers, the students and to you Al, who put so much heart into this symposium, to Peter, Eric and Adam, the two delightful young men who talked to me about their plans for the future (Eric also sent me a beautiful card), I wish to thank all of you with all my heart, I won't forget you. I wish all of you a good and happy life to be enjoyed in good health and peace.

Special greetings to your wife, Al, and to your lovely baby. Your baby seemed to "enjoy" the evening as it slept happily through all of the commotion.

Special regards to your Mayor, Mrs. Lela Irvine. She is an incredible woman. I hold her in high regard.

Looking at the Canadian Jewish Congress

Bronia Sonnenschein (1996)

AS THE OLD YEAR is coming to an end and 1997 is just about to start, I am reflecting on my association with the Canadian Jewish Congress during the last nine years.

I approached the Congress around 1988 to satisfy an overwhelming need to be useful again, to help where help is needed. I had just lost my beloved sister, Paula Lenga, to cancer. We had never been separated and I never left her side during her final year. Paula too had been a volunteer, for the Jewish Family Service, and helped in the office of Congress which at that time was led by Morris Saltzman. To offer my help as volunteer at the Congress seemed the most logical thing to do.

The Congress was never "overstaffed", quite the contrary, and could use a pair of extra hands. I was welcomed with open arms by Erwin Nest, executive director for the Pacific Region, who was later joined by Marilyn Berger as an associate director. Needless to say, during all that time I came to respect both of them highly and as the years went by I looked at them as my "Congress family", my friends.

I served my "apprenticeship" as volunteer for the Congress by "licking envelopes" as Erwin Nest jokingly called it, making countless phone calls for special events, and other odds and ends that only a volunteer could find time to do. I enjoyed it, I felt needed, and I knew it was highly appreciated by Erwin and Marilyn. Being a "Girl Friday" wasn't all that bad.

Keeping my eyes open I was also able to observe some of the mandate the Congress had been given. Not too many people in the Jewish community might know that thanks to the Congress's agenda of keeping their finger on the pulse of happenings throughout the Lower Mainland and small communities, the Congress is fully aware of the danger of antisemitic attacks, desecrating synagogues and Jewish schools, and other acts of blatant antisemitism. But it is, of course, not enough to be aware, but to actually prevent the attacks from happening. The Congress is in close touch with representatives of the government, the police, the synagogues, as well as the multicultural society. They too are affected by racist attacks. So by working closely with the Mayor and the Attorney General, and everybody concerned and ready to step in, the Congress is making us feel more secure; knowing that every Holocaust denier is under the watchful eyes of this organization, every event in the Jewish community taking place does so under police protection, is making me — and it should everybody living here — feel so much safer. Their agenda is a never-ending monitoring of everything going on inside and outside of the community. I often wonder had we in Europe had such a strong organization, would it have averted some of the problems facing us as Jews? We never had such a strong leadership in Jewish organizations, of that I am sure.

During the last four years, Marilyn Berger has taken on the agenda together with the multicultural society and the Teachers' Federation of bringing a symposium on Racism and Anti-Semitism to places like Salmon Arm, Vernon, Kelowna, Nelson, Saltspring Island, Victoria, and the latest, in November 1996, Creston. Creston was by far the most publicized event. Posters in Creston were being shown in the auditorium of the school where the symposium had taken place, stating that Creston was declared by the mayor of the town a "racist free" society. The Attorney General of B.C., the Hon. Ujjal Dosanjh, was there as well to address the public. This symposium was shown on Global TV and other TV stations. Marilyn Berger's group includes Holocaust survivors and was up until now attended by Robbie Waisman, survivor of Buchenwald, and me, Bronia Sonnen-schein, survivor of Auschwitz. Professor William Nicholls, a scholar and author who is very active in Holocaust education, also participated in many of these presentations. So far we have met with great success and been warmly received. We have met members of the First Nations addressing the problem of racism, a black man, and Doukhobors, as well as a member of the Teachers' Federation. And I know that all those listening to us will keep their promise — to remember the Holocaust and never let it happen again. This is our aim, this is our tribute to the memory of the six million who were brutally killed by the Nazis. And so whenever Marilyn Berger will call on me — so far I have been her steady companion — I will do so, I will follow her call. In a small way I am justifying my own miraculous survival.

Two years ago, Marilyn hosted the Teachers' Federation Program against Racism Training Conference held in Vancouver. The theme of the conference was Remembering the Holocaust, Promoting Peace and Understanding. I was one of the speakers as a survivor, and Prof. Yehuda Bauer addressed the audience of about 75 teachers as the eminent researcher on the Holocaust that he is. This event too met with overwhelming success.

Another highly important agenda of the Congress was organizing commemorative events like Yom Ha'Shoah and Kristallnacht Commemoration, as well as the yearly Holocaust Symposium, which lasts two days and now attracts over a thousand high school students and their teachers. All these events had to be carefully planned a year ahead, guest speakers had to be selected for each event, contacts had to be established with participating schools, and survivors approached to participate in each event. Great care was given to execute these events to the satisfaction of a large audience. Members of the Federal and Provincial Governments as well as members of the clergy, the media, and members of the Multicultural Society were invited for the solemn programs of Yom Ha'Shoah and Kristallnacht Commemoration, with invitations mailed out to them. These events were in Congress's hands for over twenty years, well before I had come on the scene. They are now handled by the Vancouver Holocaust Education Society so that Congress can look after its ever-growing agenda.

Upon Erwin Nest's invitation I became a member of the committee for each event and participated actively in them. I had stopped "licking envelopes" and making phone calls, and had gained the confidence of Erwin and Marilyn to participate in all these programs. It is not the easiest job I have ever undertaken but most definitely the most rewarding one. I am proud to be on their team.

At this point maybe it is time to introduce myself. My name is Bronia Sonnenschein and I have lived in Vancouver since 1950. In 1938 Hitler entered Vienna, annexing Austria, my former homeland, to Germany. Our lives were from that moment on changed forever. ... [*Omitted here is the material in the first two paragraphs of the Prologue — ed.*] The world fell apart for all of us Jews in 1938, after the annexation. It was also the signal that nothing would ever be the same again. At that point, the free world decided to close their doors to Jewish emigration. I will always believe that had the free world not let us Jews down, six million would not have had to die.

We witnessed Kristallnacht in Vienna on November 9, 1938; it was the beginning of the end for Europe's Jewry. Eventually every single Jew living in Austria was forced to leave, leaving all their belongings behind and without a further look at what was their beloved home. We ended up in Lodz, Poland, and were later on forced into a ghetto. The Lodz Ghetto, as it had become known, was in the hands of the Gestapo and as its "leader" a Jewish man by the name of Chaim Rumkowski was appointed. He was responsible to the German administrator, Hans Biebow, a ruthless Nazi, a killer. The conditions in the Lodz Ghetto were such that 40,000 people died of starvation and related diseases. We worked for the Germans, their soldiers and the civilian population, and received a pitiful food ration for it. We starved, but being together we never lost confidence that we would survive. It was my father who always believed that "the day will come when we will be free, there won't be borders and we will have enough bread." It was a nice dream which he never lived to see, being killed in the concentration camp later on.

In August 1944 the ghetto was liquidated on orders from Berlin and we were transported in cattle cars to Auschwitz. The trip lasted five days — there was no food, or water. After five harrowing days we arrived in Auschwitz, seeing the smoke coming out of the chimneys, the crematoria, where bodies which had been previously gassed were tossed, their lifeless bodies turned into ashes. Upon arrival it was Dr. Mengele, the so-called "Angel of Death" who performed the selection, choosing those destined for immediate death who were taken directly to the gas chambers, and those destined for slow death. Men and women had been separated upon arrival. My mother, sister and I were "selected" together with other groups for the "slow death". And that is really what it proved to be. It is difficult to describe the pain, humiliation and hunger that were forever present in Auschwitz as well as in the other camps we were taken to afterwards, like Stutthof and later on the forced labour camp in Dresden, Germany. To this day it is an unexplainable miracle, an act of God, that we survived. Nobody ever knew about our relationship. We communicated, if it can be called that, by looking at each other. My father always said while we were still in the Ghetto, "hang in, it will end sometime." Maybe we had a guardian angel. I believe we did. The same guardian angel has been with me for many years now, as the road after liberation was a rough one for me.

While in Dresden we witnessed the well-known air attack, the biggest attack on any German city. It was, as I found out after the war, revenge for the bombing of Coventry, England. It happened in February 1945. In April 1945, we were taken on another well-recorded event, the so-called death march. We marched for nearly two weeks, always along the River Elbe, flowing through Dresden. Again the only food was what we found in garbage cans. To quench our incredible thirst we were "given permission" to drink from the polluted river, the one into which the guards tossed the bodies of those inmates who had collapsed and died on the streets. At one point, as it turned out the last day of the march, Paula, my sister, whispered that she simply could not walk anymore. As a matter of fact, none of us could. She suggested for the three of us to end it all by going into the water. My mother, nearly collapsing herself — God must have given her supernatural strength to still believe in miracles — had overhead a guard mentioning the date, and whispered to us that tomorrow was Paula's birthday, maybe a miracle would happen on that day. The following day we entered Theresien-stadt, the "model ghetto" in Terezin, Czechoslovakia, where the guards left us and took off as fast as they could, the Russians being practically on their heels. They had fulfilled their order, leaving the Jews in Theresienstadt, which was to be blown up with all inmates inside. Just for once their plan did not succeed and my mother's miracle had come true. We were liberated by a lone Russian soldier on May 8, 1945. It was indeed a miracle. We were free — and so as I stated in the beginning, we eventually came to Canada, to Vancouver, in 1950 to start a new life.

The rest is, as we say, history. I am blessed with children and grandchildren; I don't want them or any other Jewish child to be called "a dirty Jew" the way I was. By sharing my experiences during the Holocaust with students, teachers, and the general public, I hope I can make at least a dent in the relationship between Jews and Christians and all other nations.

Teaching Tolerance in the Aryan-Nations Heartland

Sandy Dore (1996)

*Sandy Dore was an associate of the Program Against Racism of the
B.C. Teachers Federation, and wrote this for a BCTF newsletter.*

R ICHARD BUTLER, leader of the Aryan Nations movement in
the United States, was told of the invitation given to the
Canadian Jewish Congress's antiracist outreach education
symposium by the citizens of Bonners Ferry and Sandpoint,
Idaho. His response was, "Northern Idaho is a place where
people come to get out of the cesspool created by the blacks and
yellows and the Mexicans. The communist Jew is out to
mongrelize this part up here too. We (Aryan Nations) might go
up and monitor the speeches to counter them if we can."

Hardly an encouraging idea for the members of our group
as we headed into Idaho to discuss the Holocaust, human rights,
and antiracist education with students and citizens of Bonners
Ferry and Sandpoint, but not unexpected from Butler, a leading
white supremacist resident of Hayden Lake, about 40 miles to
the south of the two communities.

Marilyn Berger, of the Canadian Jewish Congress, had invited me to join Holocaust survivors Bronia Sonnenschein and
Robbie Waisman to travel to Idaho to discuss the concept of
racism-free schools, as counters to Butler's philosophy of bigotry
and hate.

The timeliness of the program was heightened by the fact
that in Spokane, Washington, on the days we were speaking,
trials of two suspected Aryan Nations bombers from the
Sandpoint area were taking place.

The BCTF Program Against Racism has been very involved
in the struggle against racist ideologies in school systems, and
the chance to exchange ideas and strategies with schools in
northern Idaho made me aware that our program is well known,
a comment on the work done by so many in the BCTF over
twenty-two years.

Our group flew to Spokane, where we were met by Julian Boucher, a rancher in Bonners Ferry who organized our visit.

Boucher, who has grown up in Bonners Ferry, was the first of many people we met who put to rest the racist images of Hayden Lake, Aryan Nations, and Ruby Ridge.

Boucher wanted students to discuss the Holocaust with survivors and hear their stories so that they could better understand where complacency and bystanding led when confronted by racist groups who preach the doctrine of racial supremacy.

Tension was evident as Boucher drove our team from Spokane to the Idaho border, where we were led and followed by sheriff's deputies in unmarked cars to Bonners Ferry.

The meeting room was packed with 250 to 300 citizens of this town of only 2,700 people. Security was tight, the audience was supportive, and the opening evening was a huge success without incident, although as we were leaving, I was told that two members of the Aryan Nations had been in the audience. I woke in the middle of the night to find a security person guarding our hallway, and a real sense of danger was reinforced.

The next morning, over 450 high-school seniors attended our presentation; their support and caring were overwhelming. These students were not what I had expected in this area, and they demonstrated that they are committed to antiracist, human-rights ideals by their comments, questions, and sincere emotions at the end of our presentation.

We left Bonners Ferry in positive frames of mind and drove the 30 miles to Sandpoint through a beautiful countryside, discussing the tremendous response we had received.

The citizens were welcoming, and we shared our supper with members of the Bonner County Human Rights Task Force, formed in 1992 as a counter to racist graffiti and Aryan Nations recruitment in their town.

As two of their group said, "We've always been proud of where we live, and these people (Aryan Nations) threaten our image and self-esteem. We cannot let fear alter our behavior, because if we do, we are already defeated."

We left for our community forum again with tight security and entered the town centre, where over 500 people were gathered, with many more outside the doors. The evening was a reaffirmation of the community's desire to be viewed as opposing the beliefs of Butler and his followers, and they received Waisman, Sonnenschein, and me with great warmth, hospitality, and support for our antiracist message.

The evening over, I slept — sheriff's deputy parked outside my hotel window. The next morning, as we were preparing to address the area students, the owner of the hotel appeared and said, "We have had many big-name celebrities in our hotel lobby lately (a fact attested to by the many signed photographs of well-known faces on the wall) but no one as important as you." All of us felt honoured by her statement and secure in the knowledge that our message was being well received.

Another packed audience awaited us with over 600 students in the local theatre who again received Waisman and Sonnenschein with many tears, hugs, and assurances of remembrance!

I was gratified that as in Bonners Ferry, these students also decided to implement the racism-free-schools concept and were committed to opposing the Aryan Nations philosophy of hate in every way they could.

Our group left full of the realization that we had been welcomed and well received by our host communities.

Recently we received many thanks from people in the area. The Bonner County Human Rights Task Force wrote, "You may or may not know that many more heard you than were present at the meetings; the videotape of the evening presentation ran for several days on our local cable television station. People here are still speaking about how powerful the presentation was. Thank you for coming, speaking, sharing, and meeting a gruelling schedule, for in doing so, you have made a difference!"

I was proud to represent the Program Against Racism on this team, and I will never forget the kindness afforded to us by the students and citizens of Bonners Ferry and Sandpoint.

Yom Ha'Shoah Address

Bronia Sonnenschein (1997)

Given at Beth Israel Synagogue in Vancouver.

A S YOU KNOW, Idaho is a hotbed of white supremacism, so it was with a great deal of apprehension that Robbie Waisman and I went to Idaho to be speakers at an anti-racism program arranged by the Canadian Jewish Congress. This program was facilitated by Marilyn Berger, associate director of the CJC, Pacific Region, who gave us lots of moral support. Our small group consisted of Marilyn Berger, Sandy Dore of the B.C. Teachers Federation from Kelowna, Robbie Waisman, and me. Yet this feeling of apprehension soon disappeared. We were welcomed with open arms, protected by the police, plain-clothes and in uniform, and the people of Bonners Ferry and Sandpoint in Idaho opened their hearts to us. They had awaited our coming eagerly, especially since a few weeks earlier some of them had had the opportunity to listen to us in Creston, B.C., another hotbed of racism and antisemitism. The people in Idaho, particularly these towns, had been given a bad reputation because white supremacists and militia groups had settled there.

The general public as well as the students were hanging on every word Robbie and I said during our presentations, and tears were flowing freely whether it was the general public or the students, the students asking us for autographs and treating us as very special people not to be forgotten. We proudly wore a big button given to us by a young girl who together with her classmates had joined the Bonner County Human Rights Task Force as their youngest members, and asked us to wear it during our presentation; it said "we all smile in the same language."

Young and old, all of them understood the horrors of the Holocaust. Our message came through loud and clear — as one of the local organizers wrote to me in a letter afterwards, "thank you for making our town a better place to live." It was a far cry from once being labeled a sub-human by the Nazis — it was a long way from Auschwitz and Buchenwald to Idaho. My mother and sister were among my fellow inmates who together with me survived against all odds. My father, the one who always encouraged us to hang in, was killed with so many other of my close relatives. For me, speaking out was a promise I had to keep, a promise we the inmates of the death-camps of Auschwitz and Stutthof made to each other that should any one of us survive, we would tell the world what they did to us. And for so many years no one wanted to listen.

After one of our presentations in Idaho, a policeman approaching Robbie told him, "I promise that any time I will be dealing with a racist I will think of you — no racist in my town!", while another one turned to me telling me, "you touched my heart." A Japanese woman who was previously a nun came up to Robbie telling him, "my Bishop told me the Holocaust did not happen. After listening to you I realized my Bishop lied to me." Turning to me she embraced me, tears flowing down her face, thanking me for the courage to speak. A Jewish member of the Task Force proclaimed "I was never so proud of being Jewish as I am today."

A letter I received after our return from Idaho from the Human Rights Task Force assured me that "many more heard you than were present at the meetings. The video program of your evening presentation ran for several days on our local cablevision station. I hope it pleases you that people here are still speaking about your powerful message. The courage you exemplified by telling it and the strength you summoned to meet an exhausting schedule were a sterling example for all of us."

Our trip to Idaho connecting to the people of Idaho was a monument to our people. The six million victims who perished shall never be forgotten. It was a pledge to all our children to try to do our best to erase antisemitism so that our children and our children's children will never have to face the horrors we did.

Letters to Newspapers

September 5, 1984

Dear Mr. Kaplan:

In response to your editorial (Jewish Western Bulletin, August 29), I would like to point out that although your description of the ghetto in Theresienstadt is correct, referring to it as a "model concentration camp" is not. There never was a "model concentration camp". Theresienstadt was a "model" ghetto. There is a tremendous difference between a ghetto and a concentration camp.

I was liberated in the ghetto of Theresienstadt on May 8, 1945. The few remaining Jews were the ones who gave us — with tears streaming down their faces when they looked at us — cube sugar, soup and clean clothes.

We arrived there on April 24, 1945 after being on a death march for two weeks from Dresden. (We were not the only transport arriving there.) The reason for bringing remaining concentration camp inmates to the ghetto in Theresienstadt was not to assemble us for eventual liberation. Theresienstadt with all its inmates was supposed to be blown up on, I believe, May 5, 1945.

For once the Nazis were too late to execute their diabolic plan.

Bronia Sonnenschein

Editor's Note [*JWB*]: This clarification is appreciated. Theresienstadt, the last stop for many before Auschwitz, is variously described by Shoah historians including as a ghetto (the Nazi appellation), a "model settlement" (*Encyclopaedia Judaica*) and "a model camp" (*The War Against the Jews*, Lucy S. Dawidowicz).

November 5, 1985

Editor, Jewish Western Bulletin

Dear Sir,

With reference to the article by Joanne Blaine "How one Jew fought the Nazis" published in your paper on November 1st, I bitterly resent Mrs. Moszkiewiez's words (recalling her feelings) about "how meekly most of her fellow Jews went along with the German invaders ... allowing themselves to be taken away to concentration camps without a fight. ... I never understood why the Jews did not fight, they were like sheep waiting to be slaughtered."

Mrs. Moszkiewiez has tarnished the memory of every man, woman and child who was killed during the Holocaust and cannot defend himself against her accusations of being meek or acting like sheep. She has opened up the wounds of those who survived the Holocaust — by the grace of God — and feel the anguish of being criticized by someone who had the opportunity through a chance encounter with a young Belgian soldier to be actively involved in working for the Underground. As Mrs. Moszkiewiez says, she herself was a "naive" girl when she entered the Resistance. Once there she would not have been able to leave, comparing the Resistance to a "Mafia". But even her heroic work does not give her the right to call those who were killed and tortured beyond belief meek or to compare them with sheep. Not all of us had guns or knives handy to attack the beast that tortured us.

We were herded at gunpoint to the ghettos, the cattle-cars, the concentration camps. Would Mrs. Moszkiewiez regard Elie Wiesel as meek or a sheep? Does Simon Wiesenthal fit into this category? Would thousands upon thousands of courageous people deserve to be called meek for having worn the Star of David when all they had to fight back with were only their two hands? How does Mrs. Moszkiewiez regard hostages? Are they also meek and behaving like sheep instead of fighting back against their captors with their bare hands?

I am a survivor. I had to endure Nazi atrocities from March 1938 when Hitler marched into Vienna till the day of our liberation on May 8, 1945 in Theresienstadt. I cannot take credit for having saved lives — does that make me a meek person, acting like a sheep? Or does it make me a victim who was robbed of the dignity to defend herself by having been stripped of every possible defense action.

We can't be all heroes — Mrs. Moszkiewiez must be aware of this as even her own parents perished at the hands of the Nazis.

To be courageous also means to have compassion for the less courageous ones, the "meek" ones of this world. The world does not consist of heroes only.

B. Sonnenschein

Editor's Note: See related article on p. 229.

October 26, 1990

Dear Mr. Kaplan,

In your column "Opinion" (Oct. 25) with regard to Kristallnacht, the opinion of Mrs. G—— L—— stood out reminding me again painfully that some of our Jewish friends still don't understand the magnitude of the suffering of European Jews.

The voices of six million of our people having been exterminated by the Nazis can't be heard, but the voices of survivors can. We feel hurt by insensitive remarks like the one voiced by Mrs. L—— that had "Jew and non-Jew stood up to the Government, there wouldn't have been consequences."

Does anyone really believe that anyone, especially a non-armed Jew, could have stood up to Hitler's government, the Third Reich, to every Nazi bent on killing Jews and even executing their own people if they showed resistance? How can anyone, having lived through this dark period of persecution of European Jews in relative safety, ever understand our suffering, our pain?

If anyone should have stood up to their government it was the Jews on this continent. Maybe, just maybe, Hitler's atrocities could have been avoided if the governments of the free world would have stopped Hitler — at least to a certain degree. If the doors would have been opened to us, God knows, maybe six million would not have been killed.

Thanks to the efforts of the Canadian Jewish Congress and the Vancouver Holocaust Centre Society, Canadian Jews and non-Jews alike are being made aware of what the Holocaust meant. As a survivor I wish to thank them.

Sincerely,

Bronia Sonnenschein

February 13, 1992

Dear Mr. Kaplan:

This year marked the 50th anniversary of the Jan. 20, 1942 Wannsee Conference in Berlin.

The fate of European Jewry was determined on that day and culminated in the greatest tragedy, the loss of Six Million of our people during the Holocaust. The "Final Solution" at the Wannsee Conference called for the killing of 11 million Jews.

As a Survivor of Hitler's death camps, I strongly feel that Jan. 20, 1942 should be remembered by the Jewish community and your readers reminded of this significant date in history.

Bronia Sonnenschein

Editor's Note: From 'Ideology of Death' by John Weiss: "The eventual murder of eleven million Jews was discussed, a number including those from all areas to be conquered, England as well. No voices were raised against the plan, but there was disagreement about how much 'Jewish blood' qualified one for death."

*The parts shown in italic below were edited out of
this letter as it appeared in The Vancouver Sun.*

June 26, 1997

To the Editor of The Vancouver Sun,

I wish to thank Paula Brook for her sensitive reporting on the Collins hearing. As a Holocaust survivor I appreciate it.

Although I found it impossible to attend the hearing on June 24, facing another hatemonger — I had faced so many in my life — I can't just sit back silently to let accusations regarding the Holocaust go by without reacting to it strongly. I simply have to join my fellow survivors who are as deeply affected and offended as I am, a survivor of Auschwitz and other camps.

The hurt was deep, the memory of our loved ones being killed during the Holocaust will always stay with us. Although the wounds have stopped bleeding, the scars remain and are now ripped open wide by a reporter of the likes of Doug Collins who proclaims to know the number of the victims of the Holocaust, *his rantings being published by the North Shore News religiously.* Where does Mr. Collins get his information? Certainly not from archives. It is his calculation and his calculation only, inspired by hatred.

I am deeply saddened by the attitude of these deniers, of minimizing the killings of millions of men, women and children. I am deeply saddened that hatred has found a willing ear in Vancouver, that reporters are free to spew their hatred. In my eyes this has little to do with "free speech".

When after five years living behind barbed wire I was told by the liberating forces that I am free, I am not so sure of it today. *Am I really free, or still subjected to hatred?*

Bronia Sonnenschein

November 3, 1989

Dear Mr. Hume,

I am trying to put into words my deep feelings while reading your column in the Vancouver Sun of November 3, 1989,
"It's no joking matter when roots lie in hatred."

Let me please first of all tell you that you have not only my
gratitude as a survivor of the Holocaust, but I am sure also of
those who, although not having experienced the horrors of the
Holocaust are and will remain sensitive to tasteless Jewish jokes
especially when they are told at a gathering with the purpose of
entertaining the audience. An audience that could actually see
great humour in those jokes — with the exceptions of a few.

Degrading us, making fun of us, stirring up trouble for us —
molehills can turn into mountains as history taught us — is the
prerogative of those who are totally insensitive to our — the
Jews' — feelings. You stood up for us by attacking bigotry and
hatred, by openly writing about it in a widely read newspaper
like the Vancouver Sun.

In a few days we Jews will be commemorating Kristallnacht
— the night of the broken glass. It was not only glass that broke,
our lives were broken as well. Nothing was and nothing will
ever be the same again.

And now the young generation — high-school students —
won't even be given a proper chance to learn about the horrors
of the 20th century.

Thank you for your compassion.

Sincerely yours,

Bronia Sonnenschein

August 27, 1992

Dear Ms. McFarlane,

Your article in the Vancouver Sun "Voices" on August 22, 1992 prompted me to thank you very much for your feelings of compassion and understanding.

I am not the person you saw on the bus concluding by her "badge of honour" to be a Holocaust survivor. Yet, I am also a survivor of Hitler's concentration camps and therefore appreciate your remarks more than I can tell.

Best wishes for your future,

Bronia Sonnenschein

Editor's note: Here is an excerpt from Arline McFarlane's article, "She wore her tattoo like a badge of courage":

"Suddenly into my mind flashed pictures that I had seen in magazines and documentaries on television. Nightmarish scenes of concentration camps, starving people, wide-eyed sick children with death all around. She had been there, she wore the stamp ...

She must have been a very young girl then. How much horror had she witnessed? How many loved ones had she lost? What did she have that enabled her to survive those terrible times that most of us cannot even comprehend?

The old lady became transfigured before my eyes. No longer did I see her as I had only a moment before. She sat there now bathed in the sunlight with a certain dignity about her. I wanted to go over and talk to her, but of course I could not invade her private world.

I shall never know her story but those six numbers on her arm said a multitude. She wore her tattoo like a badge of courage, which told all who saw it that here was a woman who, despite insurmountable odds, survived the Nazis.

We never spoke, our eyes never even met, yet I don't think I shall ever forget her."

Letters to Others

August 26, 1991

Dear Robert,

Let me please assure you that having participated in the seminar you gave was a great privilege. Not only was I given the opportunity to help clarify some of the feelings and emotions a survivor experiences, bearing in mind, of course, that no two people look at their traumatic experience the same way. But it also gave me the opportunity to better understand my own feelings.

I am referring specifically to two questions put to me. One, whether I was not afraid, or had actually the courage to bring children into the world, despite my past sufferings and the other one, whether or not I experienced a feeling of guilt.

Wanting children was the sign that I had not only regained my physical health, but also that I had started to recover mentally — are children not the re-affirmation of life? I believe that every survivor had asked him or herself, "why did I survive while the others did not?" This is not necessarily guilt. Would a feeling of guilt not have had a profound effect on my children? They themselves might have thought that they have to help me to carry the burden of guilt. Nothing would have been accomplished, more lives would have been ruined — needlessly. I therefore prefer to carry on the best way I can. Why did I survive? It remains an unanswered question. I feel extremely grateful, but not guilty.

I will always be available if needed — I am just a phone call away.

Wishing you and your loved ones Shana Tovah, a year filled with peace, health and happiness,

Yours,

Bronia Sonnenschein

Excerpts from a 2002 letter to a student

Dear Sheena,

Thank you so much for your delightful card and your warm words. There is never enough time or opportunity to get into all the details of one's life. Since you expressed interest about my time in New York and later on in Canada, I'll be happy to write to you about some "special" occurrences.

After leaving Israel for Canada ... we stopped for a month in Sweden as guests of good friends, where we secured a visitor's visa to the U.S. for a month reunion with part of our family who had gotten out in time. ... Regardless of having a visitor visa ... we were not permitted to disembark. We arrived on a weekend when financial institutions were closed and a security bond could not be posted for the three of us. And so we spent the weekend at Ellis Island. It was hard to believe and incredibly disappointing to us and our loved ones. We considered our- selves to still be lucky as we were given a room to ourselves. I sure had a very good look at the Statue of Liberty. Ironically, being on Ellis Island, one actually is not free. Eventually we had our reunion and a delightful time in New York. ...

Immediately after I was released from the hospital [*after the fatal car accident*] I felt fortunate to have been offered a job in the lumber company where my husband had worked, secure in the knowledge that my children were in the best care, my mother's.

A few months later an incident occurred that made me question if I would actually ever be free. A note was pushed under our door saying plainly, "Move away stinkpot Jew."

We did move to another district, but the incident is not for- gotten. There were others. The climate we live in today is not very encouraging either. But one has to go on and do the best one can do. ... My visit to Victoria, thanks to Prof. Beardsley's kind invitation, has shown me clearly that goodness and kindness still exist. Can I ask for more? ...

Fondly,

Bronia

June 1, 1992

Dear Dr. Zelman,

Through the Jewish Festival of the Arts I learned about the
Heritage and Mission — Jewish Vienna and a forthcoming exhibit
by the Jewish Welcome Service. I read the brochure and the
various articles and am looking forward to meeting Ms. Susie
Schneider, your representative.

But, most of all, it was the article about yourself that caught
my utmost interest. Our roles are somewhat reversed. I grew up
in Vienna and witnessed Kristallnacht and all the horror Nazi
Germany (and Austria) inflicted upon us. I ended up in the Lodz
Ghetto where I was with my parents and sister for four years
before being deported to Auschwitz in 1944. You, on the other
hand, ended up in Vienna after having experienced the horrors
of concentration camps.

I used to love Vienna, its music, its beauty, its charm and its
"Gemuetlichkeit", the magnificent Ringstrasse, the Staatsoper
and Burgtheater and, of course, its museums. As children, starting already in Kindergarten, we were taken to the Kunsthistor-
ische Museum and ever so often being rewarded by a visit to
the Prater. And last, but not least, the Viennese coffeehouse, the
refuge of every Viennese, where daily life centred. I applaud
you for wanting to reconstruct the Vienna of long, long ago.
Of keeping the memory of so many famous people alive that
contributed so greatly to this city. All their talents, their great
contributions, were forgotten after the Anschluss.

I visited Vienna 10 years ago together with my late sister.
(Her husband, Stan (Stasiek) Lenga was actually a native of
Lodz.) It was somehow a "bitter-sweet" trip. We wanted to
remember the laughter, the Gemuetlichkeit, the music that once
characterized Vienna. But you just can't forget the horror of
March 13, 1938, the day of the Anschluss. There was no more
Viennese music to be heard, Vienna, in no time at all, started to
march to a different tune. You know, as well as I do, that from

that day on our fate was sealed. There was no more laughter, only tears. We stayed 8 days, visiting old, familiar places — but it was not home anymore, we were just visitors, trying to recall the past.

Nevertheless, it is good to know that somebody like you wants to restore the Jewish cultural life in this city. I wish I had known of you at the time of your visit. I would have loved to meet you in person. Maybe some other time. In the meantime I am devoting my time now to Holocaust education. I frequently visit high-schools talking to students about my experiences during the Holocaust. It is important for them to know what went on and hearing it from a witness seems to make quite an impact on them.

I wish you continuing success,

Sincere greetings,

Bronia Sonnenschein

P.S. You might find it strange that as a former Viennese I am writing to you in English. I have been living here since 1950 — 42 years — it is a long time and although I won't forget my mother-language, I am not so fluent in it anymore.

November 16, 1992

Dear Professor Hilberg,

I was very happy to have been given the opportunity to meet you in person.

You probably know much more about the Lodz Ghetto than I do.

Yet, I believe there is still a difference between reading the facts that have been recorded and written about, and having actually lived through the Ghetto years.

I also wish to thank you for having addressed us. Your lecture here won't be forgotten.

I wish you continuing success, health and happiness.

Yours,

Bronia Sonnenschein

United States
Holocaust Memorial Museum

January 26, 1993

Mrs. B. Sonnenschein
4 - 6188 Willow St.
Vancouver, B.C.
V5Z 3S6

Dear Mrs. Sonnenschein,

The museum's opening date of April 1993 is less than three months away. To date we have compiled over 30,000 images in our archives, and additional photos are being added every day. Most of these photos are being entered into our computer imaging system which will be available to scholars and laymen alike.

It is with great appreciation that we received your photograph of Chaim Rumkowski and Hans Biebow via Raoul Hilberg. It might interest you to know that although we had a print of this image from Yivo Institute for Jewish Research in New York, the quality of your photo is far superior. With the help of donations such as yours, we are able to expand our photo archive in new directions. Thank you for contributing this image to our museum project.

Sincerely,

Genya Markon
Head, Photo Archives

Editor's Note: This photo is printed here on page 53.

June 24, 1997

National Hilfsfond
A - 1017 Wien, Österreich

Dear Dr. Meissner,

I hope you received both my letters from April 14 and 30th.
I am waiting with great hope to receive positive news from you.

I really find it difficult to believe that there is no trace of
me in Vienna, which I still look upon as my former homeland,
having lived there from 1916 till after the Anschluss in 1938
(as stated in Dr. Trnka's letter that I had submitted) where I was
educated and have worked.

It is for some people still inconceivable to believe that anyone having survived Auschwitz (the notorious deathcamp) had
upon liberation nothing to call its own — just the rags on ones
body given to them. I will never forget the words of the man
herding us into the ghetto — "where you are going you don't
need documents" when my mother tried to gather them.

And now 52 years later I am told that there is no trace of
me — the documents are gone, I survived.

Yours truly,

Bronia Sonnenschein

P.S. In Vienna we called it "Vogel Strauss politic" (burying your
head in the sand like an ostrich, pretending if you can't see it,
it's not here).

Excerpt from a 2003 letter to a daughter and granddaughter of Roman Kawalek

I was really happy to talk to both of you. ...

Writing about Tante Mila and Roman brought them momentarily closer to me, although they have never been far removed. Tante Mila's face drawn yet defiant, Roman's face the face of an old warrior, a lot of "piss and vinegar", a lot of "chutzpah", a lot of "old soldiers never die — they just fade away". Both of them courageous people.

I told you why I support the war on Iraq. Like Hitler in his time, a ruthless killer not only of Jews, but his very own people, so is Saddam Hussein a vicious killer, a cancer that does not go away but keeps growing day by day. I remember so clearly standing with my fellow inmates ... at the river Elbe ... where the Germans took us to wait for the end of the attack — the firebombing of Dresden. Not to protect us — just making sure we wouldn't escape. I was looking up at the sky and praying for the success of our allies, never realizing for a moment that we could be killed. Up until that moment, that day in February 1945, none of us were even aware that we had allies. Living behind barbed wire we had no information whatsoever on the world scene. It would have helped knowing we had allies.

I will never stop thanking every courageous soldier for defeating the enemy. There is not the slightest doubt in my mind that in cases like that, ruthless killers like the one today, Hussein threatening the world with mass destruction can only be defeated by force — never by "diplomacy". It took a Churchill to wake up his people, Roosevelt his, and now it's President Bush's and Tony Blair's turn to rid the world of a tyrant. You can't let a pitbull run loose. It just does not work that way. I learned to appreciate freedom only after I was robbed of it. I am aware now each day of how precious freedom is, and together with the freedom-loving world I would like to hold on to it. ...

My love to you ...,

Bronia

February 14, 2003

Dear Mr. Wiesenthal,

I have admired you for a very long time and I will never forget your words: "While others built houses I did not forget you."

I hope you will find time to read my enclosed book. It is my son Dan who encouraged me again to put on paper what I vividly remember.

Although I have lived in Canada for over 50 years, my childhood and youth in Vienna with my family will be forever my cherished memories. The "Viennese dream" ended in 1938 after the Anschluss.

But we carry on, we, the survivors have been given a second chance. You used it to bring so many criminals to justice. I simply try to do the best I can to keep the memory of the Holocaust alive.

With great respect and best wishes,
Yours,

Bronia Sonnenschein

DOKUMENTATIONSZENTRUM

DES BUNDES JÜDISCHER
VERFOLGTER DES NAZIREGIMES

SALZTORGASSE 6/IV/5
1010 WIEN, AUSTRIA

TELEFON: 0043-1-533 98 05 / 0043-1-533 91 31
FAX: 0043-1-535 03 97

BANKVERBINDUNG:
CREDITANSTALT BANKVEREIN WIEN
KONTO NR.: 0047-32608/00, BLZ 11000

Mrs. Bronia Sonnenschein
c/o Dan Sonnenschein
601 - 1089 W. 13 Ave.
Vancouver, BC   V6H 1N1
CANADA

WIEN. April 22, 2003
SW/Tr

Dear Mrs.Sonnenschein,

Mr. Simon Wiesenthal has asked me to thank you kindly for having
sent him a personally autographed copy of your book, **Victory
Over Nazism**. The volume has been lying on his desk for some
weeks now and he has repeatedly taken it up to read parts of
it. (That is also why we havn't acknowledged receipt; please
excuse us.)

Mr. Wiesenthal was not only interested in your account of your
experiences during the Holocaust but was very impressed by the
time and energy you invest in your educational work, which
reflects the aim of all of his work since the end of the war;
i.e. to make sure that the horrors and the tragedy of the
Holocaust never be forgotten and so that something similar can
never occur again. He congratulates you on the success of your
efforts and wishes you all the best for the future.

Sincerely,

T. Mergili

Trudi Mergili
(for Mr. Wiesenthal)

The article that inspired the following is available
online at www.gangway.net/1/gangway1.2.html.

March 26, 2005

Dear Prof. Haslinger,

It is not often that one comes across an article like yours,
Jewish Vienna. It only lately came into my hands.

You are my son's and daughter's generation whereas I
witnessed the annexation of Austria on March 12, 1938. My
hometown was Vienna. On that day I not only learned what
hatred was but I witnessed how the "patriotic" Viennese
surrendered their beautiful country to Germany without a
whimper. I am Jewish; I loved Vienna with all my heart, its
history, its beauty, its "Gemütlichkeit", its special flavour, the
Vienna Woods and Johann Strauss. I remember all the famous
names you quoted and all that stood for Vienna. I remember
the Vienna before 1938.

Hitler found his willing executioners in Vienna, in all of
Austria. They became first class Nazis. After liberation in
1945 we, my mother and sister, the three survivors, returned
to Vienna. A rude anti-semitic remark drove us out of Vienna
again, after spending less than a week there. I did not return
until 1982 when my sister and I went to Vienna on what we
called a "sentimental journey". We stayed one week, visited the
old familiar places, shed a lot of tears, yet also found pleasure
in recalling the good times.

It was heartwarming to read your account. Maybe your
generation can make a difference. There is always hope.

I would be pleased to hear from you. You can reach me
through my son's E-mail. I have lived in Vancouver, Canada
since 1950.

Regards,

Bronia Sonnenschein

Editor's note: Prof. Haslinger replied graciously, but unfortunately I have been unable to locate this e-mail. Part of its content may be inferred from the following.

Date: Mon, 03 Jul 2006
From: Dan Sonnenschein
To: Josef Haslinger
Subject: Re: AW: Response to "Jewish Vienna"

Dear Prof. Haslinger,

Thanks for your thoughtful reply, which my mother and I appreciate; it is good to know of the improvement in Austria.

It was certainly tragic that Hugo Sonnenschein survived Auschwitz only to die in a communist prison. My parents, who married in Prague, managed to escape the communist regime there in 1949. As far as I know, we are not related to this author, although it is still possible as my father was from Moravia (Schumperk). He died a long time ago, and his surviving brother does not seem to know of such a connection. If I find out any more on this, I'll let you know.

Best wishes,

Dan

December 27, 2005

Dear Sir Martin,

It is maybe presumptuous to send you, a renowned historian and biographer of Sir Winston Churchill, my book. It was an attempt to record my experiences during the Holocaust and subsequent rebuilding up of my life. Maybe you might browse through it.

I read your book, "Continue to Pester, Nag and Bite", and I admire you for giving us, your readers, the chance to know what greatness is all about. I also know from my experiences that it takes a lot of "biting" and determination to reach one's goal.

I wish you health, happiness and peace in the New Year and years to come.

Sincere greetings,

Yours,

Bronia Sonnenschein

March 19, 2006

Dear Sir Martin,

I apologize for my delayed answer to your letter from Feb. 21st which I truly enjoyed reading. Thank you sincerely for your kind comments about my book.

I am eagerly looking forward to receive and read your book, "Kristallnacht: Prelude to Destruction" and it is very kind of you to send it to me.

I greatly enjoyed having made contact with you by writing.

As always with sincerest wishes,

Yours,

Bronia Sonnenschein

May 19, 2006

Dear Sir Martin,

Thank you so much for your letter from 11 May. I would like to
let you know that not only was it my privilege to know "Tante
Mary" and her sister Edith (page 248 in your book) but also to
work as her assistant for at least a short time in 1938. She was
the guardian angel for the children in her care while their parents
were frantically trying to get to the free world after the annexation. Nobody could tell or read a story to these young children
like Tante Mary, nobody was loved more than she. I tried to
emulate her and she encouraged me. To this day I remember
some of them, including Herbert, a 4-year old, a beautiful boy,
and Lilly, a frail-looking little girl. Herbert was Lilly's "protect-
or", putting his arm around her when she cried listening to the
sad part — either a big, bad wolf, or a wicked stepmother. It
was a tearful good-bye when I left.

When I read her name in your book it brought a lot of
memories back. Tante Mary's violent death saddened me a lot.
She deserved the best that life has to offer and got the worst.

So you see, Sir Martin, she too came alive for me in your
pages and for that I thank you with all my heart.

Yours,

Bronia Sonnenschein

P.S. On page 8 of my book [*p. 48 in this edition*] (and enclosed) is
my picture standing in front of the house where Tante Mary's
kindergarten was located.

May 23, 2005

Dear Mr. Lawrason,

On May 19, Mr. Lemna brought his students (Grade 10) to the Holocaust Centre to view the exhibit "Lost Faces", pictures of victims of the Holocaust.

My function was to address Mr. Lemna's students about my experiences during the Holocaust. My reason for writing to you about it is to thank you sincerely for sanctioning these visits. It's never easy to talk of ones experiences during the period encompassing five years of horror.

Thanks to Mr. Lemna, whom I have known for many years, his students are exceptionally well prepared. I know because just by looking at them I could clearly read in their eyes their understanding and their compassion. I am well aware how difficult it is for them to ever begin to understand what crimes against humanity mean. Teachers like Mr. Lemna keep the memory of the Holocaust alive so that it may never happen again.

Thank you.

Sincerely,

Bronia Sonnenschein

Expulsion of Nazi Apologist

Doug Ward (1992)

This article was published in The Vancouver Sun on Nov. 4, 1992, titled "Death camp survivors welcome expulsion of Nazi apologist."

W HEN BRONIA SONNENSCHEIN reads about Holocaust-denier David Irving, memories of Auschwitz and other Nazi death camps flood back.

The ghetto, the starvings, the beatings. The smoke coming from the crematoriums.

"I am very, very angry. I just can't believe that anybody would say something like this."

During an interview Monday, Sonnenschein said she hurts each time a Nazi apologist such as Irving appears in the news. The British author's claim to fame is his view that Nazi Germany and its collaborators did not systematically destroy European Jewry.

Sonnenschein, a Jew who grew up in pre-war Vienna, said Irving is denying the hell she endured and still endures.

"Who is Mr. Irving? Was he there? Did he see our suffering? Does he know how we feel? Did he know the scars left on us? I was at Auschwitz. I was. I was. That's why I can talk about it. It's not hearsay. It's not a fabricated story."

The Holocaust ended in 1945, but the psychic wounds of the survivors continue.

"My dreams are shattered. Life hasn't been the same. Ever. You can't wash it away with soap. You try to cope and you try to make the best of it."

Leon Kahn leads a double life. He is a successful Vancouver businessperson and a Lithuanian Jew who lost his entire family in the Holocaust. Like Sonnenschein and many other survivors in Vancouver, he too is transported back to a personal hell when Irving is in the news.

"It throws it all back and brings it all into focus again. The things you're trying to forget."

When Kahn sees a freight train, he imagines his mother and grandmother being carried in cattle cars to their extermination in a death camp. When he goes on business to a slaughterhouse, he imagines the carcasses on hooks are corpses of his people.

When he thinks of Irving ...

"My whole family was picked off one at a time. I lost everybody. My father was shot with a bullet and died on my knees. My sister was bayoneted before my eyes. My mother and grandfather ... I don't know which camp they died in."

Irving, 56, is being held in a Niagara Falls jail pending an immigration hearing set for today. He had been ordered to leave Canada by Sunday night but was turned back at the border by U.S. authorities. Canadian officials say he will be sent back to England if the U.S. continues to refuse to accept him.

The British author gained notoriety for his claim that there had been no mass murder of Jews by the Nazis. Last week in Vancouver, Irving told reporters there was a Holocaust — but far fewer than the generally accepted figure of six million Jews.

Irving also denied the existence of gas chambers and crematoria. He claimed that most of the "more than 200,00 but less than two or three million" Jews who died fell victim to epidemics or slave labor treatment.

For Kahn and Sonnenschein, Irving is a reminder that the hate they survived is still out there. She worries that young people might hear him and fall victim to anti-Semitism.

"There is still that angst. You know what angst is? Scared. I'm still scared. The feeling is there. Somebody does something like that — there's the angst coming.

"If you go through such a sad experience in your life and lose so many loved ones and then Irving and Zundel and Keegstra and company say it is a hoax.

"What can make them do it?"

Sonnenschein's most precious possession is a letter she was given 45 years ago by a Christian Germany woman while waiting with other inmates of a labor camp in Dresden.

"Take it. This will protect you," the woman whispered. Sonnenschein stuffed the letter into her blouse and did not read it until after the liberation. At the top of it, in German, it said: "In the Name of the Father, and the Son and the Holy Ghost."

If you believed in its power, the letter promised, it would protect you and those around you from all harm. "I've told my children if something happens to me, they take the letter. I want to believe in the good. I don't want to believe in Mr. Irving. I want to believe in the woman who gave me the letter."

Kahn also wants to believe in things that are good. But he becomes angry when talking about Irving. "It reawakens all the feelings and the rage that I had and has slowly been going away. What you want to do on first reaction is just grab him by the throat and choke the living daylights out of him."

He added: "Sure, we live in a democratic country and we have freedom of speech. But when a man like that comes and says this to people like myself and some of my friends who went to Auschwitz — it's very hard on your psyche to listen to things like that."

Kahn said Irving is not only apologizing for Hitler, he is carrying on the Nazi leader's campaign of hatred. "He's not only politically driven, he's hate-driven. He knows that it (the Holocaust) happened. He knows all the facts and figures.

"Through people like him, Hitler is continuing on his saga that finished in 1945. By denying that it ever happened."

Canadian Jewish Congress lawyer Morris Monday said his group welcomes Canada's move to expel Irving.

"From our standpoint, what happened with David Irving is connected with the Nazi war criminals."

Meanwhile, Vancouver Jews will commemorate Kristallnacht — the Night of Broken Glass — on Monday at Beth Israel Synagogue. Professor Raul Hilberg of the University of Vermont — a Holocaust expert — is the keynote speaker.

Kristallnacht, which occurred in November 1938, was the night when the Nazis unleashed a wave of terror against German Jews. Historians regard it as the start of the Holocaust.

Holocaust Horror Stories Enthrall Teenagers

Richard Watts (2003)

Article in the Victoria Times Colonist newspaper.

A VANCOUVER WOMAN'S personal testimony of the Holocaust silenced an auditorium crammed with more than 800 teens Thursday.

Bronia Sonnenschein related her personal memories at a symposium for high school students held at the University of Victoria and organized by the Victoria Holocaust Remembrance and Education Society.

Sonnenschein's story took the teens to her own graduation in Vienna, a time before she really understood the nature of hatred. But in 1938 Austria was absorbed into Nazi Germany and Sonnenschein's life changed forever.

Her testimony took the teens to a ghetto in Poland where she spent four years. Then there was a five-day train ride in a cattle car, with no food, no water and only a bucket for dozens of people to use as a toilet.

When the train stopped and Sonnenschein stumbled out, she came face-to-face with the belching smokestacks of the Auschwitz crematoria.

Throughout her talk Sonnenschein made sure the teens got a good view of the terrible little moments, like the face of the four-year-old boy, her neighbour in the ghetto, torn from his father and loaded onto a truck never to be seen again. "I don't think that little boy had ever experienced chocolate or ice cream," she said.

And there was the experience of being stripped naked, inspected and shaved of all her body hair upon arrival at Auschwitz.

"One indignity followed another."

At the end of her talk Sonnenschein asked the assembled teens to think of her next week, on May 8. That's the anniversary of the day in 1945 when a single Russian soldier on horseback rode up and told her and her fellow prisoners they were free to go. "It was on May 8, 1945 that I really started to appreciate freedom," she said.

Sonnenschein's message drew the loudest and most visible response at the symposium. The teens all leapt to their feet at the end of her talk.

And it was the personal testimonies that seemed to strike the biggest chord.

Brianna Berbennik, 16, a student at Belmont secondary, said much of the symposium dealt with things they had already learned in school. The personal stories were, however, a more powerful matter.

"The only real part I got out of it was the real-life stories," said Berbennik.

Symposium organizers agree that keeping the story and the remembrance of the Holocaust alive is going to be tougher as survivors die.

"We have a challenge," said David Katz, past chairman of the Victoria Holocaust Remembrance and Education Society.

Katz said it's especially tough with today's teens, who are fed horrors and violence in movies and videos. "They are bombarded by so many images which are destructive they are desensitized," he said.

But as part of the symposium's effort to sensitize teens to the need to keep vigilant against hate, Victoria police Constable Paul Brookes spoke of the potential damage in symbols like the swastika and their use in hate crimes.

He warned that racist neo-nazi groups such as skinheads are also turning to more underground code symbols. For example, the number 88 is used in graffiti. The eighth letter of the alphabet being H, 88 is code for Heil Hitler. And 18 is code for Adolph Hitler, he said. "There is organized hate within our community."

His words were backed up by teens at the symposium.

"It's happening right now," said Collette Ordano, 17, of Campbell River. "You will see people walking around with Confederate flags."

Responses from Students

These pages represent a small fraction of the comments
and letters conveying similar feelings and thoughts.

O.K., I confess. I admit it. I went to this presentation with the wrong attitude. Was I prepared to learn? Not really. I was more or less content with the idea of talking with my friends and throwing spit balls at the Enderby students . . .

But when the speakers stood up, and started to relay their feelings, their terrible experiences, I was stunned. The emotions that were being handed to me were probably more than I had ever actually had to deal with.

And it was at that point that my attitude changed.

It was no longer an excuse from doing real work. It was an opportunity, perhaps a once in a lifetime opportunity, to put myself in their shoes and share the experiences of a person who had truly "been to hell and back".

And I took advantage of that opportunity.

I had never, and probably never will again, listened so intently, so carefully, to every word that reached my ears. I had never paid so close attention to every inflection, every little expression that gave me that much more insight into what these people had really experienced . . .

I will probably remember that for the rest of my life, and any time something happens to me that disturbs the even flow of security around me, I'll realize how minuscule and small my problems really are, and how awful things COULD be.

So I guess the symposium reached at least one person, me, which means that it was all worthwhile.

— Jay Schlosar

As I walked into the gym, all I thought was that this was another one of those boring presentations where someone would talk forever and a day telling us about something we already knew and could fall asleep without being noticed. But it wasn't. At the age of sixteen, I didn't understand what it was like to go through the Holocaust and live to tell my story. As the speaker spoke I knew that some people would have a hard time understanding her but for some reason I heard every word. When she finished and the next speaker presented himself, I was listening but my mind was still with the woman who just told her story. I was moved by her courage not only because of what she went through but also for getting in front of a couple hundred unknown teenagers.

My heart felt for her. I wanted to let her know that I would never forget her nor her story, but a friend of mine pulled me away to go and catch my bus. Since then when people ask me about how I felt that morning I would answer "I have never been so inspired by just one person before in my entire life." And that's just what she did. She will always be an inspiration in my life and for years to come. Her story taught me not only about the Holocaust but taught me not to lose faith in myself or God and I thank her.

— Amanda Weaver

You brought tears to my eyes when you said "we all smile and cry in the same language." It makes so much sense. I can see it when I walk through the hallways at school. We may not always look alike or speak the same language but we can always tell when someone is happy or sad.

I will remember you, your story and the saying "we all smile and cry in the same language," for the rest of my life. You touched my life in a way that no else could have. I am grateful that you and your family was saved so that you could tell us your story. I will always treasure you and your story.

— Laura Sharpe

York House

February 1994

Dear Bronia,

My name is Angela Harris and I was one of the girls you shared your story with at the art gallery. I had never heard a survivor of the Holocaust before I heard you. And although I had seen movies and read books, not until I heard you did I understand how real it was.

Your story was so amazing that one doesn't want to believe that those things actually happened in real life. But your story was indeed very real.

You are the most inspiring woman I have ever met, and I feel privileged to have heard your story. Even after all the horrifying things you have been through, it is obvious you are full of love and life. I will never forget when you said, "they never took my soul." Your beautiful soul shines through you, your name is very appropriate for you. You radiate like sunshine.

You are a very brave woman to talk about what happened to you. I can see it is very difficult for you to talk about it, but I can only encourage you by saying that you struck a chord deep within me. And I hope I can come out of my own tough times with as much conviction as you have. Your honesty was much respected, especially when you kindly answered our questions after you spoke.

I will always remember you, Bronia Sonnenschein.

May God's light always shine on you.

Angie Harris

Mrs. Bronia Sonnenschein,

Thank you so much for coming all the way to small-town Pitt Meadows to tell us your story. You have shown tremendous courage and endurance, both of which have served you well. It is amazing how you plunged yourself right back into such an overwhelming ordeal which became your life for so many years. I was truly touched and moved by your words. You have a great deal of power there. It is, as you said, unbelievable that such powerful spirits were incarcerated, and the world stood aside.

I feel that people who are lucky enough to hear your story get a lot from the experience. People start understanding, and that is a very important step. The day after your presentation, my Socials class sat around for the entire hour talking about it. There was a lot of frustration there. People want to know how other people could let something like the Holocaust happen. Although it really is easy to just let things happen, to turn one's back and pretend like everything is alright. Sadly, the world isn't so. Genocide is still a practice in parts of the world today, but most people don't really do anything about it. Sure, maybe a second thought, but actions are perhaps even stronger than words. Inside, people are very afraid. I am. I am afraid of the world, society, and myself. I am no different than the people who stood by and let the Holocaust happen. Those people did not have bad intentions. I am afraid of what might happen if I should be confronted with a war situation. I am perhaps not another Nazi prison guard, but what is it that separates them from me? Then again, maybe it's knowing: knowing that I wouldn't want to see people be hurt like that. Maybe it is my personal devotion to human rights. Maybe it's wanting safety, or security, or peace. Or maybe your words, and the words spoken by those who can no longer speak, maybe those have helped give me the strength to fight.

Sincerely,

Karyn Ho

My name is Jenna Bowers, and I am a senior at Sandpoint High School. I attended the presentation at the Panida Theatre on May 5. I want to thank you for telling your story. It had a great effect on me.

Last year in my history class we studied the Holocaust and watched several videos. Learning about it has always been disturbing and very emotional for me. I have seen "Schindler's List", and that also deeply troubled me. However, the Holocaust has always seemed very distant to me — a long time ago in a far away land. Listening to you speak of things I had only ever seen in movies made it to real to me. I want to thank you for that.

Let me say that you a very eloquent speaker. You told your story so well and I cried through the whole thing. I can't imagine how difficult it must be for you to recount your misery over and over. You are certainly one of the most courageous women I have ever had the honor of listening to or meeting. I feel that what you had to say was very important, and it definitely changed my life.

I want to extend my deepest gratitude to you for sharing your story with me and moving me so tremendously. Thank you.

— Jenna Bowers

I am writing this letter because your story touched my heart and really made me think. I thank you for opening up a chapter in your life that would probably be easier left closed. By listening to you speak about your experiences in the Holocaust, I learned in that hour and a half more than I ever have from any book or movie. I never realized how extreme the actions taken by Hitler and his followers were. I can't stress enough how pleased I was to shake your hand and I really admire you for having the courage and strength to talk about something others can barely think about.

— Mike Gray

Hello! I would like to begin my letter by thanking you for taking time out of your own busy day to come and talk to us at Pitt Meadows Secondary School. This letter will have to be a short one, for I'm sure you already have an obscene amount of letters to go through.

When we heard you were coming to speak to us about your life during the Holocaust, I know that all of my classmates, myself included, were looking forward to hearing you speak. You definitely fulfilled all of our expectations of you, and much more. Your English is impeccable, and you speak with a very keen intelligence. I noticed these things right away during the speech, but what I came to realise further into it was the horrible trials you went through to get to where you are today.

I'm sure that not more than five people in that room knew before you told us how terrible the Holocaust was and how many Jewish people died. It's hard to believe that the obscene ordeals that plagued the Jewish people could have been brought on by another human being. I believe now that Adolf Hitler set the standard for the lowest human life-form possible.

You said that your objective in delivering sermons to people all around the world was to enlighten them of the horrifying acts that went on during the Holocaust, and to prevent something like that from ever happening again. Well, you should be very happy to know that objective has been reached a hundred times over. Because when you finished speaking, there was barely a dry eye in the room, and from the number of people I spoke to, all were intent upon spreading the word about your talk. All were disgusted with — for lack of a better word — the unfair treatment of the Jews during the War and Holocaust. Mrs. Sonnenschein, you have permission to rest now, because with this information rolling around in our brains, we can pretty much guarantee that there will be no repeat or similarity of the Holocaust again — at least while our generation informs the generations to come about it.

Thank you again for your time and precious story.

— Tara Gostelow

I am a grade eleven student at North Delta Senior Secondary
and I heard you speak about your experiences with the Holocaust. I was greatly moved by your story and by the message
accompanying. I admire your courage in surviving the cruelty
brought upon you and in continuing to spread the truths of
what occurred. I'm happy to see that, although the Holocaust
happened over fifty years ago, it has not been forgotten. It was
and is a vital part of everyone's history and, as you stated so
clearly, by our knowledge and remembrance of such an event
we will have a greater chance of not letting it happen again. I
sincerely believe it won't. So many changes have occurred over
the last fifty years. So many movements fighting for equality
and human rights have planted the seeds for a more accepting
society. I thank you for reminding us what being human is all
about, giving from deep within our hearts and souls. We are not
meant to be selfish, but selfless. As well, I thank you for helping
me and my fellow students to remember that we are all part of
one race and, no matter what God we believe created us, we are
each an important part of what is called humanity. I am sorry
you were a victim of such an inhuman group of people. However, I don't think of you as a victim, rather a survivor and a
heroine who overcame the obstacles put before you.

— Sara Wickert

March 27, 1998

Dear Bronia,

My name is Marcello Gabriele and I am a student of Professor
Newton at Simon Fraser University. I recently had the privilege
of attending your discussion regarding the Holocaust. I simply
wanted to take this opportunity to thank you for sharing your
personal story of struggle. Your discussion will forever be a
valuable memory. As a historian, I have studied the Holocaust

many times and am constantly amazed at the courage and intestinal fortitude you and your fellow people displayed. I am twenty years old, approximately the age of yourself when your life completely altered. I cannot possibly imagine the horror you experienced. I applaud you in finding the strength and courage to discuss your tragic experiences with others. As you mentioned, this interaction will further educate society and hopefully prevent such a tragedy from occurring ever again. I only hope you will continue sharing your experiences with others, for your kind and gentle spirit should be witnessed by all. I recently came across a quote that I feel best describes why yourself, along with many others continue to share your horrific ordeal. The individual is named Avigdor Shachan who describes the ghettos of Transnistria. The individual states,

> To my brethren, the dead of Transnistria!
> It was with you that I marched in the death marches,
> I starved with you in the Pits of Death,
> It is with you that I carry our death
> In the fields of the Living.

I commend you on your positive outlook on life after being forced to endure such extreme hardships. You are truly an inspiration, and I am deeply honoured to have been in your presence. You have made me realize that life is a gift given to us, and as such, should never be taken for granted. You have altered my perception on life for the better, and I am eternally grateful. Once again, I commend you on your courage on behalf of my peers, I thank you for your valuable time. It is an experience that I shall never forget.

Sincerely yours,

Marcello Gabriele

I sit in Bronia's living room drinking tea and admiring the art-work. She later tells me that her daughter painted most of the pictures that are hanging on the walls. She proceeds to show me a photograph of her granddaughter and I think to myself how fortunate these people are to have such a warm, caring person in their life. I begin to let her story mull over in my mind and I wonder how she made it, how she kept on going. She answers, "Because of my family."

I look at Bronia with admiration. On the outside I notice a small, pretty, blonde-haired, blue-eyed woman. I study her eyes and I cannot help but recognize the look of pain, even when she smiles. I know I can never understand what Bronia has been through; I can only sympathize. At times, while I am speaking to her, I can feel the tears well up in my eyes and I realize how hard it must be for her to tell her story without crying. Although, at the same time I understand and appreci-ate the reasons for why she conceals her torment. I observe Bronia again, and I do not necessarily see a strong woman sitting next to me; I see a woman full of strength.

— Cristina Cavezza

How I will never forget the light of courage you shone on me and countless others. Please continue on your quest and remain resilient. You are an amazing, wonderful woman whom I admire deeply. I will never stop dreaming.

— Eric Alexander

I am so glad that you are able to talk to us about your experi-ences, some good, most bad, in the Holocaust. It really meant a lot to everyone, as I am not just speaking for myself. It is very important to remember everything that happened. I am encouraging you to write at least one book on your journey. You came face-to-face with the devil, but you were brave and courageous, and you had hope, so you turned your back on death.

— Naomi Rozenberg

How do you put onto paper what you can't even speak aloud?

As someone who is actively studying the Holocaust, and wishes to dedicate the rest of her life to it, I've read a thing or two about what went on. I've seen the horrific photographs. I've even cried over some first-hand accounts, usually written by a witness who did not live long after he had created his testimony.

But it was not until I was given the privilege of meeting and hearing Bronia Sonnenschein speak that the Holocaust suddenly became horribly and frighteningly alive. I was struck dumb by her, utterly undone by the story that she unfolded, a story that told me nothing new about the terrors of the Third Reich, but a story that nevertheless made me forget myself and my own problems so completely that even now, a week later, the thought of her and her voice come to mind without warning and make me pause in whatever I am doing.

Bronia reminded me that the huge numbers, the photographs, the printed stores — they're all real. Of course, I don't mean to say that at one point I found them not real; but I do suggest that, after one reads so much and hears the numbers so many times a strange sort of desensitization starts to creep in: thousands arrested after *Kristallnacht*, 33,000 murdered at Babi Yar, one million gassed at Auschwitz, six million exterminated between 1939 and 1945. Suddenly, the huge, atrocious numbers are just numbers. Bronia changed that; a woman with the strength to make peace with the hell she lived through reminded me that for each number, there was an individual with a life and a family and hopes and dreams. Each single number, with its story, was real, just as Bronia is real.

Words trivialize what Bronia now means to me. I simply cannot find the right words, in any language, to tell you what I feel. Suffice it to say, then, that I consider myself lucky to have shaken the hand of Bronia, a living historical testament, a mother, a Jew, a survivor, a human, a woman who looked at me with a smile filled with genuine pleasure at meeting me. And now the six million ones who died during the Holocaust are a little bit closer to real for me.

— Lauren Faulkner

I have never been at a more astonishing speech than the one you prepared for us today. I was very inspired by what you felt and how you survived through all the turmoil and disasters. I believe it must be very difficult for you to be talking to a huge group of people about your own painful past. I admire you for standing up telling us about it and letting us see what you've been through. This takes not only courage but also your love and care for our future. You want to make sure what happened to you will not occur to us and our children again. Thank you.

— Sandi Chih

I was thoroughly touched by your speech and I wish that you could have spoken to us for hours. ... I know I will never forget the way your face can light up a room. You are truly an incredible human being, in mind, body, and especially soul. May peace and harmony live with you always.

— Soula F. Parassidis

Thank you. You made the past clearer to me. The hardest steel goes through the hottest fire.

— Ashley McMullen

While taking this course, I became painfully aware of how the Holocaust continues to be felt today. I have to admit that my knowledge was somewhat naive and I was shocked to learn the extent to which the Jews have been persecuted throughout history. Besides learning a great deal of hard facts, what stood out the most for me is the Jewish unbreakable will to live. They stand as testimony to the life force that exists within the human spirit. It is this will that I find most inspiring. The effect that this course has had on me crosses intellectual borders and enters a place that is at the core of my being. It is difficult to say what I haven't fully grasped myself. My heart and many thanks go out to Bronia Sonnenschein for sharing her painful story. I honor her courage and strength.

— Kristyna Murphy

Your visit to our class as part of the course will be the memory I retain for the rest of my life. All the books, films and theoretical discussions pale in the face of your memories. Your faith, your bravery, and your love for your family are all reminders of what really matters in this materialistic world of shallow values. As you stood before us I thought of how you stood your ground in the face of insane tormentors then and how you continue to stand up for your beliefs now and I am awed by your courage.

— Grace Skinner

What impressed me most about Bronia was her strength and composure. Half of us in the crowd were breaking down in tears when she was relating her experiences. But she was strong and she did what she had to do. She told the stories to teach us, to explain to us so we could understand.

— Jenette Barry

I do not understand how people can be so indifferent about it? Do they not know the extent of the horror? Probably not. ... It makes me sad and privileged at the same time to think that we are the last generation to actually be able to see people such as Bronia speak about their loss and suffering. When they pass away, a piece of history will die with them; therefore, it is our responsibility to keep their memories alive. It is the least that we can do to honour them and their courage. If we forget, we may let history repeat itself.

— Targol Salehi

Holocaust survivors will not be around forever to share their experiences with us. Their fervent determination to educate today's young people for tomorrow will hopefully prevent a World War. Ms. Sonnenschein's efforts to prepare our generation with the knowledge and tools to stop the outbreak of another war, may pass unnoted but never forgotten.

— Raymond Gee

Mrs. Sonnenschein, Your dignity and pride may have been stolen, but your beauty of your soul and spirit will forever remind me of what these tragedies can never take away!

— Sarah A. Thorn

After listening to Ms. Bronia's moving speech on the atrocities of the Holocaust, I was deeply troubled by the experiences she described. I could not imagine that humanity was capable of inflicting such cruelties. For me, no longer was the Holocaust a statistic in history books — sadly, it was all too real.

Hearing Ms. Bronia's description of the lives of Jews in Europe during World War II made me think: why would anyone inflict this suffering on the Jews. The Jews had done nothing wrong, and yet they seemed to be the perpetual scapegoat of European society. However, that still didn't warrant such large scale concentration and extermination camps. Up until now, I am still overwhelmed by just the massiveness of this "Final Solution": six million Jews killed, many more displaced. Hitler's "Final Solution" was not a solution, but rather a manifestation of extreme sadism. Although knowing about the past is important, what is of greater importance is acting upon it. It is of no use just to listen to the presentation, be saddened, and wake up the next day as if nothing has happened. Perhaps as Professor Elie Wiesel has also mentioned in his speech in Vancouver, the lesson that we should all keep to heart is that we should not take peace for granted. In fact, we should take nothing for granted. As I have learned from this presentation, anything and everything that one owns can be snatched away in an instant — including dignity and life.

Before the presentation, I sometimes asked myself if it was really possible for humanity to become so immoral, cruel and rotten. Unfortunately, it seems, with Hitler's campaign, that is possible. My only hope is that we may correct our past wrongs and work to build and maintain peace in this world.

— Joseph Wong

The Loving Mrs. Sonnenschein

A very important lady came to our school last week, and touched many of our hearts. Mrs. Sonnenschein came to Norquay thinking it was a secondary school and found out it was an elementary school. She had a speech already planned for older kids. When Mrs. Sonnenschein saw all the younger kids I think she got a little bit nervous. Mrs. Sonnenschein told us all about World War 2 and how she felt. What I really liked about her speech was how she always had hope in herself. She knew not to give up. Mrs. Sonnenschein should be thanked for her courage and how she understood how we felt. I think that the death camps should not have been allowed to exist. If anyone had realized how the Jewish people were hurt physically and emotionally they would not have let it happen. The speech Mrs. Sonnenschein gave moved many people and some people even put themselves on the spot to think how she might have felt.

— Binita Naidu

I am surprised that Mrs. Sonnenschein can even come to classes and give these talks, considering the immense mental and physical anguish she experienced during her ordeal. I know that had I lived through such an event I would not have the strength to talk about it, especially not multiple times to schools all over the city. I suppose however that there is some logic to Mrs. Sonnenschein subjecting herself to the pain that these talks no doubt bring back, and that is that if no one was talking about the Holocaust it might just fade away. The possibility of the Holocaust fading away is a risk too great to take, no matter what personal pain people may suffer keeping the memory of this injustice alive.

— Justin S.

I admire you for your bravery and courage but I admire you most of all for your heart and faith you bestow in the younger generation like myself. Thanks again.

— Barclay Morgan

Bronia Sonnenschein: A Remarkable Woman

Shawna Lum

The events that make up history are filled with tragedy and senseless death. Take, for instance, the Holocaust. To think about how human beings treated other human beings during this time is appalling. It is frightening to learn about it, and to wonder if something like the Holocaust could ever happen again.

Bronia Sonnenschein is a Holocaust survivor and a member of the Vancouver Holocaust Education Centre. Her visit to Port Moody Secondary a couple of weeks ago really moved me. She shared with us her personal experiences: how she was forced from her regular home in Austria and sent to a ghetto, life in a concentration camp, Auschwitz, horrific death marches, and Dresden. She was about our age when all her dreams and hopes were shattered at the hands of the Nazis. She was called "subhuman" and treated even worse. I had learned this in History class, so I knew some of what happened during this time, but hearing her speak in person brought home the true tragedy of the Holocaust.

She was connecting us to the past through her words. At one point she asked us if we could imagine it. No, I could not. There was no way I could even begin to picture how I would deal with pretending to not know my own mother for fear of being separated. I could not work all day in a brutal camp without proper food or water and sleep every night in absolute terror. I do not know what it would feel like to lose my freedom.

She saw sights that no human should have to see. People who tried to escape from the concentration camp were hanged publicly, and the Jewish workers would walk by their decaying bodies for the rest of the week. Everyone was stripped down to be examined, and those too weak to work were weeded out and killed. Children were taken away in trucks, and those same trucks would return empty. She was shoved in a train cart for days, packed with so many people that they had to take turns sitting on the ground. Death was a daily occurrence for Bronia.

I cannot imagine arriving in Auschwitz and seeing the ashes fall, black smoke rising from the crematorium, and all around, dusty remnants of human life. Bronia shared all of this with us. She is an amazing individual, driven by hope. She received a letter from a German woman before beginning her march from Auschwitz. This woman, who she considers her guardian angel, secretly gave Bronia a letter filled with words of hope and of blessing. She still has this letter, and she still hopes; hopes that people can live freely, and that youth can grow up with the opportunities that were cruelly denied her. Today, we are free to live our own life, free to fulfill our own dreams. However, for the first time, I realized the importance of freedom and the price that was paid to win freedom for us today. Thank you, Bronia, for making me realize how fortunate I am.

May 8, 2005
(sent by email)

Dear Dan Sonnenschein,

I met your mother when she came to the University of Victoria
to tell us her story about WWII. I was fortunate enough to be
invited to her house to interview her for a class portfolio assignment where she showed me some of the things she talked about
in her visit to the University. She gave me her autographed book,
"Victory Over Nazism," which affects me to this day. I'm sorry
it's been so long since that meeting of ours, but I've been away
on a work placement term and am just returning now.

I was wondering if you can pass on a Happy Mother's Day
to her for me and thank her for sharing her unique story with
us. We are all so lucky to have a woman as strong and courageous as your mother to tell us of the things most others would
rather not. She has given me a gift I will always cherish — the
gift of knowledge.

I will always remember at what cost my liberty and freedom were won. I will tell the next generation, even if it's hard
to. Thank you for teaching me what V-E Day is really about.
We will never forget.

Your friend,

Rebecca Meagher

*Ed. Note: Rebecca brought two gifts to my mother on her visit, one a mug
bearing the saying, "Life is a gift, that is why we call it the present." Bronia
drank from this mug daily whenever she was at home for the rest of her life.*

A River in Germany

Krissi Hockley (1992)

Dedicated to Bronia Sonnenschein

*Then a student at Burnaby North Secondary School, Krissi wrote this poem
after hearing about Bronia's Holocaust experiences, which culminated in a
death march along the River Elbe from Dresden, Germany to Theresienstadt
(Terezin) in Czechoslovakia, where she was liberated in May of 1945.*

River of terror
river of death
the river that bleeds
of pain and human sacrifice
6 million lives

drowning
the ashes of evil
the last remains
of the Third Reich
lost forever
flowing in a river
somewhere in Germany

disguised
so innocently
don't be fooled
never be fooled by him again

"Heil Hitler ... Heil Hitler!!"
the water doth gurgle
a chant so hauntingly quiet
that even the fish
can't hear them

The screams
of the children
as they're ripped away
drowning

the fear, the pain, the sorrow
of a race
wiped out drowning
with the ashes
flowing in a river
somewhere in Germany
The Nuremberg Trials
1945 – 1949
found them guilty
murder, enslavement, looting
other unspeakable atrocities —
tortures, medical experiments, rape
these monsters of war
guilty of crimes
so cruel and unjust
sentenced
to death
yet the memories
are forever
immortal these monsters
they live on
their ashes
flowing ..... free in a river
known by the very few

as "The River of Terror"
somewhere in Germany.

Responses from Teachers

A sample of comments and letters from teachers is presented here.

The students were thoroughly impressed with Mrs. Sonnenschein's visit. They found her approachable and articulate. ... The students found her passionate account compelling, and were thrilled to shake hands with her as she left.

Thank you for once again spending time with my students. Your presence and your words have taught them more about hope and courage than any book could ever do. The students were in awe of the strength you have — the strength to have survived the Holocaust, and the strength to re-live it with each telling.

— Kelly Malone

You define the word 'courage'.

— Bob Boisvert

Thank you very much for enlightening my students on a most important topic. You imparted your message with such clarity and sincerity that I was touched and moved by your words. I feel I have gained some insight into the Holocaust that I could not have through any other form.

— Ed Hamazaki

A heartfelt and sincere thanks for your willingness to share with our York House students your personal experience of the Holocaust. As a history teacher, I especially value your words and feelings as a first-hand record of one of mankind's darkest eras.

I was touched by your humanity and warmth in approaching this frightening subject with the girls. I know that meeting you will have a positive effect on them and, I hope, on their lives in the future.

— Diane W. Wells

May 14, 1997

Dear Mrs. Sonnenschein:

Yom HaShoah was always a painful day at Hebrew Academy for our Judaic staff members who have much historical information to convey, but (thankfully) no direct personal experience from which to extract the most salient points to be transmitted to the younger generation. For several years, the only way we were able to communicate the day at all, would be to undertake a specific study of chapters of *Tehilim* (Psalms), specifically geared to the memory of the sacred *Neshamot* who perished in the name of a destructive, nihilistic ideology. ...

No textbook or tape recording (visual or audio) can ever replace the presence of a survivor who speaks for those who can no longer speak for themselves. Your hour-long session with our students in Grades Five—Seven made a strong impression. Your story, as well as your personal reflections, have made a very strong impact on your audience — both young and old alike. Your very striking presence, together with the poignant episodes you described and tailored to the age-level of your audience, were profoundly stirring. We were as affected by your quiet inferences, as by your clear, decisive conclusions regarding the executions and the "willing henchmen". You left us with much to remember and with even more to digest. Let me reassure you that your very presence was enough to remind students that in the midst of malevolent darkness, one ember alone can suffice to "cast a giant shadow".

May you continue to inspire others, as you have inspired your young audience at Hebrew Academy. You have engaged our *hearts* ... as well as our *minds*.

Sincerely,

(Mrs.) S. Feuerstein

May 14, 1997

Dear Mrs. Sonnenschein:

I am one of the teachers who listened to your talk on
Monday at Vancouver Hebrew Academy. I came over to
you after the discussion to express the feelings I had while
listening to you speak. Instead, I cried and held your hand.
I could not speak. I did, however, want you to know how
meaningful your lecture was, both to myself and to the
students who were fortunate enough to hear you speak.

I have had the occasion to listen to many Holocaust
survivors speak. Their stories portray the horrors that they
lived through. Their talks bring to the children an awareness
that otherwise they would never have. I am grateful to these
selfless individuals who spend their lives reliving the horrors
of Nazi Germany for no other reason than to ensure that our
generation never forget what "man" was capable of doing.
A lesson, that with G_d's help, will provide them with a safe
environment in which to live.

But your lecture was so different from any that I had
heard previously. I learned more than your personal story of
life during the Holocaust. You wove into your story feelings
of trust, belief in G_d, hope and *Menschlichkeit*. You spoke
with such sensitivity and insight. You provided the students
with 'real' answers, ones that would help to mold their per-
sonalities and outlook in life. And you gave them hope.

You explained to them that the Nazis (I cannot allow myself to write the name of their leader) were the ones who lost
— they are dead. You were the one who emerged the victor
and remained alive to tell the story. You were asked how
you feel about the people who lost faith in G_d as a result of
the Holocaust. Your response was, "How those people must
suffer! Life without faith is so much harder. My faith made
me strong!" I have never heard such a touching response.
You taught them about faith, yet you never judged those who
lost it.

You spoke of miracles! To us listeners it was one big horror story. To you each little ray of light — even if it was too weak to light up your dark world — was a miracle. And you waited faithfully for that one miracle that would finally liberate you. ... You taught us many things. Perhaps one of the most important lessons was how we must count our blessings. And I am sure we will from now. Our generation is truly blessed to have teachers like yourself. Thank you for all that you've taught us.

Yours Sincerely,

Shifra Feigelstock

May 4, 1995

Dear Mrs. Sonnenschein:

I would like to thank you for your participation in this year's Holocaust Symposium. Listening to you speak was an extremely moving experience, and I know that it is one that neither I nor the students who had the pleasure of meeting you will ever forget.

You challenged your audience with the words, "Can you imagine?" I know that we will never truly be able to imagine what you, and so many others, lived through. However, your great personal strength and positive energy help to reaffirm my conviction that I will always challenge my students to "try to imagine". Thank you so much, you spoke not only to our minds, but to our hearts as well. I think that empathy is the place where the true understanding of history begins.

I hope to have the opportunity to meet you again some day. Perhaps you might come to speak to my history students next year. Again, thank you. You are a remarkable woman and I will never forget you or your story. I wish you peace, health, and happiness.

Susan McIntosh

Your own personal suffering and your ability to share it with
sincerity and love was evident to all my students. If History
lives; it is because of people like you, who were eye-witness
to the atrocities that were committed by the Nazis.

Many of my students were moved to ask many questions
the next day and I believe you awakened an interest in history
that was not there before!

— Ted Golf

You have given us a remarkable and memorable gift — your
inner strength, love and wisdom will remain in all of our hearts.

— Joanna Gray

Once again you opened the hearts of my students. Your kind
and gentle manner exemplifies a way to stand up and be active
citizens. Thank you Bronia.

— Barry Krangle

[W]hen Bronia Sonnenschein spoke to us last week, I was, as
usual, profoundly moved and impressed with the power of
testimony, which I see as truth spoken out of experience.

— Donald Grayston

I just wanted to drop you a note to tell you again how much you
have impacted the thought processes of our students. We had
some trouble with a few boys at the grade 11 level making some
rather anti-Semitic comments while watching the movie "The
Pianist." When I heard about this, I immediately informed the
teacher that you were already booked to speak with my classes
and that his students should also come to hear and meet you.
Since you came to the school, their attitudes have changed and
we wish to thank you for that.

— Ross Jacobson

Introduction to a Symposium Talk

Doug Beardsley (2003)

Doug Beardsley is Professor Emeritus of English at the University of Victoria. He gave this introduction in 2003 at the annual Holocaust Symposium in Victoria. Over the years, he arranged for Bronia to speak to his class on Holocaust-related literature several times.

It's a great honour to be asked to do this introduction.

I first met Bronia when she spoke at this Holocaust Symposium five years ago. She spoke and I in the audience began writing. It was not what she said so much but rather my experience of her as she addressed you, the students, on that day. Since I wrote that poem I feel like I've been adopted ... like I finally found my Jewish mother.

Each time we meet, I have so many unanswered questions to ask her, and we never seem to find the time to get to one part of the extraordinary, multi-layered story that you're going to hear this afternoon. And that part is when she survived the fire-bombing of Dresden by the Allies in 1945.

My one great wish is that we will someday sit together and listen to Dmitri Shostakovich's Eighth Quartet which he wrote as a great homage to those like Bronia who survived.

I do know, however, that her story is always aflame with the truth of her words. I feel we are all privileged to be able to indeed hear her this afternoon: Bronia Sonnenschein.

Video clips are online at www.hopesite.ca/sympo/witness/toc_bronia_s.html.

Sardines

Doug Beardsley (1998)
for Bronia Sonnenschein

Doug Beardsley is the author of seven books of poetry, and a
Professor Emeritus of English at the University of Victoria.

On the way to the Holocaust
Symposium for six
hundred high school kids
or so it seems
in the packed auditorium
my pal Giuseppe
is understandably perplexed

his aging mother
wants fresh sardines
& won't accept the fact
they're out of season
here in Canada
the only country in the world
without sardines

except in cans
so Giuseppe sits
& wonders
while Bronia speaks
to the kids
of how she lived
in a Viennese dream

where everything real
seemed so far away
till the day she'd never seen
so many
swastikas & Jews
couldn't sit
on park benches

or in cattle cars
squeezed to suffocation
she was protected
by a *schutzpass*
from a German friend —
that was the beginning
of a world without

selection
the words spilling out
of Bronia her eyes
staring straight ahead
seeing herself
as a child
she can't see

the images on the screen behind
     her flashing like gunfire
        the Symposium Host
          mounting the stage
            to no avail
        Bronia can't stop

& Giuseppe sits forever
     in the auditorium
     & remembers nothing
      of his aging mother
her need for fresh sardines

the spools spinning on
     she can't stop
       her story
    aflame with the
    truth of her words
    the lights grow dim
    the fire bell rings

the students file out
    in rows of five
while my Italian friend
the skin falling off him
  sees only images —

books burning in a public square
 people packed in cattle cars
  mounds of murdered Jews
    a mountain of shoes
  women pulling wagons
survivors naked & starving
 partisan poets with guns
  a father losing his grip
    on a son's tiny hand

A Special Perk

*Dr. Graham Forst taught English at Capilano College. He is a
co-founder and co-chairman of Vancouver's annual Holocaust
Symposium, who was often supported at this event by his wife,
the renowned soprano Judith Forst, and other family members.*

MRS. SONNENSCHEIN CALLS THEM THE PERKS of her assignments. She is referring to the hundreds of letters, cards,
"reaction forms" and gifts of flowers and mementos she receives
for her exhausting work as an educator — specifically, a Holocaust educator. Blonde and petite, and energetic far beyond her
years, this courageous survivor talks to school groups almost
every week, her bright blue eyes flashing as she relates stories
that no one ought to have to tell. Stories that make you cry when
you hear them; that make you want to hug the tiny, eloquent
orator when she's done (and the children always do).

On March 11, 1992 while speaking to a group of twenty Girl
Guides at the Vancouver Holocaust Centre Society in Vancouver,
Mrs. Sonnenschein received a very, very special "perk". She
began by telling them that she too, had once been a Girl Guide in
Austria, and how much the Guide experience had meant to her.
Guide meetings were among the few places where she felt
accepted, where she could socialize like other little girls. So it
was hard for her, she remembers, to have to leave behind her
neat tan Guide uniform with its honor badges and its gold
three-leaf clover Guide pin (*Sei Bereit*: "Be Prepared") when she
was transported to the Lodz Ghetto in 1940.

Then came the stories — of her deportation, of humiliation
and stories of the selection and murder of children, of the ill and
elderly people. Stories we've heard, and still can't believe. As
Mrs. Sonnenschein spoke, the Guides listened breathlessly, their
leader crying quietly in the back corner chair. After forty-five
minutes, when she finished and the Guides hugged and thanked

her, Mrs. Sonnenschein noticed that one particularly small girl, blond and quiet and shy like her, had stayed in her seat.

She was fumbling slowly at her lapel: what was she doing? Then she got up and quietly walked towards Mrs. Sonnenschein. She had her Guide pin in her hands, the gold, three-leafed "Be Prepared" pin all Guides receive on their first day.

"I want you to have it," she said, holding it out to Mrs. Sonnenschein.

"You pin it on me," said Mrs. Sonnenschein.

And the picture of these two, about the same height and weight and coloring, although separated by quite a bit of time and life experience, will stay with me forever.

November 19, 1999

Dear Bronia,

I write to thank you for visiting our Collingwood School on November 10, 1999.

It was a great day for all of us; your strength, your powerful words changed all of us here at Collingwood. We realise how trivial our problems are.

Your testimony was the greatest history lesson our students were ever taught. Many of them admitted that for the first time in their lives they saw the significance of Remembrance Day, a day to reflect, a day to remember those who are not with us any more. They also saw how lucky they are living in their peaceful country, with warm homes and plenty of food around.

Dearest Bronia, it was an honour to meet. We will never forget you.

Do widzenia,

Your Polish friend,

Walentyna Karcz

Bodwell High School and Bodwell Academy
955 Harbourside Drive
North Vancouver, B.C. V7P 3S4

12 June, 2008

Dear Bronia:

We understand that you have decided to step down from your volunteer activities in support of Holocaust student education as of June 2008. We know that this decision must have been difficult.

At the same time, Bodwell wants you to know that your work with our students has been vitally important and very much appreciated. Your extraordinary ability to make connections with others has left an indelible impression on those Bodwellians fortunate enough to have met you. You have kept your promise. Together we say: Never again.

In recognition of your outstanding contribution-making to our students, Bodwell High School has declared you to be an honorary alumnus. Henceforth we will always consider you to be part of the Bodwell High School family. Mr. Chris Macintosh and Mr. Ron Smith from our Social Studies collaborative team are proud to call you 'friend'.

Please accept the attached mementoes in respect of your new status as a Bodwellian! Also enclosed is a 'Thank you' card from your last group of Bodwell High School students.

We wish you well in the future.

Best regards,

Mr. Stephen Smith
Principal
Bodwell High School

Please thank my favourite Bodwellian for visiting with my Social
Studies 11 class yesterday, in spirit. The video of Bronia's journey
was very powerful. It made a real difference for my students.
Bronia's promise will be kept in North Vancouver! Bronia's
testimony will always be an on-going part of my teaching.

— Ron Smith

Bronia after a talk in 2007 at Bodwell High School, with teachers
Ron Smith (left) and Chris Macintosh (right), and student Miguel.

Responses from the Public

January 27, 1997

Dear Ms. Sonnenschein,

Please accept the heartfelt thanks of Vancouver Post No. 1 Jewish War Veterans of Canada for your kindness in coming out to address us on Sunday morning, January 5th.

Although we have all heard, read and been told of the Holocaust, it is a subject that bears retelling over and over again by those survivors who are still with us. As I listened to your talk that morning I was struck by the dignity, restraint and moderation with which you presented your subject matter. You probably noticed the rapt attention of our members. I am sure that there were those, like myself who wondered how you were able for so many years to offer to total strangers memories of so much pain and suffering in your early years. You have our humble respect and admiration.

We send our very best wishes to you in all your endeavors, especially your efforts to keep the subject of the Holocaust alive before all peoples.

Again our thanks,

Oscar Dirnfeld, Commander
Jewish War Veterans of Canada
Vancouver Post No. 1

November 18, 1997

This morning, I listened to your interview on CBC Radio. I'd like to thank you for doing such a tremendously valuable service to humankind when you talk to people about the Holocaust and your personal experiences. People like you help to shape our human future, because you show us that we have a choice between keeping silent and blind, or speaking out and acting for respect and freedom for everyone.

Margaret Mead said: "Never doubt that a small group of thoughtful, committed people can change the world. Indeed, it is the only thing that ever has." You help create these groups of committed people. I wish you health in body and soul, and the strength to go on.

With great respect and admiration,

Barbet Schroeder

June 2, 1994

Dear Bronia,

I believe that meeting you and listening to the story of your survival has changed my life. You radiate such love and compassion in spite of the horrors you endured.

If your spirit and soul can remain so intact after such unimaginable events, then I can reclaim my own spirit and stop complaining about obviously insignificant "problems".

Life is to celebrate and you showed myself and the cast of "Canadian Stories" how one goes on beyond the boundaries of giving up.

Thank you for your courage in re-living the nightmare under Nazi rule ... you have touched all of us deeply. May we also be a witness and challenge those who would defile any human through racist word or deed.

In signing this to you the word that truly seems appropriate is ... Love,

Claudia Blackwood

December 2, 1998

Dear Mrs. Sonnenschein:

I have made this donation in your honor to thank you for touching my life in such a special way.

I had the unique opportunity and privilege to hear you address a group of UBC students November 12th in Vancouver. My daughter Jordana is studying at UBC and we went together.

Your strength, directness, straight "from the heart" address was a true testament of the special human being that you are. I will never forget the story of your life and I promise to keep its meaning alive in my life. I feel connected to you for all time.

I was very moved to hear your granddaughter introduce you. It made me feel so proud and so nourished.

Thank you again for sharing your story and encouraging others to understand and pass the torch. You are indeed an *Eshet Chayil*. You inspire others to be the best that they can be.

With warm affection,

Sandy Corenblum

From a letter to a school principal, after the writer heard
Bronia speak at Johnston Heights Secondary School.

[T]oday I heard the most profoundly effective speaker ever.
Madame Bronia Sonnenschein spoke about her survival through
the Holocaust. This lady was there in Vienna at Kristallnacht,
1938, witnessed the children 0 - 10 being carted away, travelled
in cattle carts for weeks, was an intern of at least three, maybe
four concentration camps, the death march. You could not hear
a pin drop. Her message and story was spoken with dignity and
eloquence. At the end, the students stood up and applauded and
applauded. They asked appropriate questions about her life after,
"You are free, go home."

It was so worth it. The big grade 11 boys and girls and other
grades too, many stayed after to greet her and hug her and thank
her. She was truly moved. It puts into perspective our appreciation for life and our need to be grateful for what we have and to
look after one another as humans. ...

I wanted to share this with you. If you can find time for this
enrichment for your students, I would be delighted to help
with the arrangement

All the best,
a thankful mom,

Gina Ostensen

February 20, 2000

Dear Mrs. Sonnenschein,

On behalf of the Vancouver Public Library, our utmost thanks for the author reading you gave on your book, "Victory over Nazism: A Holocaust Survivor's Journey."

It was such a privilege to hear you speak. Your dignity and courage in discussing your experiences will be remembered by all. Many spoke to us after your talk and told how much they were affected by your story.

Good luck with your book.

Thank-you again.

Yours truly,

Jean Morris,
Librarian,
Vancouver Public Library

November 1, 2005

Dear Bronia —

Thank you for the photos and pages you sent me. I cannot
express how truly moved I am. The story of the little girl who
gave you her guide pin [p. 172] actually made me cry. The letter
from Susan McIntosh [p. 167] shows how greatly you succeed in
your important endeavour. I have placed it all in your book. It
is a testimony that deserves to be preserved forever. I hope you
have made sure that copies are deposited at the National Library
and Archives in Ottawa and university libraries.

I am not exaggerating when I say that in my view, your
contribution to the task of keeping the memory of the Holocaust
alive ranks with that of Elie Wiesel and Simon Wiesenthal. In
some way you actually surpass them because you work at the
grassroot level, and your simplicity and straightforward way to
bear witness goes right to people's hearts.

Thank you Bronia for what you are achieving. We all must
be grateful to you.

Thank you again,

Gretl Keren Fischer

*Editor's Note: Two excerpts from Gretl Keren Fischer's novel "An Answer for
Pierre" are on p. 46-47, the first describing an event told to her by Bronia.*

May 8, 2006

Dear Bronia,

Oh, I think of you so often — and today, well it is the day of your release all those years ago.

As you walked the path of your new life, you shared your story. Your story shows the worst and best of what we can be as humans. Your story reminds us of the important choices we are called to make every day.

Your voice ... Choose kindness, Choose justice — Keep your eyes and your heart open.

Bronia, thank you for your courage and your generosity in sharing your story — it matters and your voice echoes.

Nancy Wyse

Nomination Letters

C ISLE Radio
Unit 20, 11151 Horseshoe
Richmond, B.C. V7A 4S5

Dear Mr. Peters,

I would like to nominate a CITIZEN OF THE DAY, a very special lady by the name of Bronia Sonnenschein. The way I see it, if anyone deserves to be a citizen of the day, Mrs. Sonnenschein is the one. And here is why I think that honor is in order to such an extraordinary person.

Recently I was privileged and honored to meet with Mrs. Sonnenschein who is a widow in her 70s, and also a Holocaust survivor. When we met I found that Mrs. Sonnenschein is not sitting at home idly and bitter because of her sufferings and emotional scars that the Holocaust left her with, by reason of being born Jewish.

No, Mrs. Sonnenschein has a mission to fulfill and that is what she has been doing. She is answering every call and making every visit to all schools, universities, colleges, wherever and whenever she is invited across the province to talk to the students. As a guest speaker (without pay) she leaves them with the message that sadly, racial, ethnic and cultural hatred and intolerance are not just history, but they are current events, and tolerance must be implemented if the "world" in which they, the students who are living today, is to survive tomorrow.

Victoria Hartman

August 19, 1998

Secretary, Tributes Committee c/o UBC Ceremonies Office
6323 Cecil Green Park Road
Vancouver, BC V6T 1Z1

Friends

I write to support the nomination of Bronia Sonnenschein for an
honourary doctorate from the University of British Columbia,
my own alma mater (BA '60).

During the past four years, I have been teaching a course
on the Holocaust in the Humanities Program at Simon Fraser
University. At the conclusion of that course, the class receives
a Holocaust survivor, who speaks about her or his experience.
Bronia Sonnenschein was one of those visitors; and her impact
on my students and myself was unforgettable. She was able to
speak both with objectivity and feeling, in a way which neither
overwhelmed us with the horror of the Holocaust, nor in any
way downplayed it. Her personal qualities and experience are
her pedagogical qualifications, and they make her an educator
of the highest calibre.

I understand that over the years she has given her historical
and personal witness to more than 10,000 students. Given that
we have not yet learned the lessons of the Holocaust, this kind
of education, which has implications far beyond the specific historical events to which it refers, continues to be urgently needed
at every level of our educational system. As a UBC alumnus, as
a Holocaust educator, and simply as a citizen, I encourage you
to support the nomination of Bronia Sonnenschein for a doctoral
degree, *honoris causa*.

Sincerely

Donald Grayston, PhD
Lecturer in Religious Studies, Humanities Program
Co-ordinator, Gandhi Project, Institute for the Humanities

February 11, 2000

To Whom it May Concern:

There is no doubt that Bronia Sonnenschein would be a worthy recipient of an award recognizing her as an amazing Canadian and an outstanding woman. She has spent the last ten years as a voluntary educator, speaking to groups of all sizes and ages in order to relay her message: humanity's need to strive toward peace and dignity. She uses her personal story of suffering and loss to move any audience she speaks to and has touched the lives of thousands of individuals.

Hearing Bronia speak is certainly a life-changing experience. For many of the people to whom she speaks, it is the first they have heard about the Holocaust, an example of the worst possible inhumanity to man. To try to explain such a topic requires bravery and strength as well as clarity and sensitivity. Bronia has all of these characteristics and that is why she touches the heart of anyone who hears her. The message she relays, although intensely emotional and tragic, transcends the horrors of the indignities and murders. She passes on, in every speech she gives, the message of hope for the future with the addendum that it is up to each of us to remember to treat others with respect and dignity in order to achieve harmony.

The courage it takes to speak repeatedly about the kind of horrors Bronia has had to endure is extraordinary. From the moment I met her in 1994 as she was preparing to speak to a very large group of university students at UBC, to this day, I marvel at her sense of purpose and strength of character. She is doing everything within her power to help children and adults, one by one, understand that the barrier between decent society and darkness is our actions as humans and citizens. If everyone did as much as Bronia to promote this important message, the world would be a far better place.

Sincerely,

Michelle Dodek

February 20, 2000

Dear Members of the Selection Committee,

Re: Mrs. Bronia Sonnenschein's Nomination for the
    Royal Bank Award for Canadian Achievement

I have been asked to provide an endorsement to support the nomination of Mrs. Sonnenschein for the above award. I am honoured to do so.

It is unlikely that a future Selection Committee will have the opportunity to consider a survivor of the Holocaust as its honoree. There are precious few left alive who have not only experienced the full horrors of the ghetto, the concentration camps, and death marches but who have survived survival as valiantly as Mrs. Sonnenschein.

Bronia was born in Vienna and still today talks of the pleasures of young womanhood in that glorious city. In an effort to rejoin family in Lodz, Poland at the outbreak of war, she was soon confined with tens of thousands of Jews to the Lodz Ghetto, subsequently deported to Auschwitz and made to perform slave labour, only to end up in a labour battalion in Dresden where she survived also the fire bombing. On a death march to Theresienstadt, she almost gave up but succeeded with her mother and sister, through mutual support, to make it to liberation.

Her husband had been murdered, as was most of her family. She emigrated to Canada in 1948 with her second husband whom she lost tragically to a car accident soon after arrival.

Had Mrs. Sonnenschein done nothing more than work hard and raise her lovely family, one would have to consider her struggle to recapture life, already an achievement of heroic proportions. But Mrs. Sonnenschein does not see herself as a heroine nor did she think it enough to care for her family and to live life as a proud Canadian. Mrs. Sonnenschein began to tell her story and to derive from it lessons so that children who heard her would be vaccinated against the types of prejudices and racism which destroyed European Jewry.

Professor Graham Forst and I initiated in 1976 a Holocaust
Education Symposium for high school students, which runs to
this day. Before long, Mrs. Sonnenschein joined us as an enthusiastic participant. She served as a featured speaker and/or as a
member on panels. How she did what she did, I will never know.

Bronia would stand straight as a candle, face 500 students,
and recount her eyewitness experiences. After her presentations,
dozens of teenagers would surround her, tears in their eyes and
promise to work to make the world a better one. Seldom have I
witnessed such an impact on students. My children have heard
her and they too have never forgotten her story and her message.

I have taught senior residents in psychiatry a special course
on "Massive Psychic Trauma," since the early 80's. The course
covers the psychiatric aspects of treating victims of the Holocaust, Dutch survivors of Japanese Concentration Camps,
Cambodian survivors, South American victims of torture, etc.
I have asked Mrs. Sonnenschein to join me on many occasions
to speak to these young doctors, generally aged about 23-35.
I attach a random selection of only five questionnaire responses
that number in the hundreds. You will note she rates 10 of 10
and has never received lower than 9.

And this result too reflects a special ability that I have
seldom encountered. Mrs. Sonnenschein can talk about the
Holocaust even to youngsters, as well as teenagers and adult
professionals and have an impact on all ages that matches or
exceeds that of the finest teachers and educators imaginable.

She is also very brave. She has spoken in communities
where right wing groups flourish. She has been in every corner
of British Columbia and even to Northern Idaho where the Aryan Nations reside. Whenever she speaks, wherever she goes,
she leaves a legacy of better understanding, a commitment to
combat prejudice and to rout out hatred from the communities.
Mrs. Sonnenschein has touched the hearts and minds of thousands and each person who has had the privilege of meeting her,
has benefited.

This physically tiny woman, who suffered so much and
has seen and faced the abyss, transcends the horrific human

(inhuman?) dimensions of her life to appear as an education giant inspiring compassion and understanding. Bronia has been faithful to historical memory, to her lost family and to her people by serving as an eyewitness.

I am so proud to be her friend and colleague in Holocaust education.

Yours sincerely,

Robert Krell, M.D., FRCP(C)

Editor's Note: Bronia didn't receive this award (also the subject of Michelle Dodek's letter) or the honorary doctorate, but did receive the BC Senior Award that she was nominated for in the letter on the next page. In addition, in 1996 she received a radio station's Citizen of the Day award as nominated by Victoria Hartman (p. 184). and in 1997 one of the N'shei Chabad "Woman of Valour" awards "in tribute to Bronia Sonnenschein whose commitment and concern for family and community in the tradition of the Jewish woman of valour serves as a shining example for all to emulate." In 2002, she was awarded the Queen's Golden Jubilee Medal for exemplary volunteer service; the photo below shows her receiving this honour from then Member of Parliament, Stephen Owen, and the last photo in this book shows her wearing the medal. Other examples of appreciation include the plaque shown in a photograph at the end of this part.

Vancouver Holocaust Education Centre

Brock House Society, BC Senior Award
c/o Mrs. Marian Pocock
3875 Point Grey Road
Vancouver, BC V6R 1B3

July 7, 1999

Dear Mrs. Pocock,

I am pleased to be submitting this letter of nomination for Mrs.
Bronia Sonnenschein, an 84 year old Holocaust survivor and
educator par excellence — who instead of slowing down, has
actually increased her efforts toward anti-racism education in
the past two years. Bronia is one of the most effective anti-
racism educators to ever address students in British Columbia
— something she does tirelessly and with great compassion and
wisdom. Besides her completely voluntary work with students
in the schools and at the Holocaust Education Centre, at age 83,
Bronia fearlessly traveled to communities inundated by white
supremacist propaganda to speak on behalf of social justice and
tolerance towards others.

   We have received literally hundreds of unsolicited letters
written directly to Bronia by students which indicated the positive effects that hearing her speak has had on them. These heartfelt and moving letters from young people are what prompted
us to submit her name for this prestigious award. ...

   Thank you for considering Bronia's application. If you have
any questions or require any clarification, please do not hesitate
to contact us.

Your sincerely,

Dr. Roberta Kremer, Executive Director
Dr. Robert Krell, Past President

A Bridge to Nuremberg

Claudia Cornwall (1996)

*This article was first published in "Zachor", the
newsletter of the Vancouver Holocaust Centre
Society, in October 1996 with the subtitle,
"The Story of Bronia and Markus". Another
of Claudia's articles is reprinted on page 63.*

"YOU HAVE TO REACH OUT," says Bronia Sonnenschein,
"otherwise the hate will never end. It will continue
generation after generation." During the past decade, Mrs.
Sonnenschein's beliefs have led her to visit schools all over
British Columbia and to speak to thousands of students about
her experiences in the Holocaust. Many of them have written to
her afterwards to say how much they appreciated her visit and
how much she has taught them. "But I never expected," she
says, "that my words would reach as far as Germany — and to
Nuremberg of all places."

Nuremberg — one thinks immediately of the huge rallies
that Hitler staged there and of the Nuremberg Laws passed in
1935 that legalized discrimination against Jewish people. One
thinks too of the fact that Nuremberg was such a potent symbol
of Nazism that it was chosen as the site of the war crimes trials
in 1946. It is no wonder that Bronia Sonnenschein should find it
remarkable that her story is now resonating in the hearts of
young Germans in that particular city.

It really started in 1993 because of a friendship that
developed here in Vancouver. In November of that year, during
Holocaust Awareness Week. Mrs. Sonnenschein was talking to a
group of U.B.C. students at Hillel House. Everyone in the room
listened carefully to what she said, but one student in the front
row was especially attentive. When Mrs. Sonnenschein had
finished speaking, he introduced himself. His name was Markus
Schirmer. "I was deeply moved by what you said," he revealed.

Two days later he phoned Mrs. Sonnenschein. In that telephone conversation she learned that the young man with the serious manner was not Jewish. He was German, in fact, and his home town was Nuremberg. He was twenty-three years old and he had come to U.B.C. to study history and English for two terms. He wondered if he could meet Mrs. Sonnenschein again. He wanted to learned more about her life and the tragic events that had overtaken it. Bronia Sonnenschein recalls, "I was a little nervous, I must admit. I wondered why he was so interested in Jewish history and whether his family had anything to hide." Nevertheless, there was something about Markus Schirmer that she found reassuring. "I thought he had a kind honest face." She agreed to see him.

Their first meeting lasted three hours. "We talked and talked. I can't remember how many cups of tea I drank," Mrs. Sonnenschein says. She told Mr. Schirmer about how she had fled her native Vienna for Poland. She recounted how there, she and her family had waited and waited for the papers that would have allowed them to emigrate to the United States. She explained that when the papers finally arrived it was too late. By that time, her family was trapped in the Lodz Ghetto. She told him about the years she had worked in the Ghetto and about the final terrible months she had spent in several concentration camps — Auschwitz, Stutthof and Pirna. She told him about the despair and exhaustion she had felt on a death march during the last days of the war. She told him about being liberated from Theresienstadt on May 8, 1945 by a lone Russian on horseback. "You are free. You can go home now," he had said.

Markus Schirmer asked if they could meet a second time and once again, Bronia agreed. The next time they saw each other was just before Hannukah and the young German brought a gift — a book of poems by Inge Israel. Published in Canada, *Unmarked Doors* explores some of the complex feelings that a Jew experiences in becoming the friend of a German.

They kept meeting. And when Markus Schirmer's parents came to visit him in Vancouver in the spring of 1994, he naturally wanted to introduce them to his new friend. *"Gruess Gott",*

Mrs. Schirmer said as she walked into Mrs. Sonnenschein's apartment. "This made me feel right at home with his parents," Mrs. Sonnenschein says. "*Gruess Gott* was what we had said in Vienna where I grew up." The four exchanged pleasantries, talked about things to do and places to see in Vancouver.

Nevertheless, it was clear to everyone that this was not quite an ordinary social event. There was something Mrs. Schirmer felt she had to say. After about an hour had passed, her face reddened and she blurted out, "You know I was only a little girl when it all happened." Bronia Sonnenschein replied, "I understand. I don't blame you."

"She was only a little girl of seven or eight," explains Mrs. Sonnenschein. "What could she have done? When I talk in the schools, the students often ask me whether I hate Germans. And I always tell them that I don't. I will never forget what the Nazis did. But I don't hold this generation responsible for what happened. They were far too young."

As the spring term wore on, Markus Schirmer continued to study and deepen his understanding of the history of the Holocaust. He told Zac Kaye, then the director of Hillel House at U.B.C. that he was also very interested in the Jewish religion. According to Zac Kaye, "Markus expressed a great interest in things Jewish and indeed attended the Seder during Passover that year at our home. He explained to me that he felt he had a duty to talk about and teach the Holocaust to German young people, that he needed to know more about Judaism and especially to dialogue with young Jews about the whole experience."

Bronia Sonnenschein recalls that he asked whether he might be able to attend a service in a synagogue. "I remember once he came to Beth Israel Synagogue with several Lutheran students. He paid very close attention to everything that was going on. And he had many questions — more questions than I could answer," says Mrs. Sonnenschein with a laugh. "I turned him over to Rabbi Solomon!"

When the term concluded, Markus Schirmer had to return to Nuremberg. "The last good-bye was hard," admits Mrs.

Sonnenschein. "But Markus promised me that he would do in Germany what I am doing here — educate young people about the Holocaust. And when he was home, he kept writing to me. After he had been back for two years, he even phoned. It was unbelievable."

Mr. Schirmer resumed his studies at the university in Nuremberg with the aim of becoming a teacher. In the spring of 1996, as part of his training, he was given the opportunity to teach at a local highschool. He included nine lessons on the Holocaust. He devoted a portion of the time to telling his class Mrs. Sonnenschein's story and also made available some material about the history of the Jewish community in Nuremberg.

"I wanted to draw the students' attention to the local Jewish history and what is left to see, Markus Schirmer recounted in a letter to Mrs. Sonnenschein. "We took a look at the sites of various former synagogues and ghettos. In the early 14th century, the local Jewish congregation with about 1500 members was one of the largest in the empire then. On our way to the present synagogue we noticed the memorial plaque of the Jewish donor of the municipal library and the wall mosaics of Theodor Herzl and Walter Rathenau in a subway station. At the end of the tour we went inside the present synagogue which is very small, according to the size of the congregation: 450 members. Still it was interesting for the students to see the Tora shrine and the balcony for the women. Something that astonished them were the security precautions they didn't expect to be necessary."

"I am happy with the result of the project," Mr. Schirmer explained. "The majority of the students were open and quite interested. Obviously, your personal account has left a mark on them." One of the students even decided to send a letter to Mrs. Sonnenschein. "In my opinion you should go on with your lectures at the university in order to tell everyone about your life and especially about the time of persecution in Germany, so that this time will always be remembered and never forgotten," Tanja Bauer wrote.

For Markus Schirmer, meeting Bronia Sonnenschein was profoundly meaningful. "My encounter with Bronia made this very dark chapter of German history much more immediate, brought it back to reality. I have learned it from schoolbooks and heard about it in university lectures. But only getting to know Bronia made it a real issue for me. It means a great deal to me that Bronia refers to our relationship as friendship. It is important for me to let her know that there are people in Germany who care and who will keep the memory of the Holocaust alive."

"He kept his promise to me," says Mrs. Sonnenschein. "He has restored my faith; I can trust again. And that is very important."

Remembrance in Nuremberg

Bronia Sonnenschein (2000)

A DISPLAY ON THE WALL, of the Wilhelm Löhe Schule in Nuremberg, Germany reads: "We have met Bronia Sonnenschein and her granddaughter Emily — and we won't forget the tragedy of the Holocaust." It also shows pictures of both of us, as well as text (see photograph on the next page).

It all came about when one student listened to the testimony of a survivor, describing life behind barbed wire in Hitler's death camps. His name is Markus Schirmer and we met at Hillel at the University of British Columbia in 1993. But he had never forgotten what he heard and when he left in 1994 to continue his studies in Nuremberg he did what he had promised to do. He became a teacher and is now teaching the Holocaust during History classes in his home town, Nuremberg.

We had stayed in touch during all these years and when I mentioned to him that my granddaughter Emily would travel through Europe upon her graduation from university, the idea to invite her formed immediately in his head and so he did. I "brokered" this invitation and no sooner had I informed Emily, her answer was as spontaneous as I knew it would be. "Of course, I will do it and what's more, I want to do it."

Emily had occasions to sit in on a class to listen to me and so she now became my "Ambassador" and no better ambassador could ever have been found, as Markus Schirmer's students wrote to me after listening to Emily telling "my story" and that of her paternal grandparents now deceased. Emily gave three 90-minute presentations in the Wilhelm Löhe Schule on May 8 and 9, 2000. I know the grade 9 students she addressed won't forget her or her powerful presentation, representing the third generation after the Holocaust.

What followed was my participation and that of my son Dan at a video-conference, where we sat in the UBC Telestudios and "got in touch" on the screen with Markus and his students and I answered their questions. A similar event — through

E-mail — occurred in July 1999 in the Neue Gymnasium in Nuremberg. The next chapter has been the display on the wall.

My deepest thanks go to Markus Schirmer, the staff and students of the Wilhelm Löhe Schule, my beloved Ambassador, Emily Herman, and my son Dan. All it took was a lot of good will of a small group participating in these projects. Margaret Mead once said: "Never doubt that a small group of thoughtful committed people can change the world. Indeed it is the only thing that ever has."

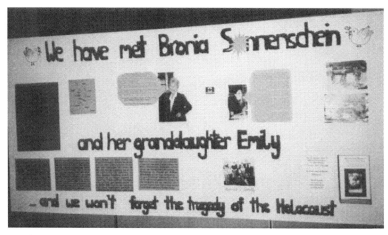

Wall display by students of Wilhelm Löhe School in Nuremberg.

To Markus Schirmer and his Students:

I regret very much not being able to be with you today. My best representative, Emily Herman, my granddaughter from Calgary, will be there instead. Emily has on several occasions been present when I addressed students and teachers, sharing my experiences during the Holocaust with them. That was when she learned in great detail of the horrors, the tragedy of the Holocaust from 1939 to 1945. In Germany it actually started in 1933 when Hitler came to power and became Reichs Chancellor. Austria's annexation to Germany occurred in March 1938. My family (my parents, my sister and myself), as well as close relatives, were from that day on considered "sub-humans" and treated as such by the Nazi regime. Emily will talk to you about it.

Like me, she has made a commitment to keep the memory of the Holocaust alive by telling her generation and all those that are interested in knowing what went on behind barbed wire in ghettos and concentration camps. The deaths of six million humans, one and a half million of them children, shall never be forgotten. Those that forget are apt to repeat it.

The war has been over for 55 years, and trust and understanding must be built and nourished. I met your teacher, Markus Schirmer, in November 1993 while addressing University students with whom I shared my experiences during the Holocaust. Both of us, survivor and teacher, have forged a bond and developed trust in each other, both of us being involved in Holocaust education, promoting understanding among all of us and so enabling us to live side by side in peace.

I am happy to know that Emily will bring this message to you and grateful to Markus Schirmer for having made it possible. Where there is a will, there is a way.

I wish you peace and happiness.

Yours,

Bronia Sonnenschein

Journey to Nuremberg

Emily Herman (2000)

NUREMBERG, GERMANY. The name of this city recalls to our minds such phrases as "The Nazi Rally City", "The Nuremberg Laws", and "The Nuremberg Trials." These phrases and their implications were at the forefront of my mind as I sat on the train headed to the infamous city. So why were Sebastian, my boyfriend, and I including it in our European backpacking itinerary? Because we had a place to stay. Seven years ago, my grandmother, Bronia Sonnenschein of Vancouver, had befriended a young man from Nuremberg named Markus Schirmer. Markus had been in the audience of a presentation my grandmother gave to University students about her experiences in the Holocaust. Compelled by her story of persecution and survival, Markus stayed after the lecture to speak with her. From then on, the two have been close friends, and from then on, Markus has dedicated much of his time to Holocaust education, working as a teacher of English and History in Nuremberg. Over time, their relationship grew to encompass Markus's parents, Peter and Ilse Schirmer, who were now opening their doors wide to Sebastian and me.

As the days before our departure from Calgary became fewer, Markus and my grandmother started talking casually about how nice it would be if I could meet with some of his students during my visit to talk about the Holocaust. I thought it was a fine idea and agreed. This casual conversation soon led to a plan encompassing two days of lectures at Wilhelm Löhe School, in which I would meet with three classes of 25 students from grades seven through ten to discuss the Holocaust.

We arrived in Nuremberg on June 7, greeted by Peter Schirmer's valiant English attempts, his wife Ilse's shy smile, and Markus's friendly embrace. After a true German meal accompanied by introductory conversations, Markus drove us around to the Nazi Party Rally sites, covering the entire history of Nuremberg in the Second World War. I was pleasantly surprised to discover that the city of Nuremberg has been adamant about keeping these landmarks in existence as a way of remembering their history and repenting for what took place here.

The next day brought the "task" of this destination. My talks with the classes consisted of the experiences of my grandmother Bronia in the concentration camps, the stories of Holocaust survival of my paternal grandparents (Benek and Sima Herman of Calgary), and an explanation of why I had come to speak to them. Ignorance regarding the Holocaust is dangerous. To ignore this one historical event and to not take from it lessons for the future is to risk repetition.

After relaying to them my information and opinions, I welcomed a class discussion. I had left quite a bit of time for this in our hour and a half slot, because I knew that if they couldn't fill the void with queries, I could. I wanted to know what they knew about the Holocaust. Do their parents or grandparents speak of it? Have they had ever met a survivor or been to a concentration camp? Do they know any Jews? Their answers were fascinating, but better yet was the enthusiasm with which they asked me questions and shared their personal stories and feelings. They told me of a grandmother who still denies the Holocaust ever happened and a grandfather who hid his four Jewish neighbours for the entire war. Some of their parents don't talk about it, and others have taken their families on trips to Dachau and other concentration camps. They wanted to know how I felt about coming to the country which fostered the Holocaust. I told them the truth. I was afraid to walk their streets and to see their people because I didn't want to discover how much hate I had within me, but when I gained Markus's friendship, felt the love of his dear parents and was greeted by their own open-minded enthusiasm, I experienced a reversal and an awakening.

This city is ashamed of how it was used and how it let itself be used by the Nazis, and now it wants its people and the world to begin to see past this reputation. The students begged me to tell them how they could make the world and other Jewish people see them as Germans, not as Nazi descendants. I had no answer, only advice. Show that you are different from what you are labelled. Meet people and help them to see who you really are and be open to seeing the same revealed in others. It's not easy for any of us to look or be seen beyond our past, but small links like the ones made from Sebastian and me, to Markus, Peter and Ilse, and the students of Wilhelm Löhe School, have shown me that understanding and acceptance are not only attainable, but deserved.

Emily speaking to a class with Markus looking on.

Absolutely Grateful for This Friendship

Markus Schirmer (2010)

*Markus is now a high school teacher (Gymnasium
— university preparation) in Ingolstadt, Germany.*

W HEN I FIRST ENCOUNTERED Bronia Sonnenschein, I instantly
realized that this was a very special moment. But I had
no idea of how important Bronia would become in my life.

I went to the University of British Columbia for two
semesters as part of my university studies to become a teacher
of English and History in Germany. Of course, I had heard and
read about Nazi atrocities before I went to Canada. But Bronia
Sonnenschein was the first Holocaust survivor I met in person.
Her vivid account of the years of horror left a deep impression
on me. Even more so her powerful personality. That was when
she gave her talk at Hillel House on the UBC campus during
Holocaust Awareness Week in November 1993. After the event I
asked her for some advice she would want to give to a future
high school History teacher for lessons about the Holocaust.
She reacted in a very warm way by telling me that I could find
her telephone number in the White Pages and give her a call.

That is what I did. We met at a tea room and she did not
become tired of answering my questions about her experiences
during the Nazi period and her family history. Then I visited her
about once a month in her home. We often had a cup of tea
together along with *Nusspusserln* — the delicious nut cookies that
Bronia made according to a traditional Viennese recipe. In the
course of time a relationship evolved that I would describe as
similar to the friendship between a grandmother and her
grandson. After two semesters at UBC I returned to Germany to
finish my studies. By now our bond has kept up for almost 17
years — through letters, telephone calls, e-mails and occasional
visits in Vancouver. Bronia has listened to my concerns and
given very valuable advice throughout the years. My letters
to Bronia had the tone of a personal log. Bronia is someone I

strongly confide in. I am absolutely grateful for this friendship and the wisdom she passes on. She often reminds me to count my blessings. In particular, at times when I did not feel so cheerful, she turned to this saying. Thank you, Bronia! Another saying she particularly likes is: It takes two to tango. She used it after some of the projects on the Holocaust with my students in Germany she was so kind to get involved in. My students were both shocked and very moved by Bronia's personal story. The fact that she responded to the questions and letters of the students brought history much more alive and made the topic a much more important matter to them as it did to me when I first met Bronia. Without Bronia's help and support — by her openness and her material in the form of newspaper articles about her, radio and video interviews — this would not have been possible. Especially her personal responses in video conferences and letters have made a world of a difference. I cannot put it in words to express how much I appreciate her steps of the tango.

So I was very familiar with Bronia's account when I visited the site of the Auschwitz Extermination Camp during a trip to Poland in the summer of 2005. With Bronia's words of a radio interview describing the selection and the subsequent inhumane treatment still resonating in my ears the visit of the site acquired an almost unbearable intensity. And this was over 50 years after the actual horror, at a museum and a place that is dedicated to keep up the memory. Thank you, Bronia for telling us what happened. I will definitely continue this important job of keeping up the memory.

I am also happy that Bronia's family have been very approachable. Since the advent of the internet a lot of our communication has happened via her son's computer, i.e., Dan's e-mail address. He keeps me posted about anything that happens in Bronia's life. Thank you, Dan! The visits of Bronia's granddaughters Emily and Claire at my parents' place in Nuremberg and their visits at my school were outstanding and very positive experiences for everybody involved. The invitation to Emily and Seb's wedding in Calgary was a wonderful sign of their friendship. Although I could not make it to the wedding,

I very much cherished their great hospitality afterwards and I was very happy to meet Bronia's daughter Vivian with her husband Ben in their Alberta home. Thanks again to everyone!

Bronia has not only become instrumental for my attitude towards Holocaust education, but also a very close friend. So I am looking forward to many more visits and cups of tea with her and her family.

Editor's Note: Markus brought this article with him when he visited Bronia and me in early September, 2010, which she was of course very pleased to read. He had made a special effort to travel to Vancouver after hearing about her injuries in a fall earlier that summer, from which she was recovering well at home after a stressful six weeks in hospital. This was to prove their final visit.

Bronia was excited about the upcoming birth of a first child to Markus and his recently married wife, Ursula. However, it was not to be that she could give her congratulations and enjoy photos. Their baby was born in April, 2011 and is named Simon. I had the pleasure of seeing the promised photo of his first smile.

Markus with Bronia on a previous visit.

A Friend in Austria

Following is the first letter from Magdalena Müllner, who since then established a regular correspondence with Bronia, and has continued her work in Holocaust education and commemoration.

2.5.1995

Dear Mrs. Sonnenschein,

As you can see on the lines down of this sheet of paper, my name is Magdalena Müllner and I am living in a little town in Austria called Laa an der Thaya. I am 19 years old and study law at the university of Vienna. Since over 3 years, that means since I was 16 years old, I spend most of my free time with research-work about the vanished Jewish community of my native place. The enclosed sheets can show you what I am doing and that I try to do this very seriously and that I also was lucky to have success with my research until now. At the moment I am in contact with 14 people who were born as part of the Jewish community of Laa / Th. and live now all around the world and I'm proud to say that I made close friends with all of them. I read your name in the computer when I visited dear friends in Maryland, who are survivors like you and born in Laa. I read in the computer that you have spent the first years of your life in Austria. There is also a family named Sonnenschein who was living in Laa. I know very, very little about this family. So I write to you in the hope that you could be a child or any relative of the family Sonnenschein from Laa. I know about following people of the name Sonnenschein from Laa ... Maybe these names help you to remember and maybe find out a relationship. With many greetings and best wishes.

Magdalena Müllner

May 22, 1995

Dear Magdalena,

Life, it seems, is full of surprises. Your letter forwarded to me by the United States Holocaust Memorial Museum in Washington, sure was a surprise. Since I don't know how much or how little information you have about me, you definitely know that I lived in Vienna and was forced to leave the city I loved so much together with my parents and sister when Hitler annexed Austria to Germany.

On May 8, 1995 I commemorated my 50th anniversary of liberation, a miracle in itself. Sonnenschein was my late husband's name and as far as I know he had no relatives living in Austria. My late husband was born in "Maehrisch Ostrau" (I don't know if it is still known by this name) and educated in Prague, the Czech Republic.

Your research into a vanished Jewish Community is indeed remarkable. There are, unfortunately, people that deny the Holocaust ever happened. Hate-mongers, they were not there, they did not witness torture and destruction. So I am really happy to know that there are young people like you who are trying to find the truth. What is so remarkable for me is that although quite a few young German students approached when I share my experiences about those frightful years in the death-camps telling me that they are ashamed of what their people did, never once did a young Austrian student come up to me.

I used to love Vienna, so did all my family, but I have lost confidence in Austrians. I hope you will understand. They have hurt us too deeply. I really welcomed your letter and interest in trying to locate and bring families together. You actually give me hope in people like yourself, the third generation after the war.

I would like to hear from you again. In the meantime I wish you the best of luck in your studies. Maybe your travels will take you once to Vancouver. I would have loved to meet you. You seem to have a lot of courage and determination.

So let's just say "auf Wiedersehen."

Sincerest regards,
Bronia Sonnenschein

The Big Lie in Laa

Magdalena Müllner (1992)

*This essay was first published in the paper, "Jüdisches Echo", in Austria.
It is reminiscent of Anna Rasmus, whose similar efforts to uncover the
truth were unwelcome by some in her town, and became the subject of the
movie, "The Nasty Girl". It is gratifying that Magdalena seems to have
met with less resistance, and in particular has a very supportive family.*

I WOULD LIKE TO TELL YOU, dear reader, a true story and hope
you will feel the same as I did. The story deals with a big Lie,
a Lie which nearly was strong enough to obliterate and destroy
the memory of 26 families.

Today everybody knows about the Holocaust. It is, or it
should be known to all of us, what happened then, 50 years ago.

We know that all this happened in our country, and nobody
in his right mind can and should deny the existence of the crimes
and genocide which happened in Mauthausen and all the other
concentration-camps! Where did all those millions of victims
come from? If you ask today an average citizen, he will tell you:
"from Poland and naturally from the big cities like Vienna or so."
But does this statement of Mr. or Mrs. X or Y really reflect the
truth?

Now back to the actual story, which deals solely with Laa, a
little town on the river Thaya in the most northern part of the
County of Lower Austria (Nideroesterreich) situated directly on
the Czechoslovakian border; the population have the typical
friendly and easygoing nature of the Austrians of this area with a
slight anti-foreigner disposition caused by the recent influx of
Czechs and Poles since the opening of the borders, although this
tendency is only very little. Nobody would guess that there is
something here which none of the young people, or those who
were born after 1938 know about. Over five decades an
unbelievable Lie has been told here. It said: Jews? No, we never

had any Jews living here. What an unbelievable LIE!!!, and those who told this lie nearly succeeded to uphold it until none of the community will be old enough to remember and talk about the 26 Jewish families who lived here in Laa until 1938 and were known to all the community. Everybody knew them, everybody shopped in their shops. This is now told by many who now at last have agreed to talk about it. Even a Synagogue was here and always there was a Rabbi living in the town. They have been respected people, but nevertheless this big Lie has been told for so long. I bet, that at least 80% of today's population never even dreamed or knew about this part of the past. How could they have known about it when this Lie has been so well dispersed within the whole area. There are only two written sources of a few sentences in books from the beginning of this century, available where the Jewish community of Laa is mentioned. It is also written there that already in the years of 1294 and 1337 Laa witnessed 2 pogroms on the Jews, and now they nearly got away with murdering the truth of 1938.

Some of the people who now talk are actually afraid to do so. One should think that in a democracy you can freely talk without being afraid, but I have learned differently. There is a 65 year old lady who was willing to remember and talk, but only with tape recorder switched off. She remembered that a woman farmer from an outlying farm, who purchased something from a Jew, was chased around Laa with a shield about her neck. What was written on this shield, the woman, even now after 50 years, was afraid to tell me. Not only in Vienna, but also in Laa it happened, but "We never had any Jews here". The Laa'er Nazis also distinguished themselves by forcing Jews to scrub the sidewalks; it even was said that the Nazis put some acid into the water, so that hands of the Jews would be burnt.

The relationship between the Jews and the Christians in Laa was always prior to 1938 apparently very friendly. The children went together to the same school, the farmers brought their harvest to the Jewish vegetable and fruit shops, and if one wanted to buy something good and nice, you went to a Jewish shop to buy it and even paid it in deferred payments. I even heard about two Jewish-Christian weddings. Last week I found some Jewish graves in Mistelbach's Jewish cemetery where some of "my Jews" found their last resting place. (I call them "my Jews" because I am the only one who cares for them.) Nobody can imagine how it feels to see for the first time the names engraved on the tombstones of people whose existence has been denied. It is impossible to describe this feeling, I just would have loved to embrace with my arms all those tombstones one by one.

It is not much, which I was able to find about the darkness of this history. There is a lot to learn about this darkness, and I will probably not find everything, but I will do my very best to discover as much as possible, because I cannot hear this Lie anymore.

Magdalena in 2010 at the engraved stone for Laa at Yad Vashem.

Why it is Important to Remember

Magdalena Müllner (1998)

F OR ME it had been always important to keep the memory of the Jewish community of Laa an der Thaya alive. There are several reasons for this.

First I believe that you don't die and vanish totally from this world as long as you're remembered by at least one person. Being forgotten is kind of a second death. One could say that this is a natural process: who remembers the grandfather of his great-grandfather? In the case of the Jewish community of my hometown, the situation is quite different. They were driven away or killed. Those who committed the crimes or just stood by and did nothing survived to form the older generation of Laa. To forget the Jewish people of Laa is like agreeing to the expelling and killing. Keeping the memory is also a way of restoring to the Jews of Laa, a fragment of the *heimat* they were robbed of.

Furthermore, I see Laa as an example of the processes that happened in so many little towns all over Europe 60 years ago. Seen from that point of view, Laa is not just a tiny spot on a map. It represents the weakness of human kind in certain situations. It confronts us in a deep and difficult way with how we would react in a situation when the law itself becomes unjust. It's not only important that people from Austria know this story but also that people all over the world know.

Finally I want to quote a story that shall explain why it is important to carry the story of the Jewish community into the 21st century (from Arthur Kurzweil's *From Generation to Generation: How to trace your Jewish genealogy and family history.* New York: Harper Collins, 1994):

Elie Wiesel, a survivor of the Death Camps, taught a course at City College in New York on the Holocaust. ... "But, since we weren't there, what should we say to the next generation?" a young man asked. "You have said that we will never understand what happened. If so, how can we tell people about it?" "Yes," Wiesel said. "You will never know. But you will know that there was something. You will know one incident. One tear. That will be yours to tell." Wiesel went on. "In my books, I don't like to repeat stories. Once I did. One story I told in two books."

He then told the legend, a Chassidic tale. It was a tale that contained many of the Chassidic masters. It began with the founder of the Chassidim, the Baal Shem Tov, the Master of the Good Name. It seems that when there was a disaster about to strike, the Baal Shem went into a certain spot in the woods, lit a candle and said a prayer — and the disaster was prevented. Then, a disciple of his was faced with a disaster. He knew where the special spot in the wood was located, he knew how to light the candle, but he did not know the prayer. But the disaster was averted. Then another disciple was faced with calamity. He knew where the spot in the wood was located, but he did not know how to light the candle, and he did not know the prayer. But the disaster was prevented. Then a final disciple was faced with a disaster. He did not know how to light the candle, he did not know how to say the prayer, and he did not know where the spot in the woods was located. All he knew was how to tell the story. And then, too, the disaster was avoided. ...

"What can you tell your children? Tell them that you knew the last survivors. As the survivors were alive when it happened, you were alive to hear their story ... Tell them that: you knew the last survivors. They will listen. And they will ask the same question: What shall we tell our children? They will tell them: We knew people who knew the last survivors. We heard the story from people who knew the last survivors. We heard the story from people who heard the last survivors. ... And the question will again be asked. And the story will be told. Again and again. It will be told."

Editor's Update:

Magdalena is now a school teacher in Munich. Since the time of the preceding letter and articles, she, along with her father Franz, have accomplished a great deal to carry her initial work forward. They formed Lead Niskor, a Society for commemoration of the expelled and murdered Austrian Jews, with Mr. Müllner as its Chairman. The Society helped create in Laa a dignified granite memorial engraved with the names of the 33 Jewish families who lived there before the war; it was dedicated on June 19, 2005. Below is an image of the memorial (Einladung) from a colour painting.

One of the ongoing activities of the Society is maintaining the Jewish cemetery in Laa. An excellent website, www.lead-niskor.org, was also set up, with an English version containing much of the content of the German version. Included on this extensive site are many historical details with photographs of Laa and its former Jewish community, descriptions of contacts with survivors and their relatives, texts of speeches, and various articles.

On February 17, 2010, Magdalena and her parents were awarded the Marietta and Friedrich Torberg medal by the Jewish Community of Vienna.

On August 19, 2010, the official ceremony of the engravement of Laa an der Thaya in the Valley of the Communities at Yad Vashem in Jerusalem, Israel, was held. The Müllners rightly view this engravement as a great achievement.

A photograph of Magdalena in front of the engravement appears on page 209. Further photos and much more may be found on the Lead Niskor website.

Bronia in Sandpoint, Idaho (p. 113–117). On the right is Jenna Bowers (p. 150).

With students after a talk at the University of British Columbia.

After another talk at UBC, with Zac Kaye, then the director of Hillel there.

With students, teacher Philip Paul, and mothers in Kamloops, B.C.

Image of Bronia with *Schutzbrief* which accompanied the article on p. 63 (photomontage by Bill Keay).

At the Vancouver Holocaust Centre in 1995, after givng a talk there (photograph by Laureen Moe).

Markus Schirmer and his mother, Ilse, visiting Bronia.

Bronia's younger grandaughter, Claire Herman, speaks to one of
Markus Schirmer's classes at a school in Nuremberg, in June 2002.
Her friend, Naomi Rozenberg (p. 154), helped in giving this talk.

Bronia's grandson, Jonathan Herman, then a student at the Emily
Carr Institute of Art and Design in Vancouver, helped in 2004 to
develop a logo for the Vancouver Holocaust Education Centre.

Bronia with students after her last presentation at the annual Vancouver Holocaust Symposium in 2008, before retiring.

Bronia with students of Susan Cox, standing second from right, from her ethics class at the University of British Columbia.

Bronia being visited at her home by teacher Fred Lemna, some of his students, and a mother, Susan Major.

Fred brought an appreciated Sacher Torte from his trip to Vienna, shown here with Susan and her daughter Candra.

Bronia with plaque from teacher Fred Lemna and his students:

With Profound Respect
And Admiration
Bronia Sonnenschein
We will bear witness
as will
our children and
our children's children.

From the Young
Men and Women of
Sardis Senior
Secondary School
With Whom
You've Shared
So Much Today.

May 1, 1997

Part 4

A Full Life in Vancouver

A Full Life

Dan Sonnenschein (2003)

A S MY MOTHER HAS SAID, she became "in a way, the guardian of my people". She has worked diligently and conscientiously at this task, for over a decade, and continues to do so. Bronia Sonnenschein has won the respect, admiration, and gratitude of her people, as well as many in the wider community.

Clearly, the title of this book alludes not to military victory but to psychological and religious victory, as well as physical. My mother's spirit was not crushed. Working hard for her living as a young widow, she raised a Jewish family and has three Jewish grandchildren. Through the educational activities she has been invited to participate in, she has become a dignified and respected ambassador of the Jewish people. Herr Czarnulla's prophesy about my mother has come true.

I would like to share an episode she never mentions in her talks. She always pays tribute to her mother, who encouraged her daughters to carry on one more day, and to the German lady who risked her life to give her a mystical letter of protection. My mother is too modest to mention a time when she, in effect, risked her life to save her mother and sister. The incident occurred in a hell-hole of a camp at Pirna, a dying field of mud to which prisoners had been herded after the bombing of Dresden. It involved the same Herr Czarnulla, who came by candlelight to select laborers to take back to Dresden to rebuild the munitions factory. He picked Bronia, but not her mother and sister, which would have condemned them to a certain death. She revealed the relationship and said she would not leave without them. Mercifully, he agreed to take all three. Bronia says now that she had no choice; she knew she wouldn't survive without them.

It is fortunate that Czarnulla was a less cruel Nazi than some, and could still show kindness. His decision was a risk, because as a member of the S.A. he was outranked at the Pirna camp by a female member of the dreaded S.S. In a bizarre scene, this fanatic gave the assembled, miserable, starving prisoners a lecture about how she had given up her husband and family to follow the *Führer*. Bronia wryly comments that she was thinking something like, "Good for you, lady." To be in a position to look back upon such an event with a measure of humor is indeed a victory.

Another victory is involved in one of my mother's most significant childhood memories, the prayerful words she read in a Purim play while playing the role of Jewish hero Mordechai (p. 86). Perhaps her teacher who wrote this had some premonition of a future Haman (an enemy of the Jews in ancient Persia who had plotted our annihilation, and whose defeat is recounted in the Book of Esther).

We must be concerned not only with Hamans of the past, but of the present as well. Jewish tradition teaches that "in each generation, Amalek will arise to destroy you". It's clear that in the earlier part of this century, Amalek was the Austro-German Nazi empire. Subsequently, the Soviet empire and some of its allies took over this role. Today, along with increased dangers of antisemitism in the former Soviet Union, other nations and forces threaten the Jewish state with mass destruction. While history may never repeat exactly, we can try to understand and apply its lessons. We must remember the past in spite of those who would prefer to falsify it, or just let it lie and fade away.

My mother's work as a witness to history has not been easy, but she has kept her promise to her former inmates. Her rewards include the numerous letters and comments she has received, and the many fine people she has met. In 1995, Bronia was appointed a Life Fellow of the Vancouver Holocaust Centre, in recognition of outstanding contribution to Holocaust education. In 1997 she was among those who received a *N'Shei Chabad* (Women of Chabad) award with a plaque that reads, "To a Woman of Valor — many have done worthily, but you surpass them all." Another plaque was given to her after a presentation organized by dedicated teacher, Fred Lemna, and is inscribed: "With profound respect and admiration, Bronia Sonnenschein, we will bear witness, as will our children and our children's children. From the young men and women of Sardis Senior

Secondary School with whom you shared so much today, May 1, 1997."

The year before, Bronia had travelled to Salmon Arm, B.C. for a talk, and she treasures the eagle feather given to her there by Rosie McLeod-Shannon on behalf of the First Nations. Rosie told her that the three colored bands on the feather represent her compassion, inner light, and courage. May her light continue to shine and inspire, and bestow its blessings upon her family and friends.

Bronia after a presentation at a Catholic elementary school in Cloverdale, B.C. in June, 2002. At the left are a grandmother and mother with their child in the middle. To the left of Bronia is teacher David Pistrin, and on the right are parents with their son. The father told Bronia, "You are a mother to us all."

Bronia Made a Difference

Paulette Cave (2010)

*Paulette is a long-time volunteer at the Isaac Waldman Library
in Vancouver's Jewish Community Centre. This article is for
the next edition of her book, "Women Who Made a Difference".*

I ENROLLED IN A HEBREW COURSE at Vancouver's Jewish
Community Centre. "Now, I go for a swim," announced Fay,
the instructor, after the first lesson. Thereafter, I brought my
bathing suit.

Among the pool regulars I observed a woman swimming
gentle laps without disturbing a hair of her neatly coiffed head.
Fay introduced us in the changing room.

"She's a Holocaust survivor," Fay had told me. "And she
speaks to the students at local high schools."

Ah, I knew about her. My late husband, who had taught at
Princess Margaret Senior Secondary School in Surrey, described
a petite Jewish woman, with a soft voice, who had spoken to the
students about her wartime experiences in a prison camp. Was
that you, Bronia? "Probably," she said. "My dear — so many
schools." While Bronia was enduring the experiences she
described to students, my English husband had been doing his
bit to defeat Nazism. He joined the R.A.F. at eighteen and flew
many missions over Europe as a navigator in Mosquito Bombers.
In that sense, his and Bronia's lives were connected — fighter of,
and resister of the common enemy.

"Skipping ropes! You, too!" exclaimed Bronia.

We were sitting on Bronia's sofa, sharing childhood
memories. There were some things in common, but nothing in
my life compared to what Bronia described as "growing up in
the most beautiful city in Europe." A large, extended family
provided a sense of belonging and, from an early age, Bronia
absorbed the culture of her beautiful Vienna. She attended a
French kindergarten, had piano lessons and visited the Museum
of History of Arts. "As students we attended performances at

Vienna's State Opera House — mind you, standing in the fourth gallery! We used opera glasses and the acoustics were wonderful. Pogroms in Russia and the Spanish inquisition were things we read about. They did not affect us. I had Gentile friends. We never dreamed ...!" The Anschluss of March 13, 1938 put an end to all that. In "Victory Over Nazism", Bronia tells her story from that time on. Hopefully, the summary I present will inspire readers to buy her book.

Bronia and her family were taken to the Lodz Ghetto in Poland. They concealed their relationship in order to prevent Nazi captors from sadistically executing one family member in front of the others. In 1941, twenty thousand more Jews from Vienna and Prague arrived at the Ghetto. The quota of watery soup, rotten vegetables, occasional bits of horse meat and a loaf of bread was meant to last a week, but never did. Food rations were not increased to accommodate the newcomers. Half-starved ghetto inhabitants worked twelve hour shifts producing furniture, machinery, clothing and toys. Those too weak to work were deported and killed. In the Lodz Ghetto, families were together. In 1944, those who survived were still together as they crowded into cattle wagons, heading for Auschwitz. Of the one hundred sixty thousand who had entered the Lodz Ghetto, only sixty thousand were left. At Auschwitz, the naked prisoners were paraded past the infamous Dr. Mengele. With a flick of his hand, he gestured those deemed unfit for work towards the left and the gas chambers. The Auschwitz band played Bach and Beethoven as prisoners were fed into the ovens. Survivors were handed ragged clothing. Bronia describes interminable roll calls, standing in the hot sun, in rain, in snow. They subsisted on one daily serving of watery soup, one slice of bread and a bowl of coffee. The smoke never stopped coming from the ovens which turned to ashes innocent human beings. "My mother, my sister and I survived because we were together." They never revealed their relationship. The sadistic captors would have delighted in killing one family member in front of the others. The prisoners were moved to Stutthof, a camp ill equipped to accommodate masses of prisoners. "We ate and slept on the floor." Sanitation was minimal. Paula came down with scarlet fever. Bronia and her mother propped her up during roll call. She recovered. At night, Russian and Allied bombs rained down on Dresden, destroying the factory where the prisoners sorted bullets. The prisoners were taken to Pirna, then back to Dresden to resume working in what was left of the factory. The Russians advanced ever nearer. S.S. men herded the prisoners together. There followed twelve days of marching without food, water, or shelter. The bodies of those who died were thrown into the Elbe river. "Paula and I decided to end it all. Being so close to the river, drowning in it seemed to be the simplest way." Their mother begged them to wait just one more day. April 24 was Paula's birthday. Thus, they made it to Theresienstadt. The Germans had planned to concentrate as many as possible Jews into the camp — then blow it up. Fortunately, they ran out of time. On May 8, 1945, their German captors fled. "My mother, my sister and I were blessed to hear the young Russian soldier who entered the camp announce, 'You are free. You can go home now,'" The Russians handed out bread. Bronia described eating a chunk of bread, "any time we wanted to!"

After a spell in hospital, Bronia made it to Prague. She wore the clean clothes given to liberated prisoners. Along the way, she obtained food which was distributed at train stations. She found temporary shelter and looked for work. Not knowing the Czech language, she settled for a factory job stuffing vanilla baking powder into packages. She spent every free moment learning the language. Bronia's knowledge of French and English, and growing fluency in Czech, enabled her to land a position at a hops exporting firm. Things were looking up! Then communist Russia took control. Her job was gone. "It was almost like 'deja vu'," wrote Bronia in her book ... "dictatorship all over again ... Yet luck was with me — or was it maybe a miracle?" Bronia was hired to work with the American Joint Distribution Committee. This was a Jewish organization set up to help Jewish people reach the free world, providing they had relatives there to sponsor them. During this time, she met Dr. Kurt Sonnenschein. They were married on Dec. 28, 1948.

The political situation in Prague was untenable. Bronia and her husband set their sights on Israel. Getting there became a bureaucratic nightmare. The Sonnenscheins pulled it off, arriving in Haifa in May of 1949. They found themselves in the chaos of a new country taking in refugees and Holocaust survivors. Dan was born in Israel, by which time Bronia and her husband had decided to move to Vancouver. Dr. Sonnenschein's brother was already in Canada and he agreed to sponsor the family. The Sonnenscheins travelled to Vancouver via Sweden, where they visited with Dr. Sonnenschein's friends. In New York, the couple visited with Bronia's relatives. "(The ones that got away in time.) The three of us arrived in this beautiful city (Vancouver) in July, 1950." Bronia's mother, sister and brother-in-law arrived soon after. Bronia's husband found work in the office of a lumber company. Bronia's daughter was born. Things were looking up. Then, in 1952, the car in which Bronia and her husband were riding was involved in a head-on collision. Dr. Sonnenschein was killed. Bronia and her son survived. Their baby girl was safe home with Bronia's mother.

Bronia became the breadwinner. She worked, for twenty-five years, in the office where her husband had been employed. Acceding to her children's wishes, she retired. What was she to do? Her mother had died in 1977, her sister ("my very best friend"), in 1986. "I couldn't just sit around!" Bronia joined the Vancouver Holocaust Centre Society — a logical step considering her status as a Holocaust Survivor. She accepted an invitation to speak to students about her experiences. There was another invitation, then another. During the next twenty years, she would tell her story to thousands of students. "I spoke in Idaho!" she told me as we swam side by side. White supremacy was on the rise in that part of the United States. Bronia was not about to be scared off! A letter of thanks from a senior student at Sandpoint High School is included in Bronia's book. "We have to keep the memory of the Holocaust alive so that it may never happen again."

In 1993, during Holocaust Awareness Week, Bronia spoke at the University of British Columbia. A young man in the audience, listening raptly, happened to be from Nuremberg, Germany. He contacted Bronia two days later. Could they meet? She agreed, albeit a tad nervously ... Nuremberg, after all ... Hitler's rallies. Well, one meeting led to another, and another. She met Markus Schirmer's parents when they visited Vancouver. Markus, interested in Jewish religion and culture, attended services at Beth Israel Synagogue. Once, he brought a group of Lutheran students. Bronia said he had more questions than I could answer. "I turned him over to Rabbi Solomon!" Markus returned home resolving to do in Germany what Bronia was doing in British Columbia. He taught nine lessons on the Holocaust in his student practicum. He told Bronia's story. He made them aware of landmarks throughout Nuremberg — sites of former synagogues and other buildings significant to the Jewish people. He and his students visited a synagogue. He spoke to this group and that. Bronia's message was rippling out — and out.

Now and again, I have been privileged to visit Bronia in her apartment. While she makes the tea, I look around. Among the pictures and ornaments, there are plaques and other mementos from her public speaking days. An eagle's feather from the Native band of Chief Dan George gives an idea of the cross-section of society to whom she passed on her message. We sip tea, eat bakery pastries and chat at her dining room table. Bronia has firm ideas about the younger generation and how it needs to shape up — in general. She knows young people, her grandchildren included, of whom she approves.

I and another volunteer at the JCC Isaac Waldman Library lead a weekly conversation session where new Canadians can practice using English. Bronia joins us. Her syntax is flawless, only the faint accent indicating English is not her first language. *L'chaim* is a Hebrew expression meaning "to Life!" Bronia did, indeed, choose life. I will add Dale Carnegie's, "When fate hands us lemons, let's try to make lemonade." Bronia did that — in buckets! Thank God she and her sister listened to their mother, on that prisoners' march and did not throw themselves into that river.

Surviving Victimization

Diane Rodgers (2012)

Diane is President and Project Coordinator of the BullyFreeBC Society, which is dedicated to eliminating workplace bullying and harassment in British Columbia. She has done extensive research on the Holocaust.

IN 1985, BRONIA READ AN ARTICLE entitled "How one Jew fought the Nazis" about a Jewish woman who had joined the underground during the Second World War and actively resisted the Nazis. She was disturbed that the former fighter reflected on "how meekly most of her fellow Jews went along with the German invaders ... allowing themselves to be taken away to concentration camps without a fight. Then another quote from the article: "I never understood why the Jews did not fight, they were like sheep waiting to be slaughtered."

As a survivor of the Lodz ghetto, Auschwitz and Stutthof concentration camps, Bronia resented this rebuke from another survivor. As she stated in a letter to the editor of the publication (see p. 119): "I had to endure Nazi atrocities from March 1938 when Hitler marched into Vienna till the day of our liberation on May 8, 1945 in Theresienstadt. I cannot take credit for saving lives — does that make me a meek person, acting like a sheep? Or does it make me a victim who was robbed of the dignity to defend herself by having been stripped of every possible defense action. ... We can't all be heroes. ..."

In fact, recounting what happened to the Schwebel family in those years makes it difficult to see how Bronia did not consider herself and her family to be heroes for managing to save their own lives.

Under the brutal measures of the Nazi regime, between March 1938 and May 1945 they were dispossessed of their home and belongings, forced to flee from Austria, then terrorized, overworked and starved on a daily basis in Poland for more than four years through a genocidal process of slave labour imprisonment in the ghetto. From there they were crammed into box cars for deportation to concentration camps and for labour in a Dresden factory where they were bombed. Finally they ended the war down to skin and bones, heads shaved and dressed in rags — dragged by the guards on a death march along the River Elbe from Germany to Czechoslovakia with 3 meals of watery soup in 12 days. Around them people were dropping dead in their tracks and the bodies thrown into the river. At that point Bronia and her sister Paula were broken, desperate for release from the unending misery, ready to commit suicide. Their mother Emilia said, 'Wait.' It was April 1945 and the next day they arrived at Theresienstadt which was under control of the Red Cross. The Germans fled.

Their father Abraham did not survive with them. He had died several months before, in Stutthof, a victim of the Holocaust, like millions of other civilians who perished because the Nazis despised Jews and because the cloak of war gave them the freedom of action required to commit genocide. Of the 200,000 estimated souls to have passed through the Lodz ghetto, probably less than 10,000 survived.

Obviously a middle-class family from Vienna had no hope of fighting back against this magnitude of force. As Bronia said: With what? How?

But even after the passage of more than 25 years since the writing of the article and her letter of bitter protest to the editor, a dark thread of victim blaming still winds through Holocaust discourse and distorts the field of inquiry. Instead of facing up to Nazism, even today, people persist in trying to find out what the victims did wrong, looking for fault in the ones who were targeted for destruction.

This impulse to avoid confronting evil leaves survivors knowing horrifying truths that others prefer to ignore, dismiss and dispute. And so people like Bronia, whose life experiences can reveal cause and effect of mass human failure, are instead re-victimized for surviving the inescapable.

The darkest aspect in this assignment of blame to Holocaust victims is an unnoticed step of casting the Nazi regime into the background, in order to assess how people responded to dehumanizing persecution. Oddly, these discussions sometimes use the term "Jewish honour" as though victims of genocidal atrocities let down every other Jew by not fighting back harder... So after the Nazis set out to destroy their lives, posterity stands in judgement of how they performed while undergoing the hellish process.

Regardless of the ethics and value of such discussions, they do nothing to address the real question of how everyone else in Europe and around the world failed so many helpless individuals who had no chance to save themselves.

Writer's note:

I met Bronia in 1994 when she came to the Jewish Historical Society of BC where I was community archivist. Over the next many years she visited sometimes for a chat after her swim at the Jewish Community Centre. Our conversations continued after I left that position in 2006 and began organizing local advocacy against workplace bullying and harassment in BC.

Given her experience in the ghetto of slave labour, when I started doing research for this initiative I asked Bronia about working in the Lodz Judenrat office. As one of the secretaries she came in direct contact with Nazi administrators which is the extreme situation of a hostile workplace.

Recalling those times, in her peaceful sunny garden apartment in Vancouver, she shared painfully illuminating stories of an environment where workers were openly hated and might survive for another day if they earned favour in a system designed to destroy them.

Her courage, grace and resilience throughout those years and after continue to be an inspiration.

Apfelstrudel

Susan Cox (2012)

*Susan is an Associate Professor and Michael Smith Foundation
for Health Research Scholar at The W. Maurice Young Centre
for Applied Ethics at the University of British Columbia.*

*"The language of Friendship is not words, but meanings.
It is an intelligence above language." — Henry David Thoreau*

I T IS LATE AFTERNOON, a grey February day, almost snowing. I think of Bronia and the promise of new friendship that seemed such an unexpected presence one spring day some nine years ago. I rummage through several boxes in my office to find my copy of the second edition of *Victory Over Nazism*. I reread the careful inscription, "To Susan, So generations will never forget what so few lived to tell. With best wishes, Bronia Sonnenschein." It was dated March 3, 2003, the first of many occasions when I was invited for tea at Bronia's cosy apartment.

We had a lot of things to discuss that day. Bronia wanted to know about the students in my Genetics and Ethics class. In February I had taken them to the Vancouver Holocaust Education Centre to see the exhibit *Ravensbrück: The Forgotten Women of the Holocaust* as part of the seminar I was teaching on Genetics and Ethics. Most of the group of 10 or 12 students were in the genetic counseling program at the University of British Columbia and it was important that they learn about the history of eugenics as part of the curriculum. We were so very fortunate that Bronia was also there to speak about her experiences as a Holocaust survivor.

In hindsight, I could not have imagined anything more welcome than the phone call I received from Bronia a few days after we had visited the VHEC. This is Bronia Sonnenschein. I met you the other day with your class and I would like to invite you to tea. Please call me and let me know if you have time in your busy schedule. I so look forward to hearing from you.

Reflecting on her meeting with my class, Bronia recalled that one of the students was from Iraq. The student had, until she met Bronia, been extremely reluctant to say that this was her homeland as many people seemed to react with such prejudice. The authenticity and power of Bronia's testimonial had, however, created such a deep feeling of respect and trust that she decided it was safe to open up and say more about who she really was. Others in the group soon followed suit sharing with Bronia their innermost thoughts. Bronia casually dubbed the discussion that day our United Nations meeting and she could not have been more right.

When the Ravensbrück exhibit first opened, I attended a tour that was for teachers who planned to bring their students to visit. The docent explained the unique aspects of this particular concentration camp; how it was built exclusively to house female prisoners, and that it had the highest percentage of murdered prisoners of any concentration camp in Germany. Yet Ravensbrück, and the women imprisoned there, remained relatively unknown. By reproducing the drawings, poetry and even a recipe book made by the women inmates, the exhibit explored the strategies that the women imprisoned there used to survive.* As we heard, it was friendship and solidarity as well as their determined resistance to the destruction of mind and spirit through creative and intellectual activities that allowed them to survive. What struck me most about this opening, however, was the social time that followed. In a room adjoining the exhibit,

---

* The recipe book belonged to Rebecca Teitelbaum. As a forced laborer in Ravensbrück, Teitelbaum "managed to steal paper, pencil, needle and thread to write and sew together a tiny, 110-page book of the recipes she recalled from home. The women around her found comfort in reading the recipes aloud to one another. Teitelbaum lost the book during her forced evacuation from the camp, but a stranger found it and succeed in returning it to her in Belgium, where he located her two years later. The book is now housed in the Vancouver Holocaust Education Center."
(See: http://truthpraiseandhelp.wordpress.com/tag/ravensbruck.)

there was a display of books and a long table filled with tea and coffee and pastries. At one end was what appeared to be a special cake being served in very thin slices. Imagine how it must have tasted to learn that this *Gateau à l'orange* was made from a recipe written in painstakingly small letters in the recipe book featured in the exhibit! The survival of this recipe, like so many others that the women of Ravensbrück recited to each other was evidence of extraordinary resourcefulness and courage. I had never encountered a cake so intensely infused with meaning, so emblematic of the power of women's friendship and solidarity in the face of such utter brutality.

I learned fairly quickly that Bronia had a sweet tooth. And when I had occasion to visit the beautiful city of Vienna, in 2005, I knew that I had to visit the Hotel Sacher and sample the famous *Sacher-Torte*. Though Bronia said she had no intention of ever returning to Vienna, she retained an astounding wealth of memories about the city where she enjoyed a happy childhood. While checking my email late one night in my tiny hotel room next to Stephansplatz, I received the most eloquent travel guidance. Listen to some extracts from this delightful message as Bronia walks with you through the streets of Vienna!

> ... We walk along the Ringstrasse where you can't miss the Votivkirche, one of the many splendid churches in Vienna, the Burgtheater where classical plays were performed, the magnificent Rathaus and the lovely Rathaus park. A stroll around it, weather permitting, would delight you.
>
> ... Coming to the Volksgarten, another one of Vienna's beautiful parks, you will find the small Theseus Temple. (My memory of this beautiful Temple is falling down the stairs attempting to jump from it. I ended up with a chipped tooth and a not so warm welcome at home. The things you do when you are a child not fearing anything.)
>
> ... A visit to the Stadtpark will be greatly rewarded by looking up to the lifesize statue of the waltz king Johann Strauss playing on his violin the Blue Danube waltz. My feet kept dancing just looking at it. Did you know that

Vienna was called the music capital of the world? No
wonder, wherever you went you heard the gentle tunes
of Viennese music, and in spring there was the smell of
lilac in the air.

... And now on to Vienna's magnificent St. Stephan's
Cathedral. It was badly destroyed during WW II but carefully restored to its old majestic beauty. In Vienna they don't
tear down houses, not even schools, as my granddaughters
can confirm having visited the elementary school I attended.
Emily was in Vienna in 2000, Claire in 2002. That's one of
the things that make Vienna unforgettable.

... From all the wandering around we need a break and
visit to one of Vienna's many konditoreis. I recommend the
"Demel" on the Graben, where you can also see the "Pillar
of the Plague". But first let's eat the delightful little open-
faced sandwiches, each looking artful, have a coffee with
whipping cream and one of the best pastries Vienna has to
offer. We get ready to see the Opera house that still bears
memories of the Emperor Franz Joseph and his Empress
Elizabeth. And while we are there, there is the world-
famous cafe Sacher where Anna Sacher once ago created
the Sachertorte, for the Emperor who reigned for 60 years
(no bodyguard) and was beloved by everybody.

... And there is more, so much more to feel and experience in Vienna, the Vienna I loved before 1938 and my
Viennese dream collapsed. But I am happy to remember
the good times and will always love the memory.

Bronia was very pleased to see a pale pink Demel's box tucked
under my arm the next time that I visited for tea. Another time
when I visited, I made the *Sacher-Torte* myself and was delighted
to find that Bronia and Dan had a big bowl of whipped cream
all ready to serve with it. This is apparently the world's most
famous cake, a luscious chocolate creation with apricot filling,
smothered in dark chocolate. Bronia assured me that it was
also quite fitting to add a big dollop of cream to your coffee!
No wonder the Viennese walk and bicycle everywhere.

But, oh for a piece of Apfelstrudel! As Bronia explained to me, the real "Apfelstrudel" is a "far cry from the humble apple pie." It is packed with thin slices of apple, raisins, sugar and cinnamon and encased in a light and airy blanket of unleavened dough. There is nothing else like it.

I have not yet attempted to make it though I know I one day will.

In Bronia's dining room, about to enjoy Susan's *Sacher-Torte*.

Before a Concert of Ghetto Music

The first item is an excerpt from the introduction by festival co-organizer Janos Maté before a performance by the klezmer group "Brave Old World" on March 5, 2005 at Vancouver's Chan Centre on the University of British Columbia campus.

L ADIES AND GENTLEMEN, tonight's performance of Songs of of the Lodz Ghetto is most timely as this year we commemorate the 60th anniversary of the liberation of Auschwitz and the other death camps, as well as the final defeat of the Nazi regime.

For many of us here tonight, whose families were shattered by the Holocaust, these songs are a direct connection to our loved ones who perished. These songs grew out of their culture, their world, their stories. The very existence of the songs, and the interpretation that Brave Old World brings to them, is a profound defiance of the monstrous plan that would have eradicated our people and erased our culture.

We are so indebted to our poets, song writers and composers. They spark eternal flames that glow *so* brightly that not even the deepest darkness can extinguish them. And we are so fortunate to have great artists, the guardians of these flames, who enable us to bridge our past with the present.

Ladies and gentlemen, a few weeks ago I had the privilege to meet a truly remarkable person. One, who as a young woman fled Vienna with her family when the Germans took over Austria in 1938; lived through four years of excruciating hardship in the Lodz ghetto; and between August of 1944 and her moment of liberation on May 8, 1945, survived Auschwitz and Stutthof concentration camps, the fire bombing of Dresden, and a 12-day death march from Dresden to Theresienstadt.

Of the 250,000 people transported to Auschwitz from the Lodz ghetto in 1944, she was one of the 877 that survived.

She has real life memories of the songs we are about to hear tonight, *as* they were sung on the streets of the ghetto by the people who wrote them. She vividly remembers the songs as a source of strength, courage and entertainment for the starved and tortured population of the ghetto.

She also remembers the moment when, at a point of near death, she made a solemn promise that if she were to survive she would never forget, and she would never let the world forget. And she has kept that promise. Over the years she has given hundreds of talks in schools and in the community at large. Her story has reached thousands of people, young and old alike. She has been interviewed on TV and radio, as well as for Stephen Spielberg's Shoah project. And she has faithfully recorded her story in a very personal manuscript, aptly entitled: "Victory over Nazism: The Journey of a Holocaust Survivor".

She receives volumes of letters of appreciation. One person who heard her speak on CBC wrote: "People like you help to shape our human future, because you show us that we have a choice between keeping silent and blind, or speaking out and acting for respect and freedom for everyone."

Ladies and gentlemen please rise and share with me the honour of welcoming an amazing woman, an outstanding human being, Bronia Sonnenschein.

Bronia's Words of Introduction

It is my privilege to be here tonight to pay tribute to my fellow inmates, my family included. We lived in the Lodz Ghetto for four years behind electric barbed wire. We worked together, we starved together, and together we dreamed of freedom. Together we mourned when in September 1942 the Gestapo rounded up thousands of children up to 10 years old and men and women over 60, deported and killed them brutally.

The street musicians, Jankele Herszkowicz and Karl Rosenzweig lit up our life with their gift of music, the songs of the Lodz Ghetto. Tonight, 60 years later, I will be hearing the songs of the Lodz Ghetto together with you and my son and grandson at my side. I look upon it as a special gift for which I thank the Brave Old World with all my heart, as well as Janos Maté for his kind words of introducing me. Thank you.

My Mother

Vivian Herman (1998)

Vivian is a former librarian who has since then pursued her creative interests in the visual arts. She lives in Calgary, Alberta with her husband Ben, a retired family physician. They have three children and five grandchildren.

M Y MOTHER IS AN EXTRAORDINARY PERSON whose strength of character and moral conviction is evident in every aspect of her life. She has continually amazed me with her ability to face the most difficult challenges in her life, loss of home, spouse, family, and illness. Her devotion to Danny and me, and the preservation of family were her sole concern in the early years of rebuilding her life after the Holocaust and the death of my father. I know that my wonderfully supportive grandmother played an enormous part in her life as well as my own. She was a tremendous role model and teacher. It was through her we all learned of strength, dignity, humor and grace. Mom was also greatly encouraged throughout her life by her sister, my Aunt Paula. She was a vibrant and caring woman, a selfless and devoted sister and friend. I know that Mom will forever be linked to these two courageous women who were so instrumental in her physical and emotional survival. Their spirit is forever with her, as it is with me. Despite losing them, as well as other close family members, Mom has always persevered with fierce determination to be there for Danny and me and her grandchildren. I think that her appreciation for the blessings she has found in her life, and her ability to see the beauty in life, has helped sustain her optimistic spirit.

Teaching the Holocaust to thousands of children and teachers has been a demanding and difficult task. However, there doesn't seem to be a challenge too great if Mom sets her mind to it. It has been an experience with many rewards and it has made me extremely proud to know that in her senior years she can find such meaningful work and gain great personal fulfillment. The countless letters and personal messages from students and teachers that Mom receives express such gratitude. They speak of the privilege to have been touched by her words and story of survival. I know that she has made a difference in the lives of so many young people.

Mom has always longed to be a little taller in stature, but in my eyes and in my heart she is a giant. Through her life I have learned of courage, integrity, love and devotion. She has shown me the beauty and joy of motherhood which I too have been blessed to share with my children.

Together on Vivian's wedding day on August 17, 1975.

My Grammy

Emily Sztabzyb (1998)

Emily is Bronia's eldest grandchild. She is a university arts graduate with experience in theatre, singing, and dance. She lives in Calgary with her husband, Sebastian Sztabzyb, and her two children.

S HE IS MY LITTLE GRAMMY, but she is one of the strongest women in the world. Each day she is busy; she speaks to groups about the Holocaust, visits with friends, spends time with her son, talks to us on the phone (in Calgary), reads books. I've never met any other woman her age who swims and goes for walks every day. She is what I would like to be one day.

She tells me to count my blessings, and I do. I see that she takes her own advice. Despite a significant amount of difficulty and tragedy in her life, she still has a positive spirit. She believes in finding the good in people and she always searches for the bright side. Her focus on the happy details of her life are what keep her the smiling, laughing, young-living Grammy that I love.

She speaks so many other words that must be remembered. So many times I have wanted to stop her, mid-sentence, and grab a notepad to write down every syllable. Her words are like poetry. It is impossible for me to remember them all at one given time, but they always seem to come to me when I need them.

A part of her life that shaped her greatly was the Holocaust. I have often tried to imagine what this time was like for her and for my Baba and Zeida. I love my grandparents so much and I want to understand, but I cannot. I can only listen to their stories, remember them, and pass them on. To forget or to deny is to open the door to reoccurrence. For this reason, my Grammy has dedicated much of her life to Holocaust education. She wants to protect her children, grandchildren, and our children from the terror she faced. Thank you Grammy. I promise to continue with what you are doing.

My Grammy is one of my best friends. In many ways she is a typical Grandma; she hates loud music and she still worries about me driving in the dark, but in many more ways, she's not so typical. We talk on the phone like two friends would, we have so much fun when either of us comes to town for a visit, and she understands me so well, sometimes better than I understand myself. I learn from her, I confide in her, I find comfort and happiness in her, and I love her. She is my little Grammy.

Two days before Emily's wedding, in 2002.

Acknowledgements

Bronia Sonnenschein (2003)

A ND NOW THAT ALL IS SAID AND DONE, all the information fed into the computer, all the pictures scanned in and this book is almost ready to be printed, I would like to add my final thoughts. My thoughts about the way my life has been, the highs and the lows, the despair and the struggle to have reached this point in life when I can truly say: After all it's been a good life. Having always been blessed with a family that was loving and caring, and having experienced the great joy of my family during the raising of my children, Dan and Vivian, has enriched my life more than I will ever be able to tell. Ours was and is a family that never quarrelled, that understood and respected each others feelings, and that is why I can say, "I made it from the horror of the death camps to the love and security my children and grandchildren, Emily, Claire and Jonathan, as well as Ben, my son-in-law, have always given me. They are proof that one can rise above oneself and truly mean it. I did it, I have been victorious. There is no bitterness; sadness, yes, but when we are together my children and grandchildren feel and know that I have protected them by showing them the right way to live one's life. And so my thanks are to my children for having helped me along the way.

How do you thank your son, who has put his life on hold to finally convince me to let him produce this book about me. It is not so much a story, as tracing through my writings the years before, during and after the Holocaust. He had no outside help whatsoever to do it, scanning all the pictures that I had received after from some of my relatives who had gotten out in time. He did the arranging, the layout, the word processing, the editing, selecting the cover of this book, and finally putting it all on a disk to be given to the printer. Is there any proper thanks for that? The love I have showered him and Vivian with, the love both of them received from their "Granny" (my mother), my sister Paula and her husband Stan, bore fruit in the way they are today. And so Danny, I thank you with all my heart for having undertaken this project, for always being there when I need you. You have never let me down.

But I can't just let it end here. My deepest thanks to all my friends whom I have been so fortunate to meet during the last 10 years since I began my work in Holocaust education. Among those who were instrumental in bringing Holocaust education to its present wide state of recognition are Dr. Robert Krell, founder and first president of the Vancouver Holocaust Centre; my fellow camp survivor and educator Robbie Waisman, current VHC president; Dr. Roberta Kremer, VHC director; Rita Akselrod, director of the VHC Outreach Program; Erwin Nest and Marilyn Berger, director and former associate director respectively of the Canadian Jewish Congress, Pacific Region; Dr. Graham Forst, a co-founder of the annual Holocaust Symposium at the University of British Columbia and co-chairman for the last 23 years; Professor Emeritus William Nicholls, founder of the Department of Religious Studies at UBC and another Symposium co-founder and participant; and Professor Chris Friedrichs, a historian at UBC and long-time chairman of the Kristallnacht Commemoration Committee.

It is not possible to mention everybody by name but your friendship means a lot to me. I thank all and each of you for your encouragement. I wish to thank all the teachers and professors, all the educators who invited me to their classrooms to share my experiences with their students. Their support too was greatly encouraging and continues to give me hope that together we will reach our goal, our hope and our promise — Never again will there ever be another Holocaust.

Bronia celebrating another Chanukah in freedom (5754 / 1996).
On the wall are two of her awards, one being the eagle feather.

At the Quarry garden in Queen Elizabeth Park, Vancouver, beside
a plaque honouring a Holocaust hero, diplomat Raoul Wallenberg.

Bronia and her children, at Vivian's home in Calgary in 1995.

Bronia at her grandson's Bar Mitzvah. Standing from left to right: Claire (granddaughter), Dan (son), Vivian (daughter), Ben Herman (son-in-law), Emily (granddaughter), Peter Kavalek (first cousin), Jonathan (grandson).

Three generations under the traditional *huppah* (canopy) just before Emily's wedding ceremony.

Bronia with her extended family including new grandson-in-law, Sebastian Sztabzyb.

With Emily just before her wedding.

L'Chaim!

(To life!)

Bronia with her grandchild, Emily, and great-grandchild, Annie.

Four generations: Bronia with her daughter, granddaughters, and first great-granddaughter, at Claire's wedding in 2007.

Bronia admiring her second great-granddaughter, Makena, with the happy parents, Claire and Lou Kolman.

Four generations: Bronia, Vivian, Makena, Claire in July 2009.

Bronia and great-grandson Leo, with Emily, Makena, and Claire at a dinner the evening before Jonathan's wedding, in May 2010.

Bronia at the marriage of her grandson Jonathan to Jackie Berger, along with her children and son-in-law.

Bronia enjoying tea with Paulette Cave in May 2010.

Bronia on her patio (her "summer residence") with
Rosemary Fitzgerald and son Michael, in Oct. 2010.

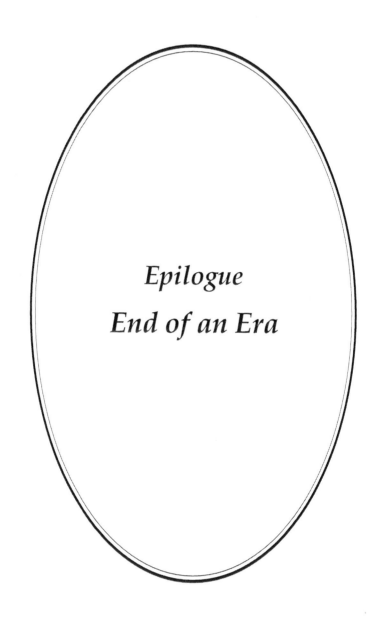

Epilogue

End of an Era

Bronia's Magnificent Legacy

Chris Friedrichs (January 28, 2011)

*Following is the eulogy movingly delivered to a full
chapel at Bronia's funeral at the Beth Israel Cemetery.
Professor Friedrichs is a historian at the University
of British Columbia who is very active in Holocaust
education, and was a long-time friend of Bronia.*

I AM DEEPLY TOUCHED to have been asked to give expression to some thoughts that everyone in this chapel must share. I will not attempt to recount Bronia's whole life. You do not have to be told who Bronia was. You are here because of who she was. Rather, I hope to find the words to express not only what we have lost, but what so many others far beyond this chapel and far beyond our own Jewish community have lost through the death of this matchlessly unique human being.

We all know that Bronia's long life went through many phases in remarkably many places. There were the happy years of her childhood and adolescence in Vienna. There were the years of the Holocaust with that long, grim list of places that Bronia never forgot — Lodz, Auschwitz, Stutthof, Dresden, Pirna, and then the death march to an unknown destination which turned out to be Theresienstadt — years during which every single day was spent on the knife's edge between death and life. Then there was the liberation and the search for a renewed life in Austria, Czechoslovakia, Israel and finally, via Sweden and New York, Vancouver where Bronia and her husband found the home they had longed for. But then the happy years of a new beginning were brutally interrupted by the sudden death of her husband. Bronia had to create an entirely new life of work and devoted single motherhood. And then, finally, during what for most people would be years of comfortable retirement, there was an entirely new career as an educator — a teacher not to hundreds or thousands but to tens of thousands of young people in British Columbia and elsewhere.

At every step of the way on this incredible journey, the core of Bronia's existence was the sustaining love she received from and gave to her family. In every crisis or challenge of her life, it was family that gave her strength. At that desperate moment on the last death march, when Bronia and her sister were, after all they had gone through, finally at the point of giving up, it was a few simple words from their mother that persuaded them to go on for just another day — and that one more day opened the door to liberation and life. Her husband, her mother, her sister, her son and daughter, her three grandchildren, and then even great-grandchildren — these were the anchors of Bronia's life. To sit in Bronia's cozy living room in the Willow Gardens and hear her talk about her grandchildren was to watch the world become brighter. For decades Bronia lived for her mother, sister, children and grandchildren. But she did not live through them. Rather, her love for her family and their love for her gave her the strength to do all those other things that made her life so remarkable. This was, I think, the secret behind the amazing impact Bronia had in her last career, as a Holocaust educator. Without the support she got from Dan and indeed her whole family, Bronia could never have found the strength to do what she did, over and over, for more than twenty years.

Everyone who ever had the privilege of hearing Bronia Sonnenschein speak to an audience of students will never forget the experience. Whether it was a group of twenty students in a classroom or hundreds of students in a huge lecture hall, as soon as Bronia began to speak she became the focus of intense attention. There was a rapt, unbroken silence as the young audience listened to this tiny woman with a European accent tell, quietly but with uncompromising clarity, exactly what happened to her between 1940 and 1945. When she finished speaking, the silence was suddenly broken by thunderous applause, a standing ovation. And then — who could forget the long line of students who would come up to Bronia afterward, just to shake her hand or ask for a hug or simply to look into her eyes to show how much it meant to them to have personally heard and met a human being who lived through things like this.

What was it that made Bronia such a uniquely compelling communicator? We know some of the ingredients. First, there was Bronia's honesty. Without any dramatics or overemphasis, she simply told the students the raw facts about what happened to her and other human beings in the ghettoes, in the camps, and on the death marches. There was Bronia's dignity, the uncompromised dignity of a person who had experienced unspeakable things which, in the end, had degraded only her tormentors and never herself. And there was her generosity of spirit, which was so evident when Bronia answered a question that came up almost every time she spoke, by saying simply, "No, I do not hate Germans. I hated Nazis. But there were good and bad Germans." Considering what she had experienced, it was a remarkable statement, and her young audience knew it.

But there was one more thing that created an instant bond between Bronia and the students of every colour and background who heard her speak. Yes, they saw in Bronia something they had never seen before, a survivor of the worst inhumanity ever inflicted on other human beings. But at the same time they saw something utterly, compelling familiar. Her accent was different, her story was unique. But for an hour, for an afternoon, this woman became a grandmother to hundreds of children, a grandmother who had experienced what was almost beyond description but wanted to tell them about it because she loved them and wanted to help them become better human beings.

When we say that someone has left a legacy, we normally think of things said and done, things created or written. And there are indeed countless concrete legacies of Bronia's remarkable life and her career as a Holocaust educator. There is an incredible archive of thousands upon thousands of letters written by students who heard Bronia speak and wanted her to know how her words had affected their lives. But there is also a vastly greater and even more important legacy, an *invisible* legacy of things *not* said and *not* done by the young people of our province and elsewhere — the racist remarks that were not made, the jokes that were not laughed at, the gangs that were not joined. This too is part of Bronia's magnificent legacy.

Every one of us in this chapel has a reason to mourn our loss. We will miss Bronia's vital presence, her strong opinions, her energy, her voice, her love. But we mourn not just for ourselves or our community. We mourn as well for the whole generation of schoolchildren who, because of the inevitable and inexorable passage of time, will not have the opportunity to share the experience of those tens of thousands of young people who will never forget the day they met and heard and came to love Bronia Sonnenschein. The work will continue, but it can never be the same.

Every year there are certain days on which the Holocaust is recalled with particular intensity. On Yom Hashoah we look inward. On that day the Jewish people mourn their own loss. But on January 27, the International Holocaust Remembrance Day, we reach out. For on that day the rest of the world is summoned to join with us in remembering the Holocaust and reflecting on its meaning. And it was on the very eve, the *erev* of that day, that Bronia's long life came to an end. We do not know how and why the Almighty summons anyone to eternity. But we do know that the work was finished, and the timing of Bronia's death was a remarkable echo of her life. As for us, we are left with the memories. May Bronia's memory be as a blessing to us all.

A Granddaughter's Tribute

Emily Sztabzyb (January 28, 2011)

*Emily is the elder granddaughter of Bronia, who held her
minutes after her birth and felt a special bond right away.
Emily delivered this speech in Vancouver's Beth Israel
Synagogue to conclude a religious service after the funeral.*

I KNOW, as I look out at all of you, that each and every one
of you feels you could be standing where I stand now —
speaking about Bronia Sonnenschein, with love, admiration, and
deepest respect. Because that's what my Grammy brought out
in every person she interacted with.

She had a way of making you listen to what she had to say,
a way of making you feel like, in that moment, you were the
only person she wanted to be talking to; a way of capturing a
moment, a thought, a feeling, with such poetry and wisdom.
And she kept those abilities — that knack, right up until last
week. And for that, we are so grateful: that we — all of us — got
to celebrate her life, bask in her love, learn from her, and laugh
with her, for 95 years (now the secret is out).

Yes, we will all miss her so much — but there isn't one of us
who wasn't inspired and changed by her — challenged by
witnessing her strength, courage and optimism ... mother,
grandmother, great-grandmother, and friend.

Obituary

B RONIA died in Vancouver on January 26th, 2011. She was raised in Vienna, Austria and fondly remembered her youth there, despite the vicious persecution of Jews that followed Germany's annexation of a welcoming Austria on March 13, 1938. Bronia and her family ended up in the Lodz Ghetto in Poland for five years, followed by transport to Auschwitz, then Stutthof concentration camp (where her father perished), and on to a factory in Dresden. With her mother and sister, Bronia survived the fire-bombing of Dresden by the Allies. Later, with the Russians rapidly advancing, the three were sent on one of the notorious "death marches" and made it to the Theresienstadt ghetto (near Prague) where, on May 8, 1945, they were officially liberated by a young Russian soldier on horseback, who told the Jews greeting him, "You are free, you can go home again."

Describing this scene ("but we had no home to go to") was an essential part of talks to students, teachers, and others that she started giving in 1987 until retiring in 2008. She always said that without her family she would not have survived, a favorite quote being, "He who has a why to live, can bear with almost any how." During her late-life career as a Holocaust educator, she addressed tens of thousands throughout British Columbia (and one trip to Idaho), receiving awards such as the Queen's Golden Jubilee Medal for exemplary volunteer service.

Bronia survived many other ordeals, including the death of her husband in a car accident in 1952, leaving her a widow with two infants. She became her family's breadwinner, helped by her mother, sister, and brother-in-law to raise her children. Despite the hardships, she was known for her cheerful, upbeat attitude and counted her blessings, chiefly her family: son Dan and daughter Vivian (Ben) Herman; the Hermans' children, Emily (Sebastian), Claire (Lou), and Jonathan (Jackie) — who all considered Bronia "a cool Gramma"; and her three great-grandchildren, in whom she took such delight.

Bronia was bright, stylish, funny, and warm. She was engaged with the world, devoted to her *National Post*, although often riled by its content and venting her anger by scribbling wisecracks or "vitriolic comments" on the pages. Bronia was a remarkable person and left a magnificent legacy. We will always remember her vitality, courage, and deep love of family. A quotation that gave her some solace is: "Radiant days — do not weep that they are gone, but smile that they have been."

The family thanks Dr. Monte Glanzberg for his long-time, excellent care, Professor Chris Friedrichs of UBC for his very moving eulogy, and Bronia's many other admirers for their outpouring of love, appreciation, and respect.

This obituary is online at legacy.com, with photos and Guest Book comments.

A Cousin's Tribute

Peter Kavalek (January 28, 2011)

M Y EARLY RECOLLECTION OF BRONIA is a bit vague and is limited to "the two girls" (being Bronia and sister Paula) my parents spoke about, and photos in the family album.

This became more frequent during and at the end of World War 2, the concern about their welfare, or rather the lack of it, and finally when the tragedy of the Holocaust came to light.

The only good news was that "the two girls" and their mother Emy survived.

Next came their arrival in a refugee camp in Israel about 1948/49: Bronia with recently married husband Kurt Sonnenschein, Paula with husband Stan, mother Emy Schwebel, and Stan's brother with wife.

All were accommodated in a hut the size of a small room constructed of a wooden frame with canvas walls and some sort of roof. Sleeping facilities were camp beds and bunks.

The location was on top of beautifully scenic Mount Carmel above the city of Haifa.

I am mentioning this as I visited there frequently and was a guest in their temporary home gaining the right to sleep on the floor or a vacant bunk if one could be found and eating in the communal dining room, for free, which added to the great time we had. We really had a good time.

This was when I got to know this family I had only ever heard about previously.

Danny was born in 1949 and the family left for a new life in Canada shortly thereafter.

Vivian was born in Vancouver and tragically husband Kurt was killed in a car accident.

Bronia took charge of a very difficult situation, went to work, bought a house and with mother Emy running the household established a warm and beautiful home.

The first time I visited twenty years later I saw what Bronia created. Happy children, and a welcoming atmosphere, obviously done with love and dedication.

Bronia was entirely and totally unselfishly devoted to her family. Fortunately she was rewarded, blessed with her children, three grandchildren, saw them married and lived to become a great-grandmother.

Her work for Holocaust memorial is well known and documented and would take a few more pages. I restricted myself to the more personal recollections.

The end of an era — a fruitful and full life. Always remembered.

Bronia and Paula in the refugee camp in Ahuza, Israel.

Paula and Stan in Ahuza. Photos by Peter Kavalek.

Letter from Bodwell High School

February 28, 2011

Vancouver Holocaust Education Center
5 - 950 West 41st Avenue
Vancouver, British Columbia V5Z 2N7

Dear Advisory Council and Board of Governors,

All of us at Bodwell High were deeply saddened by the news of Bronia Sonnenschein's passing. Her legacy at Bodwell will be sorely missed. She was liked and respected by all those who knew her, and the students who had a chance to see her and listen to her experiences have been touched by just being in her presence.

When the news of Bronia reached our school, it hit many of us with a tremendous impact. We were saddened, and her death will leave us a void that can never be entirely filled. In this time of sorrow, our only consolation is the knowledge that we were privileged to have known Bronia, if only for a short time in her long and wonderful life.

During the time that our students had the opportunity to know her, we came to know Bronia as a person of intelligence, integrity, always willing to help, whose life and career were, indeed, an inspiration to all of us at Bodwell. The results of her outstanding life and the beneficial influence on students will always live on. The people whose lives she touched, will always be monuments to Bronia's life and dreams.

Sincerely,

James R. Burnett,
Interim Principal

Letter from Austrian Ambassador

Ottawa, May 20th, 2011

To the Family of Mrs. Bronia Sonnenschein,

We have belatedly learned about the demise of Mrs. Bronia Sonnenschein on January 26th of 2011.

As the Austrian Ambassador in Canada I wish to express to the entire family of the late Mrs. Sonnenschein my heartfelt sympathy for this terrible loss.

I know that Mrs. Bronia Sonnenschein grew up in Vienna and despite the vicious persecution by the Nazi regime fondly remembered her youth in Austria.

To inform people about the crimes of the Nazi regime and to raise awareness of any forms of anti-Semitism and racism remains an important task. I know that Mrs. Sonnenschein, as a dedicated and tireless Holocaust educator, made a most valuable contribution in this regard reaching out to thousands of people in British Columbia with this important message.

Yours sincerely,

Werner Brandstetter

Tribute from a Hillel Director

Eyal Lichtman (February 2011)

Dear Dan Sonnenschein and Family,

We were very deeply saddened to learn of the passing of your mother, Bronia. We especially regret that we did not receive your message in time to attend her funeral.

Your mother was an individual of outstanding courage and spirit. So tiny in frame but so enormous in character, we were blessed to know her and so much more blessed to see the powerful impact that she had on the lives of so many Jewish and non-Jewish young people. Through her interactions with succeeding generations, your mother put a necessary face to the 20th century story of our people. History is an abstraction for many students, but your mother ensured that thousands of young people would carry with them and pass down to future generations the power of hearing that history from an eyewitness. We were honoured to have Bronia as a guest of Hillel students over the years and we know that her presentations at the annual high school symposium reached so many more non-Jewish students.

We can tell you about one particularly moving impact that your mother had, which truly changed the world. You may recall that, several years ago, an anti-Semitic incident occurred at the prestigious Lester B. Pearson College of the Pacific, on Vancouver Island. In an admirable response, the school approached the Jewish community and a week-long program was developed, in Vancouver, to educate the four young men who were involved. Like everyone at the international school, these young men were chosen because of their scholarship and character, and received full scholarship in the belief that they would return to their home countries and become leaders with a broad understanding of the world and its peoples. The student who had been the motivator behind the incident, in which graffiti was chalked around the campus while the Israeli ambassador was visiting, was a promising young student from Mauritius.

Part of a week-long itinerary of volunteer work, seminars and educational events included a meeting with your mother. To witness the dawning of understanding on the consciousness of these four young men during their time with your mother was an example of the magnitude of her life and her experiences. Telling her story and that of her family and community opened the minds of these young men in ways no history lecture possibly could. Each of them, now long returned home to Malta, Uruguay, Mexico and Mauritius, will carry with them forever the compassion they learned from meeting your mother. Indeed, they fell in love with her and she with them, despite the unfortunate circumstances that had brought them together.

This is a single example of the impact she had on younger generations of strangers. It does not take into account the joy she brought to family and friends, of which we know she had an adoring many. We know that she considered Canadian Jewish Congress a part of her family because that was the organization under whose auspices she arrived in Canada.

Through the years of interaction with our students and the admiration and love felt for her, we hope she felt part of the Hillel family as well. We certainly feel like we have lost a beloved friend.

The irreplaceable Bronia will be deeply, deeply missed. May her memory be for a blessing.

On behalf of the Hillel mishpachah,

Eyal Lichtman,
Executive Director

Condolence Messages

This is a sample. We again thank all who expressed condolences in any way.

She always had a smile and a wonderful outlook on life.
— Ethel Karmel

She was a jewel in our community and leaves a legacy for us all.
— Cathy Golden

Bronia has left an amazing legacy which will never be forgotten.
— Rome and Hymie Fox

It was an honour to know her, to hear her life story, to learn from her.
— Golriz Boroomand

Bronia was a truly remarkable person, whose warmth, graciousness and inner strength drew the admiration and love of everyone who met her. She captivated the hearts and imaginations of countless students by turning her dark history into a powerful force for good in this world.

— Frieda and Danny Miller

Her passing marks the end of an era for us all. Bronia was a founding member and life member of our society but above all, our most inspirational of teachers and our dearest friend.

— Ed Lewin and the VHEC
Board of Directors
Frieda, Rome, Nina and Staff

Those who have had the privilege of knowing her are enriched as a result. Her passing has left a hole in our community and she will be missed tremendously.

— Jody Dales

She lived up to her name — a ray of sunshine despite her painful past. We are grateful that we had a chance to meet this wise and sweet woman.

— Jana and Ken Abramson, and Claire

I will miss her warm smile, her sparkling, wise eyes, and her warm hug.

— Geoffrey Druker

Her memory will live on in the thousands of students and teachers who had the privilege of meeting her during her decades as a VHEC Outreach Speaker. We miss her warmth, humour and grace.

— Nina Krieger

I'm so moved by your mother's death. ... The eulogy is remarkable — magnificently written and a splendid testament to your wonderful mother. ... So she has made the best possible contribution to our community and to young people and that is that she was able to live on and love on to the end of her life even though she suffered so.

— Ingrid Schossleitner

Our deepest condolences to you and the family on the passing of your very ordinary and very extraordinary mother. It was an honour and joy to have known her for a little while. ... May Bronia's legacy live on.

Dearest Bronia,

Thank you for having an open heart despite a history that easily could have rendered you bitter. Like the ever-present glow of your reading lamp through the January rain, your sunshine will continue to travel — with verve! — through the many thousands who heard your messages.

— Rosemary Fitzgerald

[Y]our mother ... was my first introduction to a survivor. Even at the tender age of 14 I could tell that your mother was a great and heroic woman. The world is a lesser place without her.
— Mark Weintraub

Bronia was an amazing and remarkable woman who touched the lives of all who knew her — myself included. I will always remember her and the impact she had on my life. I'm so thankful and appreciative that I met and got to know Bronia.
— Romy Ritter

Bronia was the liveliest soul we knew. Her legacy is her life which she lived to its fullest. Thousands will remember her.
— Jean and Harvey Gerber

We are truly saddened by your mother's passing. We admired her strength and enthusiasm and her love for her family.
— Robert and Elke Mermelstein

Our deepest condolences on the loss of such a wonderful mother and grandmother. We are so lucky to have such fabulous memories to remember her by.
— Wendi and Barry Vaisler

From light to dark, and then to light again. May your Mother's inspiration keep shining on us all.
— Birgit Westergaard and
Norman Gladstone

She was a delightful lady and will be greatly missed.
— Rita Propp

She was an absolutely wonderful human being. We hope you find inspiration in your life from this role model.
— Violeta Moutal, Carol and Nadia

Bronia was a true hero for her family and for the Jewish people and a great humanitarian. ... We recall hearing her speak in person ... Her images, her story, her animated oratory are so moving to hear. Her memoirs, which we have read and shared with our daughters and other family members, will have a permanent place in the testimonies of Holocaust Survivors.

— Mitch and Marg Weiss

I did not have the honor of knowing your mother, but I did read her obituary in the National Post. With her passing, she has left her family a precious legacy. Her perseverance and determination in the face of evil should remain a source of inspiration to all of you.

— Sam Mitnick

[W]e hope you find comfort in remembering what a strong and positive woman she was, a real inspiration to our generation as well as our children's.

— Raquel and Rafael Hirsch

Bronia was a special friend and inspiration to me and I know to a great many others. I cherish her memory very deeply and feel so very lucky to have known her.

— Susan Cox

I am sorry for your loss, but glad that you had such an inspiring inheritance, which you clearly appreciate. Her spirit goes on, which must have been profoundly satisfying to her. What a beautiful and powerful soul she had.

— Barbara Kay

Bronia, a beautiful lady, will forever be remembered for her courage, her friendship, and her remarkable ability to enrich so many lives.

— Isabel Lever

Bronia was very special in the life of the community and a very dear person to us. ... She was an invaluable source of information and inspiration both in our personal conversations and in her untiring efforts to bring the message to the Jewish community and the community at large. ... Bronia was small in stature but she cast a giant shadow of knowledge, comfort, strength, determination and love.

— Zev and Phyllis Solomon

Peace be with her. What a great woman she was. ... [S]he created unforgettable memories for my students on so many occasions.

— Donald Grayston

An incredible life, and I'm sure that her willingness to share her experiences has had an incredibly profound effect on many. For that, we should ALL be grateful: those who do not remember the past are condemned to repeat it, and Bronia clearly ensured that the people she spoke to would remember.

— Alain Maissoneuve

[S]he and I used to travel together to schools in various cities in the interior [of British Columbia] to teach students about the Shoah. ... Through our travels together I got to know her better, and came to understand what a noble soul she was. Again and again she re-lived her own pain so that later generations would know the truth ... I also saw what a lovely person she was herself, and I came to have a great affection for her. She has left a gap that can never be filled, and I will always miss her.

— William Nicholls

To me, she was a monumental personality, committed to her family and to being a witness to the brutality she experienced when young. Personally, I will always remember Bronia as an optimistic yet practical person who clearly saw people as individuals with both strengths and weaknesses. I will miss her.

— Diane Wells

What a warm, courageous and spunky person she was and she was able to give a voice to that. To hear what she endured throughout her life left me mesmerized. She was a true gift and I consider myself fortunate that I met her even that one time.

— Toby Kolman

I, like so many, am so privileged to have known her. She is a beautiful soul and was the most purely good human of her generation that I ever knew. ... I know she had an amazingly positive impact on the world around her. ... There is something special that she brought to the world that is still very much alive.

— Julia Segal

This [obituary] was a most moving tribute to a woman who was a tour de force. I regret not knowing her sooner and know that her legacy will reach far beyond our time. *Zikhrona Livrakha*, May her memory be an everlasting blessing and inspiration.

— Michael Zoosman

I know that by sharing her stories, and almost as importantly, showcasing her consistently positive and upbeat attitude, she taught university students more about life and living in an hour spent with her, than perhaps they had learned to that point. It was always a joy to be in her company and I will never forget her. May your family be comforted knowing that she touched the lives of so many people who will, undoubtedly, keep her memory alive. That's a remarkable legacy.

— Gabe Meranda

I am comforted with the knowledge that she led a life of strength and love. ... Please know that Bronia's work has not passed with her. In my classroom, I continue to relate her story and teach her lessons of hope, determination, and tolerance. Her passing has only underscored the need to continue her work so that future generations are aware.

— Kelly Malone

It was a pleasure to have met you and your family during your short stay in the hospital. I hope that you are now at peace and thank you for your contributions to humanity and your bravery in sharing your stories.

— Dara Lewis

We are touched by Bronia's death as we were by her life. She will always be an inspiration for us.

— Ronnie and Karen Cahana

We know that Bronia was an exceptional individual, blessed with a great ability to make connections with young people. She helped us to value freedom's precious gifts.

— James Burnett

I had the honour of meeting Bronia when she was asked to speak to employees at WorkSafeBC as part of a series of events organized by our Diversity Committee. The grace and humanity with which she wove her own story made a lasting impression on so many of us. Dan, thank you for bringing your mother to our doorstep and for helping her to remain such a ray of light for the world. I had the great pleasure of being invited for tea with your mother one afternoon. It is a memory I shall always treasure.

— Pamela Cohen

Hello Dan and Vivian,

Your Mom and I shared a very special relationship, and I will miss her presence, but she will live forever in my heart, spirit and life. ... Bronia was one of the truly happiest people that I have ever encountered, WOW what a lady!!!!

Bronia loved you both with all her heart and soul and her true gift from God was her grandchildren and their children. She showed me how to count my blessings through her stories of all of you. Thank You, Thank You, Thank You, my dear friend.

— Debbie Maki Mazzei

Your mother was a tiny lady but a giant in many ways. She was articulate, influential, and charming. She will be missed by many.
— Evelyn and Irving Goldenberg

Bronia sounds like a truly amazing woman. I wish I had had the privilege of hearing her speak about her experience.
— Rachel Fisher

A "one of a kind" elegant, charming lady who made an indelible mark on those around her. I remember how much I enjoyed her phone calls and her enthusiasm. She was a very unusual person.
— Harriet Abramson

I was very sorry to see your Mom's obituary in the paper and feel fortunate to have known such a lovely lady.
— Lois McPherson

One of my favourite people, she had a sort of twinkly intelligence.
— Kathy Evans

Words cannot express how privileged we feel having met your wonderful mother. Her contribution to humankind cannot be measured. When our grandchildren are older, they will learn her story.

We will never forget her story, in part because we have her book, but more importantly the wonderful opportunities we had over the years to chat with her. We will never forget her. Thanks to her efforts to educate people about the Holocaust, there will be many more who remember.
— Dan and Carol Lundine

We are so happy that we got acquainted with Bronia. She was such a dear and warmhearted person. We admired her ability to work such a long time as a Holocaust educator. We will honour her memory.
— Ilse and Peter Schirmer

I was really saddened to hear that Bronia had passed. ... Your mother was such a well-loved and well-liked and respected person, so there will be a lot of people who have appreciated all that she contributed to her immediate community and to the larger community around her. Thinking of you and feeling sad, but also feeling so grateful that your Mom lived so long and did so much and was such a beautiful person.

— James Mullens

What a great lady she was. She contributed so much to the world and we are all the better for it. She impacted so many of our lives. I have great memories of her.

— Karen Corrin

I am so very sorry to hear of Bronia's passing. She has been such an inspiration and will continue to be a powerful voice in Holocaust and tolerance education.

— Sheila Hansen

I am sure you have been comforted by all the wonderful memories of your mother and by the impact that she had on so many people. She was tireless in sharing her story, and lit up the room for young people, who absolutely adored her.

— Zac Kaye

She was a gracious, charming lady who was an inspiration to us all in how she lived her life.

— Rochelle Rabinowitz

When we lose someone who has made such an impact on the world, it is as if a great gift disappears and leaves a great hole in our soul. Your mother's passing must leave a great hole in your soul but I hope that you can now see her as a star shining brightly in the heavens.

— Sandy Corenblum

I only met her at the event commemorating the work of Raoul Wallenberg, but she struck me as a gracious, intelligent, and interesting lady. And your preface to *Victory over Nazism* makes it clear that she was tireless in her efforts to make sure that the lessons of the Holocaust are not forgotten.

— Len Berggren

I am sorry not to have had the opportunity to meet your mother who must have been a very remarkable and unique personality.

— Michal Unger

I feel so fortunate to have had the opportunity to meet with her and learn about her experiences!

— Maija Sharrock

She was always very kind to me and I feel honored to have known her and grateful that she shared her history.

— Claus Jahnke

Your Mom was such a very special lady, somebody I'll remember forever. ... I continue to teach my students about your Mom.

— Marilyn Berger

Bronia was (and remains) to me a very special, sweet, and strong woman who I am honoured to have known.

— Craig McAdie

Bronia was a special person, beloved and respected by many. I think of her with warmth, as I know do many others.

— Renee Switzer Guarino

I always remember your mother for her warmth, understanding and generosity and I offer my heartfelt condolences together with my profound hope that her remarkable legacy will endure forever.

— Mark Steven

Notes

xi   At his son's *bris* (circumcision ceremony), Lou Kolman spoke of the meaning of the names he had been given, the first being for his grandmother, and the second as follows:

> "Asher's middle name, Bradley, is in memory for Claire's grandmother, Bronia, whose first *yahrzheit* is observed this week. Bronia was a strong survivor of life's challenges and she always celebrated the richness and goodness in life. Her first-most love was her family and she cherished her grand-children and great-grandchildren. Bronia lived a life of dignity and was a beacon of light, hope, and courage. Her love for her family and our love for her gave her the strength to do all the things that made her life so remarkable. Her honesty and generosity of spirit are among the many qualities we wish for our son."

The *yahrzheit* is the anniversary of death in the Hebrew calendar. The Hebrew names of Jonathan's and Jackie's daughter, Felicity, are Aliza Bracha, the first to honour Jackie's deceased maternal grandfather, and the second to honour Bronia, whose Hebrew name this was and which means "blessing".

7   Philip Kawalek was once the mayor of Husyiatin, Poland. He died many years before his wife, a murder victim of the Nazis, who is pictured here in a later photograph.

In some records, the name 'Emilia' is spelled 'Emilie'. She was born in Husyiatin, Poland in 1892. She received training in French language, piano, embroidery, and other skills considered suitable for a cultured woman of the time.

Abraham Schwebel was born in Siekirzynce, near Lemberg in Poland in 1885. He obtained a law degree from the University of Lemberg and was an officer in World War I. After moving to Vienna with his family (where his law degree was not valid), he worked in the textile industry, often traveling to Lodz, Poland on business. His connections there facilitated his escape to this city soon after Germany's annexation of Austria, where he was joined one by one by his family, who then tried to get exit visas.

11   The entire period of horror was over seven years, from the Nazi annexation of Austria on March 12, 1938 to May 8, 1945.

16   In the abstract of a talk Michal Unger gave, *After an Alibi: Hans Biebow and the Rescue of Three Jewish Groups from the Lodz Ghetto (1944 - 1945)* (available at www.fondationshoah.net/FMS/DocPdf/Coinchercheurs/UNGER.pdf), she writes that:

> "Hans Biebow ... realized very quickly that Jewish forced labor was a potential 'gold mine'. He turned the ghetto into an important factor in the German war industry, and a source of personal profit not only for himself but for several high ranking German officials as well.
>
> Due to the enormous profits that these Nazis gained from Jewish forced labor, the Lodz ghetto was not liquidated along with the other ghettos ... and continued to operate until August 1944.
>
> During the last period of the ghetto's existence, Biebow and his close associates — especially Erich Czarnulla and Franz Siefert, fearing that they would be forced to enlist to the army, and be sent to the front, planned a way to protect themselves and their interests."

Their plan was to re-locate two factories from the Lodz ghetto to Germany, the second being a munitions factory, for which about 500 Jews, mostly metal-workers and their families, were first deported in late August 1944 to Auschwitz

> "where its members remained together without going through selection. To the best of our knowledge, this is the only group that arrived in Auschwitz, which did not go through the selection process, and remained intact. Most of the members of this group were transported from Auschwitz to concentration camp Stutthof and in late November 1944 reached Dresden where Biebow and his associates set up a munitions plant known as Bernsdorf & Co. Despite their suffering, mainly in Stutthof, most of its members survived and were liberated in Theresienstadt in May 1945."

Bronia and her family were added to this group later, and did undergo the dreaded selection upon arrival. Roman Halter, one of the initial 500, tells in his book, *Roman's Journey*, of how after many of the original group had died "from beatings, starvation, infection from vermin, and the terrible Baltic winds", more were requisitioned as "the original order had been for a transport of 500 slave laborers, [so] 500 it had to be, not one more and not one less" as the SS was "punctilious as always about such things".

Unger concludes her summary by describing how Hans Biebow continued to implement

> "his policy of using Jews and Jewish forced labor for practical reasons ... first of all to protect from being sent into combat at the front. The main reason however was to

furnish himself and his close associates with an alibi to avoid punishment for their war crimes. The paradox is evident: this Nazi war criminal, who participated in the annihilation of the Jews of the Lodz ghetto and other ghettos in the Warthegau, rescued a large group of Jews as the war wound down. ... [Their fate] depended on the personal interests and initiatives of a corrupt German merchant and war criminal. ... It is through this extraordinary episode that we may observe the last stage of the heightened tension that existed between the SS ideology of total annihilation of the Jews, and the more practical policy of exploiting the Jews for the benefit of the Reich and for personal gain."

A reinforcing comment in McKale's *Hitler's Shadow War* is:

"[S]ome local German officials and economic experts in Poland did everything in their power to prevent the destruction of the ghettos. Their motives ranged from trying to use underpaid Jewish labor to produce essential goods for large profit to taking bribes from the Jews, which helped produce a good life, and the fear that with the destruction of the ghetto many such officials might be sent to serve at the front."

18 Paula's description of the incident of scarlet fever is on p. 42.

21 The name of the woman who gave the Schutzbrief to Bronia was Mrs. Upschat (see p. 65). In late 2012, I was gratified to learn (as my mother would also surely have been) that this incident was cited in the German scholarly book by Pascal Cziborra: *Frauen im KZ: Möglichkeiten und Grenzen der historischen Forschung am Beispiel des KZ Flossenbürg und seiner Aussenlager* (Women in Concentration Camps: Possibilities and limits of historical research by example of Flossenbürg concentration camp and its satellite camps). The relevant online excerpt was found by doing an Internet search on the keywords, Schutzbrief and Upschat.

23 This was written in German and translated by us in 1999.

25 Horwitz in *Ghettostadt* describes the hospital atrocity, in part:

"That same apprehension quickly turned to panic when they saw the Germans roughly forcing patients out of the buildings, even pushing some children from the windows, and piling them onto the vehicles. Stunned, bystanders soon realized that they were witnessing not just the closure of the hospitals but the beginning of the wholesale deportation of the patients."

27   The reference to 30,000 people killed was Bronia's best estimate
      at the time. In the book *The Lodz Ghetto* compiled by Adelson
      and Lapides, the numbers during this particular deportation,
      as stated by Rumkowski, were 21,000 (14,000 children and 7,000
      adults). Many more were deported at other times.

31   Issues about the controversial Rumkowski are explored in
      Unger's monograph, *Reassessment of the Image of Mordechai Chaim
      Rumkowski*, and also in the play by Avraham Cykiert, *The Emperor
      of the Ghetto*, compellingly performed by actor Alan Hopgood.

32   About Jakob Edelstein of the Theresienstadt (Terezin) Ghetto, in
      a position similar to Rumkowski's, Ruth Bondy concludes that
      his "chief error ... lay in his logic":

      "He, like all the Jews — true to their education and reasoning
      — assumed that the Germans needed as much manpower as
      they could get in their war against the three great allied
      powers, Britain, Russia, and the United States. It never
      dawned on them that the hatred Hitler and his Nazi ideo-
      logues bore the Jews, and their desire to destroy them once
      and for all, took precedence even over their desire to win the
      war, and only increased as all hope of victory diminished.
      Edelstein, like all the Jews, believed wholeheartedly in
      Hitler's inevitable defeat, and the Allies' certain victory.
      It was merely a question of time. They had to hold out
      another day, another week, another month, until the spring,
      the winter, next year. Had the war ended in 1943, as the
      British General Staff had anticipated, or even in 1944 — as
      indeed it might well have — the stubborn optimism shown
      by the Jews would not have seemed so painful or so naïve."

35   Shmulek's father lost the will (or heart) to go on living. Others
      killed themselves, as recorded in the following example from
      The Chronicle of the Lodz Ghetto (edited by Lucjan Dobroszycki):

      "Oct. 22, 1942. The bridge in Koscielna Square again became
      the scene of a suicide. Frajda-Ruchla Dobrzynska, age 45, ...
      jumped off the upper level of the bridge to the street below
      ... Her husband, Icek Dobrzynski, age 46, committed suicide
      yesterday by jumping from a fourth-floor window ... The
      cause of both suicides are the deportations, several weeks
      earlier. Their two children were taken away."

36   At the same time as Mila was taken, so was Bozena Strauss, the
      mother of Bronia's first husband, Erich Strauss, whom she had

..

married in the Lodz Ghetto. He also perished in Stutthof, as did Bronia's father. Mila's husband, Janek, had died of a heart attack in Vienna after being summoned to the Gestapo.

48   Her employer, a Dr. Trnka (see p. 132), didn't want to let her go, and offered to rehire her when she contacted him after the war.

53   A number of photos from the Lodz Ghetto of Bronia, her sister, and one of their father, are online at the Yad Vashem archives at http://collections.yadvashem.org/photosarchive/en-us/. These were recently discovered there by Diane Rodgers. We had been aware of three of these, two having come into our family's possession after the war, and two having been printed in Dobroczyki's English-language edition of *Chronicle of the Lodz Ghetto*. The photo of Bronia's wedding to Erich Strauss, in a double ceremony with Mary Schiflinger's wedding (to Ignatz Yelin), was given to her by Dora Burstin, a fellow office worker there whom she happened to meet after the war.

The photos of Bronia are from the above-referenced archives with the given website address and the following identifiers:

5732949_7262714.html   5732949_5741356.html
5732949_7262735.html   5732949_5741358.html
5732949_7262748.html   5732949_5741366.html
5732949_7262755.html   5732949_5741368.html
5732949_5741364.html   5732949_5741350.html
5732949_5741363.html

The photo of Paula modeling clothes is one of many online in the Yad Vashem archives at the same base directory, completed by one of the following identifiers:

5732949_7192038.html   5732949_6997873.html
5732949_7192046.html   5732949_6997888.html
5732949_7192457.html   5732949_6997893.html
5732949_7192820.html   5732949_6997945.html
5732949_7192859.html   5732949_6997986.html
5732949_7192883.html   5732949_6998001.html
5732949_7194045.html   5732949_6998022.html

In his book about war-time Lodz, *Ghettostadt*, Horwitz writes:

"Mainstays of a ghetto workforce dedicated as well to the production of ladies' apparel, Jewish women applied themselves and their talents with all necessary diligence to the unwelcome task of catering to the requirements of German fashion. Ghetto photographs reveal some of these Jewish women modeling for the camera a selection of articles of ghetto manufacture, among them robes, suits, dresses, and coats. Standing atop a stool placed in a hallway or a table in the corner of a room — in one series of photographs a closed doorway is visible behind them — young ladies display these creations with a suggestion of big-city sophistication. Rarely smiling, they assume elegant, mannequin-like poses, simulating the mannerisms of models in a magazine ..."

In an audio interview in 1978, Paula said that she also designed clothes. They had to work seven days a week and were always hungry, but as a bonus, workers were able to keep samples, and so she got to have some "really fantastic clothes".

The photograph of Biebow and Rumkowski was obtained from a relative of Stan Lenga, Paula's husband. It is one of the prints produced by Mendel Grossman and given to his fellow inmates.

Biebow was found in Bremen, Germany after the war, then tried and executed (hanged) by a Polish court.

In addition to books named in the first bibliography, extensive information on the Lodz Ghetto may be found at the web site www.shtetlinks.jewishgen.org/lodz/holocaust.htm.

57   In Prague, Bronia contacted an old friend of her deceased first husband, a Dr. Ota Rais, who with his wife, Nina, extended her great kindness and helped with the rebuilding of her life. Dr. Rais passed away some years ago but Mrs. Rais and Bronia kept in touch by mail. Bronia always kept a tremendous affection for Prague and the Czech people.

58   Kurt Sonnenschein had a doctoral degree in law, from the University of Prague. He escaped Czechoslovakia in time, and eventually fought in North Africa with the Jewish Brigade of the British Armed Forces. His younger brother Eric survived Theresienstadt and Auschwitz, moved to Vancouver (where he lived until his death in 2009), and sponsored his brother to come to Canada.

60   The quote is, "he who has a why to live, can bear with almost any how."

61   *Wienerisch* is Viennese dialect.

62   *Zählappel* is roll call, and K.Z. stands for *Konzentrationslager*, concentration camp.

65   Here's the basic *Nuss Pusserln* recipe:
Beat 2 (or 3) egg whites with ½ cup sugar until stiff.
Fold in 2 ½ cups of finely chopped walnuts.
Add a little vanilla extract (or other flavoring).
Mix and form into cookies.
Maybe add a chocolate chip to the top of each cookie.
Bake at moderate heat (say 325 d.) for 10-15 minutes.

Thanks to Claudia Cornwall, the recipe is now posted on the Internet, at emomrecipes.com/recipe/388. Claudia commented on the site: "Bronia Sonnenschein was a friend of mine and a Holocaust survivor. At the end of the war, when she was liberated, she bought herself a red dress to celebrate. She was a gallant lady and an inspiration to many."

75   The photos of Emily Schwebel and her daughters, and the one of Paula above it, were probably taken by Stan Lenga. Stan was also a survivor of the Lodz Ghetto and Auschwitz, and contributed much to the happiness of our family life.

76   The family photograph is by Peter Kavalek, Bronia's first cousin. (He changed the spelling of his last name to reflect the original pronunciation, while first cousin Roman kept the spelling but with an Anglicized pronunciation.) Ann was Emily Schwebel's younger sister. With her husband, diplomat Alfred Moscisker, she escaped Austria to New York where they lived (under the last name Morse) for many years until his death, after which she moved to Vancouver (where she changed her first name from Hania to Ann). Most of the early photographs printed in this book were saved by her, and some by Peter's mother, Grete. The photograph with Emily is by her mother, Vivian Herman.

83   "invisible barrier between myself and the Christian world." These words were written while the wounds were still raw, and Bronia wanted it made clear that she did regain trust.

85   In 1996, Bronia was videotaped for the Shoah Project. *Shoah* is the Hebrew equivalent of Holocaust, and means annihilation.

86   Bronia sent this article to Robert Krell, who thanked her in a letter calling her description outstanding, and asking permission to publish it:

"In doing so, you would be setting a very important example of what a survivor can do to remind and inspire our Jewish children who get far too little by way of Holocaust education."

Condolence messages by at least two of those who heard Bronia speak at Camp Hatikvah, Mark Weintraub and Romy Ritter, are included among those printed in this book, on p. 272.

99 Mr. Simpson's reference to Bronia being tattooed is an incorrect assumption. In her case, the number she was given was only sewn on her blouse. Tattooing was not a consistent policy, as described in Olga Lengyel's memoir, *Five Chimneys* [p. 118-9]:

> "In the camps of Auschwitz-Birkenau and, later, everywhere, many stories circulated about the tattooing of the prisoners. One would think that all the internees were tattooed upon arrival. Some believed the tattooing safeguarded one against being sent to the gas chamber, or that, at least, a special authorization from Berlin would be necessary before a registered-tattooed internee could be put to death. Even in our camp many were convinced of that.
>
> Actually, as in so many matters, there was no fixed regulation. Sometimes all deportees were tattooed when they arrived. Then again there was laxity, and over a period of months the ordinary deportees were not tattooed at all.
>
> The inmates of Birkenau were directed into their camps without matriculation numbers. Undoubtedly such formalities appeared superfluous even to the Germans, for these people were merely to be fuel for the crematory ovens."

118 The traditional Germanized name, while naturally resented by Czechs at the time, is useful to indicate the town under Nazi occupation, during which time it did not function as normal. Upon liberation, Theresienstadt again became Terezin.

No other ghetto seems to be referred to as a concentration camp. Some distinctions are that ghettos were pre-existing parts of towns (or the entire garrison town of Terezin in this case) with the local non-Jewish populace being evicted, and with "normal" infrastructures for dwelling (although crowded much beyond normal capacity), unlike barracks and latrines built for those purposes in camps. Ghettos also had some semblance of normal society, with a Jewish administration and permitted cultural activities. A website, www.brundibar.net (no longer existing), quoted this comment by Hanno Loewy:

> "[V]arious publications prefer the term "concentration camp," dropping the term "ghetto," which faithfully reflects the sources. This is generally done in the belief that the term "ghetto" would cover up the actual conditions in Theresienstadt. And in fact the conditions in the ghettos are comparable in many ways to those of certain concentration camps.

If, however, we prefer "ghetto" here, that isn't because we don't recognize the meaning of "a part of the city in which Jews live" as a euphemism in this context. Nor is there any suggestion that "Things weren't all that bad" in the ghetto. Existing differences between Theresienstadt and the types of camps in the Nazi system become all the clearer that way. It is hard, even in this area, to demand a sophisticated view. But anyone who postulates exact observation should not stop short at terminology. Despite all the similarities there was in the ghetto an ultimate sort of free space that no longer existed in the concentration camp. In the ghetto 'a complete microcosm arises, a pretended normality of everyday life that not only serves physical survival, but increasingly becomes a place of psychic refuge, a self-nurtured illusion, the escape to which represents the only protection that is still left.'"

And Schneider, in *Exile and Destruction*, writes:

"Kaltenbrunner persuaded Himmler shortly after his promotion to do away once and forever with the entire ghetto system, most probably realizing that despite the harsh conditions in the ghettos, there was a sense of some autonomy, no matter how precarious. As long as families could be together, they could nurture each other and find the strength to face each day. By moving them into actual concentration camps, their physical and psychological breakdown was much more rapid and thus hastened the process of their destruction."

119   There was some notable military resistance by Jews. Also, any criticism of "insufficient" military resistance must keep in mind the savage Nazi reprisals against families and communities of the resisters, such as those perpetrated against Czechs after the assassination of perhaps the worst Nazi of them all, Reinhard Heydrich. For grim details, see books like Callum Macdonald's *The Killing of Reinhard Heydrich* or Michael Elkins' *Forged in Fury*.

The reference to hostages includes those on hijacked airlines, and may be applied to the hostages on board the four airplanes intended as terrorist missiles on September 11, 2001. It was primarily Todd Beamer and some others on board his flight who "resisted" and heroically averted another disaster, because theirs was the only flight that learned what was going on. Although the Allies knew a fair amount about the Holocaust by 1942, they did not broadcast this news. In a relevant comment on "the final solution", Ruth Bondy has written:

"Many, many Jews never knew of such a plan, not even during their last moments, when they stood in the gas chambers. The idea that people could be gassed to death like insects never crossed their minds. ... [T]hose who know that Auschwitz, Treblinka and Sobibor did in fact exist, and that death factories are conceivable, can no longer comprehend the naïveté of the Jews before the deluge. Post-Auschwitz man can only try to understand, telling himself over and over again that they never knew that mechanized murder was possible."

138   After I notified Sir Martin Gilbert of Bronia's death, he replied: "Your mother's help was very special to me."

141   Unlike those of Irving's ilk, real Nazis don't deny the Holocaust but boast of it when they can, like Adolf Eichmann's right-hand man, Alois Brunner, did from his long-time sanctuary in Syria.

166   *Neshamot* are souls.

167   *Menschlichkeit* means "human-ness", as in having good character.

179   *Eshet Chayil* is Hebrew for "Woman of Valor".

188   In his letter of Aug. 11, 1992 to Bronia thanking her for talking to one group of residents in psychiatry, Dr. Krell wrote:
"I was particularly moved by one comment which reads as follows. 'I particularly would like you to convey further appreciation to Mrs. Sonnenschein for her very moving narrative. I cried for her, for me, for everyone — that such things could occur.'"

202   See the top of page 287 for Bronia's *Nusspusserln* recipe.

206   Another German student, Silja Kotte, met Bronia after a talk at the UBC Hillel and, like Markus, also became a friend, keeping in touch after her return to Germany. She is now on the faculty of the Institute for Psychology at the University of Kassel, and was active in a German-Israeli leadership development program.

210   *Heimat* conveys the nostalgic feeling of an idyllic but real home.

213   In the top photo, Bronia is wearing the button "We all smile in the same language" given to her by Ashley Howell, youngest member of the Bonner County Human Rights Task Force.

221 S.A. was the *Sturmabteilung*, Storm Detachment, and S.S. was the *Schutzstaffel*, Protection Squad, the sinister core of Nazism.

In his book, *Roman's Journey*, Roman Halter wrote that:

"Czarnulla ... was a kind of [*Oskar*] Schindler figure. It was in fact Czarnulla who obtained Himmler's consent for us 500 metalworkers to be sent to Dresden on November 23, 1944. Czarnulla was captured when the war ended and was taken to Poland, sentenced to death. ... Czarnulla had a dual personality. On the one hand, he was responsible for terrible things in the Lodz ghetto, such as fleecing the Jews of Luxembourg, etc., channeling the booty through the metal factory. On the other hand, on a personal level, he was capable of doing some good for a few individual Jews."

Czarnulla was executed on March 27, 1948 in Lodz.

222 On December 16, 2002, Bronia received a Queen's Golden Jubilee commemorative medal for her outstanding volunteer service. In the last photo in this book, she is shown wearing this medal shortly after getting it. (She did not make a practice of this!)

223 Markus Schirmer attended this event and took the photograph.

235 A documentary film, interwoven with another performance of Brave Old World's concert of these Ghetto songs, is described at www.songofthelodzghetto.com.

242 *Baba* and *Zeida* refer to Emily's paternal grandparents, Sima and Benek Herman, who were saved by Oskar Schindler.

247 Raoul Wallenberg was a Swedish diplomat in Hungary who saved many thousands of Jews. Imprisoned by the Soviet Union after the war, he presumably died there. For details and articles on this hero, one online source is www.raoulwallenberg.net.

275 The word *mischpachah* means "extended family".

297 Clare's book, *Last Waltz in Vienna*, meant a great deal to Bronia, describing so well her experience in that city. Here is a quote:

"We did not close our eyes to what was going on in the Third Reich, but we did not open them too wide either. And even had we looked with wide-open eyes we would not have seen much, for the writing on the wall for the Jews was still in virtually invisible ink."

Bibliography

Introduction to the First Edition

M ANY PEOPLE HAVE COMMENTED that the impact of hearing my mother makes it all so much "more real than books". Of course, I know what they mean. However, once one has awakened to the reality of these events, there is a great deal that can be gained from the right books, and in some cases this is the only way to obtain information.

Two bibliographies are provided, including some books and authors mentioned in this book. This introduction provides a little guidance on suitability for various audiences, as well as comments on how some of the material relates to this book.

The first bibliography consists of books of particular relevance or special interest to Bronia. Of the two on the Lodz Ghetto, Dobroszycki's *Chronicles* is an encylopedic collection of diaries and other first-hand documents perhaps more suitable for researchers; Adelson and Lapides credit him with being central to the compilation of their book, which was made into a film and is available as a videotape.

One of Bronia's favorites is the literary memoir, *Last Waltz in Vienna*. Another is the more scholarly but also highly readable *Vienna and its Jews* which quotes Clare's book frequently. Clare describes how the Nazis in Germany implemented their anti-Jewish measures gradually, carefully testing the waters. In contrast, the assault on Jews that took place immediately after a rapturous Austrian welcome for the Nazis and Germany's annexation of Austria, was described by Berkley as a *Blitzverfolgung* (lightning persecution). In general, Berkley makes a good case that Nazism was an Austro-German phenomenon (elsewhere he has called it a Bavarian-Austrian phenomenon).

Of course, there's plenty of blame to go around, since there was a fair amount of support for the Nazis' anti-Jewish policies throughout much of Europe and elsewhere in the world. This is discussed in such books as those by Abella, Perl, Pool, and Rossel.

With regard to Rossel's book, *The Holocaust: The World and the Jews, 1933 – 1945*, classifications can be misleading or incomplete. This book's Cataloging-in-Publication category is "Holocaust, Jewish (1939–1945) — Juvenile Literature". Firstly, although it uses a documentary and review approach designed for teaching young people, there is much of interest for adults as well. Elie Wiesel called it "thought provoking, informative, and stimulating. ... one of the best books in the field."

Another classification issue is the time period. Doug Ward states on p. 143 that "historians regard [Kristallnacht] as the start of the Holocaust." The *Anschluss* (annexation of Austria), also in 1938, could be considered a starting point, as can earlier stages, going right back to Hitler's election. This last time frame is expressed in the title of Rossel's book, and in others such as *Perpetrators, Victims, Bystanders: The Jewish Catastrophe, 1933–1945* by Raul Hilberg. and *The War Against the Jews, 1933–1945* by Lucy Dawidowicz.

A book highly recommended by Hilberg is *Ideology of Death* by John Weiss, of which he says that "for many readers this book can safely take the place of an entire library."

In an excellent chapter on the subject in *Just Because They're Jewish*, Hirsh Goldberg characterizes the Holocaust as "history's culmination of ignorance and the hatred that ignorance can arouse. The centuries of misconceptions, stereotypes and falsehoods about the Jews caused a slow, but inexorable, murder of a people's image. The Holocaust brought the vicious process to its illogical conclusion."

The Jewish people has been the object of the most outrageous slander throughout the centuries and to the present day. My mother was once startled after a talk by a young boy; he told her of a letter from a puzzled friend in Ontario who had heard another Holocaust survivor speak there but had seen no horns, and then asked his friend, "where do Jews have their horns?" While such instances of lingering, medieval delusions are rare in North America, they are unfortunately much more popular in some areas of the world. The "blood libel" (that Jews ritually kill for blood) is being preached by some Islamic clerics. A forthcoming book from the Simon Wiesenthal Center entitled *In Their Own Words* will document this disturbing situation. On a positive note, we should not forget the refreshing phenomenon of philosemitism, many examples of which are quoted in Gould's compilation, *What Did They Think of the Jews?* This book also has examples of transitions both from anti-semitism to philosemitism and, less encouragingly, vice versa. (Often it's a failure in proselytizing to Jews that brings the latter on, as in the case of Martin Luther.)

Two inspiring books are *The Triumphant Spirit*, a collection of professional photographs and brief descriptions of many Holocaust survivors (including a foreword by Thomas Keneally, author of *Schindler's List*), and *Hasidic Tales of the Holocaust*, an artistic portrayal of inner resilience and spiritual resources based on interviews with survivors. In the tale, *A Sign from Heaven*, one of them says, "You see, in order to survive you must believe in something, you need a source of inspiration, of courage, something bigger than yourself, something to overcome reality." This is reminiscent of one of my mother's favorite quotes, "he who has a why to live, can bear with almost any how."

Introduction to the Second Edition

NEW TO THE FIRST BIBLIOGRAPHY IS *With a Camera in the Ghetto* by Mendel Grossman, a professional photographer who made it his mission to document the horrors of the Lodz Ghetto. His surviving photographs powerfully convey the misery of ghetto life.

Among changes to the second bibliography is the addition of Norman Cohn's *Warrant for Genocide*, a history of the forgery, "The Protocols of the Elders of Zion", promoted over the years by many rabid antisemites including American industrialist Henry Ford (who was very popular with the Nazis). More recently, this classic of Jew-hatred was promoted in a Saudi-financed series on Egyptian television. The back cover of the 1996 Serif edition notes that "even before Hitler came to power, the Protocols were one of the cornerstones of Nazi propaganda" and claims that *Warrant for Genocide* "remains one of the key books for understanding the murderous folly of the twentieth century."

The little-known story of "righteous gentile" Frank Foley is told by Michael Smith in *Foley: The spy who saved 10,000 Jews*. Another relatively obscure part of the history of the times is the attempt by Peter Bergson and his friends to save European Jews, as described in *A Race Against Death: Peter Bergson, America and the Holocaust* by David Wyman and Rafael Medoff.

The cover of Perl's *The Holocaust Conspiracy* effectively conveys the complicity of many nations in the Nazi war against the Jews, including the Allies even as they were waging war against Nazi imperialism. It shows a swastika composed of the flags of several nations: Britain, America, Canada, Switzerland, and the Soviet Union (not a complete list of course). The book also describes active collaboration among Axis powers, such as the leader declared an "Honorary Aryan" by the Nazi regime for his enthusiastic support of the Final Solution. This was the Grand Mufti Haj Amin el-Husseini, who set the tone for the ongoing Arab war against the Jews. His toxic influence is also discussed in the books by Bernard Lewis and Robert Wistrich.

Introduction to the Third Edition

The previous introduction to the Bibliography ended with a mention of the influential Arab Nazi, Haj Amin el-Husseini, a fanatical supporter/inciter of the so-called Final Solution. He is the subject of several books, including *Icon of Evil: Hitler's Mufti and the Rise of Radical Islam* by David Dahlin and John Rothmann. Not included in our bibliography but worth mentioning is a similarly titled, and seemingly more scholarly book: *A Genealogy of Evil: Anti-semitism from Nazism to Islamic Jihad* by David Patterson. Finally, this monstrous Nazi collaborator features prominently in Jeffrey Herf's *Nazi Propaganda for the Arab World*, a book that follows the author's acclaimed *The Jewish Enemy: Nazi Propaganda during World War II and the Holocaust*.

In the latter, the author documents the huge amount of demented, Jew-hating vitriol produced and pervasively distributed by the Nazis. He writes: "From the foundation of the Nazi party to Hitler's rantings in a Berlin bunker in 1945, the key themes in the regime's anti-Semitic story line were righteous indignation about victimization at the hands of a powerful and evil foe, promises of retaliation, and projection of aggressive genocidal intention onto others." About the subject focused on in his subsequent book, Herf writes: "Not only did the Nazi regime fiercely oppose the establishment of a Jewish state in Palestine and lend support to anti-Zionist Arabs, but in the positive reception it afforded al-Husseini it effected a rapprochement between Nazism and Islamic fundamentalism in its early years."

This connection up until more recent years is covered in Matthias Küntzel's *Jihadism and Jew-Hatred*, a book that the author claims "demonstrates that al-Qa'ida and the other Islamist groups are guided by an antisemitic ideology that was transferred to the Islamic world in the Nazi period." He states that "the history of the Muslim Brothers shows that revolutionary antisemitism is no mere supplementary feature of modern jihadism; it is its core." Also, "[p]rior to the consolidation of Soviet influence in Egypt, the country's new rulers had made no secret of their Nazi sympathies. It was not by chance that Egypt became the El Dorado of former Nazis who decamped there in droves in the 1950s."

More directly related to the events in this book is Gertrude Schneider's first-hand, vivid account, *Exile and Destruction.* Writing of the assaults on Jews in Austria that began immediately with the *Anschluss* in 1938, she writes: "Even the newly arriving German soldiers could not get over the ferocity of these anti-Semitic Austrians and the treatment they meted out to their momentary captives." It could have been my mother speaking when she writes of being sent from a ghetto (in Riga) to a concentration camp (in Kaiserwald): "If we had thought our life there had been a hard one and at times unbearably so, we now realized that by comparison it had not been that bad at all. While families lived together, they could communicate, they could embrace each other, they could sustain each other, and when they closed the doors at night, they could have a little privacy." Bronia also agreed that after the war, "the effervescent, enlightened, and creative Jewish presence in Austria was for all purposes lost and would never again give Vienna that special, cosmopolitan flavor."

Voyage of the Damned is about the ill-fated journey of refugees on the St. Louis, memorialized in Canada by the "Wheel of Conscience" in Halifax, one of the ports where they were callously turned away. The authors state that "the survivors tend to have one thing in common: a love of life and an enthusiasm for living it every day to the full. Having been near death, escaping through a miracle of chance, they realize how precious and precarious life is."

A Holocaust book that deserves to be better known is *Hitler's Shadow War* by Donald McKale, in which the author makes the case that the Nazi exterminationist war against the Jews was the primary war, waged under cover of the more obvious war to expand the German empire. He writes: "[A]s far as the Nazi leadership was concerned, the problems in the war seemed only to make Germany's most critical wartime task, the extermination of the Jews, more urgent." Like Schneider's comment quoted earlier, he writes that "[t]he Nazis noted with satisfaction the magnitude of popular support the Kristallnacht received in Vienna. Anti-Semitic violence there was much greater than in any other city in Germany." It is also worth quoting McKale's concluding remark: "Perhaps most important to realize is that numerous prejudices from Western history combined together by the twentieth century to make the Jews, in the view of many Westerners, the most hated and dangerous enemy of not only the world, but of all mankind. The Holocaust was inconceivable without the presence of such deep-seated intolerance. A persistence of similar hatred today among some Westerners, and its intensification elsewhere in the world, as, for example, in the Middle East and portions of Asia, is both highly problematic and ominous."

Helping to keep the Nazi war against the Jews in the shadows was the influential and widely over-rated American newspaper, the New York Times. *Buried by The Times* is Laurel Leff's indictment of this newspaper's *de facto* policy of downplaying news of the Holocaust while it was being perpetrated and often air-brushing out the Jewish identity of the Nazis' "public enemy number-one". She also makes the case that if not actually a policy, this approach was based on the un-written mentality of the paper's Jewish owner, tacitly understood by his underlings. As she writes, "the story never received the continuous attention or prominent play that a story about the unprecedented attempt to wipe out an entire people deserved."

A fascinating and highly readable book that supports McKale's thesis of annihilation of the Jews being the primary Nazi aim is *Ibsen and Hitler* by Steven Sage. In his conclusion the author writes: "Both scripts [of Ibsen plays], as adapted by Hitler to the world stage, inexorably decreed a war against the Jews to override all else. Even territorial expansion was subordinate. The Greater German Reich turns out to have been but a means to achieve the apocalyptic end."

First Bibliography

Adelson, Alan and Robert Lapides (ed.). *The Lodz Ghetto: Inside a community under siege.* New York: Viking, 1989.

Berkley, George E. *Vienna and its Jews: The tragedy of success, 1880s–1980s.* Cambridge, Mass.: Madison Books, 1988.

Clare, George. *Last Waltz in Vienna: The rise and destruction of a family, 1842–1942.* New York: Henry Holt and Co., 1989.

Cornwall, Claudia. *Letter from Vienna: A daughter uncovers her family's Jewish past.* Vancouver: Douglas & McIntyre, 1995.

Dobroszycki, Lucjan (ed.). *The Chronicle of the Lodz Ghetto, 1941–1944.* New Haven: Yale University Press, 1984.

Fischer, Gretl Keren. *An Answer for Pierre.* Ottawa: Borealis Press, 1999.

Frankl, Viktor E. *Man's Search for Meaning.* New York: Washington Square Press, 1985.

Gilbert, Martin. *Kristallnacht: Prelude to disaster.* London: HarperPress, 2006.

Grossman, Mendel et al. *With a Camera in the Ghetto.* New York: Schocken Books, 1977.

Horwitz, Gordon. *Ghettostadt: Lodz and the making of a Nazi city.* Boston: Belknap Press, 2008.

Levi, Primo. *Survival in Auschwitz: The Nazi assault on humanity.* New York: Macmillan Publishing Co., 1961.

Orenstein, Henry. *I Shall Live: Surviving against all odds, 1939–1945.* New York: Simon & Schuster, 1989.

Pisar, Samuel. *Of Blood and Hope.* Boston: Little, Brown, 1979.

Schneider, Gertrude. *Exile and Destruction: The fate of Austrian Jews, 1938–1945.* Westport: Praeger, 1995.

Unger, Michal. *Reassessment of the Image of Mordechai Chaim Rumkowski.* Jerusalem: Yad Vashem, 2004.

Second Bibliography

Abella, Irving and Harold Troper. *None Is Too Many: Canada and the Jews of Europe, 1933 – 1948*. Toronto: Lester & Orpen Dennys, 1983.

Alexander, Edward. *The Holocaust and the War of Ideas*. New Brunswick, NJ: Transaction Publishers, 1994.

———. *The Resonance of Dust: Essays on Holocaust literature and Jewish fate*. Columbus: Ohio State University Press, 1979.

Altshuler, David (ed.). *The Precious Legacy: Judaic treasures from the Czechoslovak state collections*. New York: Summit Books, 1983.

Anissimov, Myriam. *Primo Levi: Tragedy of an optimist*. New York: The Overlook Press, 1996 (Translated by Steve Cox).

Beller, Steven. *Vienna and the Jews, 1867 – 1938: A cultural history*. Cambridge: Cambridge University Press, 1989.

Berkley, George E. *Hitler's Gift: The story of Theresienstadt*. Boston: Branden Books, 1993.

Bondy, Ruth. *"Elder of the Jews": Jakob Edelstein and Theresienstadt*. New York: Grove Press, 1989 (Translated by Evelyn Abel).

Cohn, Norman. *Warrant for Genocide: The myth of the Jewish world conspiracy and the Protocols of the Elders of Zion*. London: Serif, 1996.

Cohn, Werner. *Partners in Hate: Noam Chomsky and the Holocaust deniers*. Cambridge, Mass.: Avukah Press, 1995. (Available online at wernercohn.com/Chomsky.html.)

Dahlin, David G. and John F. Rothmann. *Icon of Evil: Hitler's Mufti and the rise of radical Islam*. New York: Transaction Publishers, 2008.

Dawidowicz, Lucy S. *The War Against the Jews, 1933 – 1945*. New York: Bantam, 1986.

Del Calzo, Nick, et al. *The Triumphant Spirit: Portraits and stories of Holocaust survivors ... Their messages of hope and compassion*. Denver: Triumphant Spirit Publishing, 1997.

Des Pres, Terrence. *The Survivor: An anatomy of life in the death camps*. New York: Oxford University Press, 1976.

———. *Writing into the World: Essays, 1973–1987*. New York: Viking, 1991.

Eisner, Will. *The Plot: The secret story of the Protocols of the Elders of Zion*. New York: W. W. Norton, 2005.

Eliach, Yaffa. *Hasidic Tales of the Holocaust*. New York: Vintage, 1988.

Elkins, Michael. *Forged in Fury*. New York: Ballantine Books, 1971.

Fackenheim, Emil L. *To Mend the World: Foundations of post-Holocaust Jewish thought*. New York: Schocken, 1989.

Friedrich, Otto. *The Kingdom of Auschwitz*. New York: Harper-Collins, 1994.

Fromm, Bella. *Blood and Banquets: A Berlin diary, 1930–38*. New York: Simon and Schuster, 1990.

Gilbert, Martin. *The Holocaust: The Jewish tragedy*. London: Collins, 1986.

Goldberg, M. Hirsh. *Just Because They're Jewish: If anything can be misconstrued about the Jews, it will be ... and has been*. New York: Stein and Day, 1979.

Goodrick-Clarke, Nicholas. *The Occult Roots of Nazism: Secret Aryan cults and their influence on Nazi ideology*. New York: New York University Press, 1992.

Gould, Allan (ed.). *What Did They Think of the Jews?* Toronto: Stewart House, 1991.

Halberstam, Yitta and Judith Leventhal. *Small Miracles of the Holocaust: Extraordinary coincidences of faith, hope, and survival*. Guilford: The Lyons Press, 2008.

Halter, Roman. *Roman's Journey: An extraordinary odyssey of Holocaust survival*. New York: Arcade, 2012 (reprint).

Hazzard, Shirley. *Countenance of Truth: The United Nations and the Waldheim case*. New York: Viking Penguin, 1990.

Herf, Jeffrey. *The Jewish Enemy: Nazi propaganda during World War II and the Holocaust*. New Haven: Yale University Press, 2006.

Hilberg, Raul. *The Politics of Memory: The journey of a Holocaust historian*. Chicago: Elephant, Ivan R. Dee, 1996.

Kelley, Douglas M. *22 Cells in Nuremberg*. New York: MacFadden Books, 1961.

Klarsfeld, Beate. *Wherever They May Be*. New York: The Vanguard Press, 1975.

Küntzel, Matthias. *Jihadism and Jew-Hatred: Islamism, Nazism, and the roots of 9/11*. New York: Telos Press, 2007.

Langer, Lawrence L. *Art from the Ashes: A Holocaust anthology*. Oxford: Oxford University Press, 1995.

Leff, Laurel. *Buried by the Times: The Holocaust and America's most important newspaper*. Cambridge: Cambridge University Press, 2005.

Lengyel, Olga. *Five Chimneys*. Chicago: Academy Chicago Publishers, 1995.

Levi, Primo. *The Drowned and the Saved*. New York: Vintage, 1989.

Levy, Alan. *The Wiesenthal File*. Grand Rapids: Wm. B. Eerdmans Publishing Co., 1994.

Lewis, Bernard W. *Semites and Anti-Semites: An inquiry into conflict and prejudice*. New York: W. W. Norton & Co, 1986.

Loftus, John and Mark Aarons. *The Secret War Against the Jews: How Western espionage betrayed the Jewish people*. New York: St. Martin's Press, 1994.

McKale, Donald M. *Hitler's Shadow War: The Holocaust and World War II*. New York: Cooper Square Press, 2002.

Nicholls, William. *Christian Antisemitism: A history of hate*. Northvale, NJ: J. Aronson Publishing, 1993.

Perl, William R. *The Holocaust Conspiracy: An international policy of genocide*. New York: Shapolsky Publishers, 1989.

———. *The Four-Front War: From Holocaust to promised land*. New York: Crown Books, 1978.

Pick, Hella. *Simon Wiesenthal: A life in search of justice*. London: Weidenfeld & Nicolson, 1996.

Pool, James. *Who Financed Hitler: The secret funding of Hitler's rise to power, 1919 – 1933*. New York: Pocket Books, 1997.

Prager, Dennis and Joseph Telushkin. *Why the Jews?: The reason for antisemitism*. New York: Simon & Schuster, 1983.

Pringle, Heather. *The Master Plan: Himmler's scholars and the Holocaust*. Toronto: Viking, 2006.

Reichel, Sabine. *What Did You Do in the War, Daddy?: Growing up German*. New York: Hill & Wang, 1989.

Rossel, Seymour. *The Holocaust: The world and the Jews, 1933–1945*. West Orange: Behrman House, 1992.

Sage, Steven F. *Ibsen and Hitler: The playwright, the plagiarist, and the plot for the Third Reich*. New York: Carroll and Graf, 2006.

Schneider, Gertrude. *Journey into Terror: Story of the Riga Ghetto*. Madison: Praeger, 2001.

Smith, Michael. *Foley: The spy who saved 10,000 Jews*. London: Hodder and Stoughton, 1999.

Thomas, Gordon and Max Morgan Witts. *Voyage of the Damned*. Chelsea: Scarborough House, 1990.

Weiss, John. *Ideology of Death: Why the Holocaust happened in Germany*. Chicago: Elephant, Ivan R. Dee, 1997.

Wiesel, Elie. *Night*. New York: Bantam, 1982.

Wiesenthal, Simon. *Justice Not Vengeance*. London: Weidenfeld & Nicholson, 1989.

Wistrich, Robert. *Antisemitism: The longest hatred*. London: Thames Mandarin, 1992.

———. *Hitler and the Holocaust*. New York: Modern Library, 2001.

Wyman, David S. *The Abandonment of the Jews: America and the Holocaust, 1941 – 1945*. New York: Pantheon Books, 1984.

——— and Rafael Medoff. *A Race Against Death: Peter Bergson, America and the Holocaust*. New York: The New Press, 1998.

The Partisan Song

Hirsh Glik (1943)

Written in the Vilna Ghetto, this song spread rapidly to other ghettos as well as partisan groups, becoming the anthem of the underground resistance movement. Glik set his Yiddish words to a stirring melody by Russian brothers, Dmitri and Daniel Pokras. Today this is sung at the conclusion of many events commemorating the Holocaust. Bronia once wrote, "It is significant to survivors whose spirits were not broken and to all those who remember and never forget."

Never say this is the final road for you,
Though leadened skies may cover over days of blue.
As the hour that we longed for is so near,
Our step beats out the message — we are here!

From lands so green with palms to lands all white with snow,
We shall be coming with our anguish and our woe.
And where a spurt of our blood fell on the earth,
There our courage and our spirit have rebirth.

The early morning sun will brighten our day,
And yesterday with our foe will fade away.
But if the sun delays and in the east remains,
This song as password generations must maintain.

This song was written with our blood and not with lead,
It's not a little tune that birds sing overhead.
This song a people sang amid collapsing walls,
With grenades in hands they heeded to the call.

Therefore never say this is the final road for you,
Though leadened skies may cover over days of blue.
As the hour that we longed for is so near,
Our step beats out the message — we are here!